MW01003055

YOU ONLY
GET WHAT
YOU'RE
ORGANIZED
TO TAKE

LESSONS FROM THE
MOVEMENT TO END POVERTY

YOU ONLY GET WHAT YOU'RE ORGANIZED TO TAKE

LIZ THEOHARIS AND NOAM SANDWEISS-BACK

BEACON PRESS, BOSTON

BEACON PRESS
Boston, Massachusetts
www.beacon.org

Beacon Press books
are published under the auspices of
the Unitarian Universalist Association of Congregations.

© 2025 by Liz Theoharis and Noam Sandweiss-Back

All rights reserved
Printed in the United States of America

28 27 26 25   8 7 6 5 4 3 2 1

This book is printed on acid-free paper that meets the uncoated paper
ANSI/NISO specifications for permanence as revised in 1992.

Text design and composition by Kim Arney

*Library of Congress Cataloging-in-Publication
Data is available for this title.*
ISBN: 978-0-8070-0864-5; e-book: 978-0-8070-1090-7;
audiobook: 978-0-8070-1830-9

We dedicate this book to Liz's parents,
Athan G. Theoharis and Nancy Artinian Theoharis,
and Noam's aunt, Adina Back.
May their memories be a blessing.

The poet was as true to common sense as to poetry when he said, Who would be free, themselves must strike the blow.

—FREDERICK DOUGLASS,
West India Emancipation Speech, 1857

I went down to the rich man's house and I took back what he stole from me. I took back my dignity. I took back my humanity . . . Ain't no system gonna walk all over me.

—"RICH MAN'S HOUSE," written and composed by Minka Wiltz and the Economic Human Rights Choir of the New Freedom Bus Tour, 1998 (sung to the tune of the church hymn "Enemy's Camp")

CONTENTS

AUTHORS' NOTE

This book was written collaboratively. The pages that follow reflect our shared conversations and insights. Most of the stories and personal reflections are drawn from Liz's life and leadership within the movement to end poverty over the last three decades. When we use first-person singular, it is Liz speaking. When we use first-person plural, we are referring to both of us, or to larger groups of people, depending on the context.

INTRODUCTION

"**I** lost the van seats."

Wiping the sleeplessness from my eyes, I blurted these words out to my boss at the community service office where I would work as a student all four years of college. He wasn't happy.

It was the late spring of my sophomore year, 1996, and the sun had just begun to peak over the horizon. We were waiting to board an early morning bus bound for Washington, DC. My boss and I had organized a group of students to travel south from Philadelphia for a rally to protest the passage of welfare reform, which threatened the lives of millions of children and their families. An unholy marriage of neoliberal politicians and Christian extremists had gained power on the national scene, exemplified by Newt Gingrich's 1994 Contract with America, a highly influential Republican legislative agenda, and Ralph Reed's similarly titled 1995 book *Contract with the American Family*. Reed, who is still a leading figure on the Christian Right, used his book to lay out an agenda that, like Gingrich's, advocated sweeping cuts to government programs by deploying religious and moralistic language.

Democrats were also being drawn into this reactionary moment, though they did so through the more buttoned-up language of "personal responsibility" and market liberalization. It was the Clinton administration, after all, that ultimately passed welfare reform in the name of rightsizing bloated government—even though the welfare programs they targeted accounted for less than 2 percent of federal spending as a percentage of GDP.[1] In stark contrast to this supposedly necessary fiscal austerity, bipartisan public investments in "law and order" were on the rise. Just two years earlier, then senator Joe Biden authored the 1994 crime bill, funneling billions of federal dollars into prisons and police departments.

In 1996, politicians on both sides of the aisle regularly invoked the bogeyman of "big government" in order to justify shrinking the social safety net and deregulating key sectors of the market. But although they argued that an economy unshackled from the government would benefit everyone, it mostly just benefited corporate profits and set the country down the path toward the Great Recession a decade later. A new, crueler, and more fragile version of American democracy was taking shape.

A year before the rally, I moved from my childhood home in Milwaukee to Philadelphia to study at the University of Pennsylvania. During my freshman year I began working with the National Union of the Homeless (NUH), a group of unhoused people who were taking over vacant homes across the country.* The NUH was not a charity, a service provider, or a professional advocacy group but rather a political organization led by and for unhoused people. The roots of the organization reached back to the early 1980s, when people circulating in and out of Philadelphia's patchwork shelter system

---

* In this book, Noam and I refer to people without housing as *unhoused*. For years, organized poor people have fought for this descriptor to replace the word *homeless* since it helps shift the focus and blame from impoverished individuals to the systems that produce their deprivation. Still, we occasionally use the word *homeless*, especially when referring to organizing in the 1980s and 1990s. This was how unhoused organizers described themselves at the time, and it was a radical reclamation of language that was used to demean and diminish them. The NUH was known to carry banners that read: "Homeless Not Helpless." This reclaiming of identity—from hostile implication to liberatory possibility—was not unique to the NUH. Oppressed people are constantly negotiating and reimagining the language society imposes on them.

began organizing themselves into communities of mutual aid and solidarity. In 1983, unhoused leaders, including Chris Sprowal, Tex Howard, and Franklyn Smith, founded the Committee for Dignity and Fairness for the Homeless. Within a year they had recruited over five hundred members across the city and were operating out of an autonomously run shelter called Dignity Shelter. By 1986 they had created the Philadelphia/Delaware Valley Union of the Homeless, which aimed to unite poor and unhoused people across lines of difference like race, gender, sexuality, and religion. By the end of the 1980s, they had gone national, with close to thirty thousand members in twenty-five cities.

I was introduced to the NUH on my first day of college. I had arrived for a pre-orientation program and that night we gathered to learn about grassroots efforts to confront inequality in the city. Among the speakers were Ron Casanova, known as Cas, the vice president of the NUH; and Kathleen Sullivan, a Penn alum and a leader with Empty the Shelters, a national organization of students that partnered with the NUH and other poor people's organizations, including the Philadelphia-based Kensington Welfare Rights Union. Casanova was a sincere, tenacious, formerly unhoused Nuyorican man in his mid-forties who had previously been a leader in the Tompkins Square Park rebellions in the East Village of Manhattan during the late 1980s. By the time I met him, he had served countless roles with the NUH: strategist, agitator, takeover expert, mentor, cook, and confidant to many. He was also a brilliant artist who painted vivid and impressionistic depictions of the struggle for housing and dignity.

Standing beside Casanova was Sullivan, a study in contrast. She was a white woman in her early twenties and had recently graduated from Penn. Originally from California, she was introduced to the world of homeless organizing and welfare rights activism when she moved to Philadelphia. During her undergraduate years, she became a leader with Empty the Shelters, founded in response to the limitations of traditional, campus-based community service organizations, which often treated poor people with paternalistic pity and offered only to help ameliorate and manage the worst effects of poverty. By the time I met Sullivan, she was deeply connected to many of Philadelphia's poorest residents, comfortably biking across the city, between college campuses and unhoused communities. She was a gentle, unassuming presence, but when I heard her speak that first night it was also clear that she was guided by a fierce and unflinching moral compass.

Casanova and Sullivan were a revelation. They described the grassroots organizing they were doing and what it meant to build power among the poor—to support everyday people coming together to create deep and lasting change in our society. These two organizers, from very different walks of life, were not simply bemoaning homelessness and poverty nor were they asking for sympathy. They had a deep analysis of the situation, its systemic causes and its history, as well as its solutions, which started with poor and unhoused people taking action together. In hindsight, the timing of my introduction to these two organizers was immensely tragic: just a few months later, Sullivan was killed by a drunk driver while biking home from her job at the Cheesecake Factory. The night I met her, though, she was all hope and possibility. Listening to her and Casanova, I was fired up. Within a few months, I joined the movement, and I never left.

Which brings me back to the van seats. One of my jobs at the community service office on campus was to coordinate a fleet of fifteen passenger vans. This was an incredibly convenient job for a young organizer. Outside the official channels and hours of the office, I commandeered the vans for all manner of Empty the Shelters business, from transporting supplies between the homes that unhoused people were occupying to staging public actions and protests alongside my classmates. The night before the rally, I spent the midnight hours driving around West Philadelphia, picking up loose furniture and odd appliances that students had left on the curb at the end of the semester. Most of the discarded items were perfectly functional, some quite nice and practically new, and I knew my unhoused friends would put them to good use. To make room for all the stuff, I removed the van seats and hid them near a classmate's house, planning to pick them back up at the end of the night. I didn't think anyone would steal a set of van seats with no van attached, and I even asked some community members to keep an eye on them. But when I circled back a couple of hours later, they were gone.

My boss was understandably upset when I tried to explain myself the next morning. He would now need to requisition new seats, which meant paperwork and added expenses. But beyond the logistical headache, I could see that my mistake had unsettled him, and I think it was because it diverged from his image of me as a rule-abiding and trustworthy young woman. I didn't come off as a typically rebellious student. At the community service office, I completed my work earnestly, with a deep sense of responsibility ingrained in me by morally rigid parents who embodied an ironclad immigrant work ethic passed down to them by their own parents. But now my boss was recognizing another truth about me. I wasn't just a concerned, community-conscious student. I was also a stubborn, sometimes foolhardy, young organizer who was more than willing to navigate the early morning streets of the city in a van with no seats.

I lived a double life in college: working student and street organizer. I spent my weekend nights in homeless shelters doing art projects with kids and organizing among the temporary residents. I received good grades, even when it meant pulling multiple all-nighters in a row after protests or handwriting my term papers in tent encampments. And rather than being dissuaded by the van seat incident, I was still willing to use whatever resources were at my disposal to support the organizing efforts of unhoused people. One summer, I took some of the money I received from an undergraduate research grant and bought bolt cutters and other supplies for our next housing takeover, candidly reporting it on my expense report. On the eve of Christmas break another year, my friend and I handed out children's bikes to unhoused kids. The bikes were donated by "Skinny" Joey Merlino, Philly's Italian mob boss at the time, in an attempt to rehabilitate his image in the eyes of a city prosecuting him for racketeering.

During my four years of college, the movement to end poverty became the most important place of learning in my life. Its leaders and members were my professors and classmates. It was in Philadelphia where I discovered how it feels to reclaim a vacant home for a family in dire need of shelter; how it feels to march through the streets with people for whom you would do anything, and who would do anything for you; how it feels to know that this mutual commitment is strengthening a life-sustaining muscle called solidarity. By the time I graduated, the movement had placed me on an inescapable path: the path of fighting for a society in which everybody has the right to live and thrive, the path that would become the work of my life.

After thirty years of walking down this path, I find myself reflecting on what I've learned along the way. This book is an attempt to capture some of the lessons that the movement to end poverty has taught me about the world and the work of transforming it in the image of justice and abundance for all. These lessons, I hope, are evergreen. For me, they ring with especially sharp resonance in this moment.

Today the world is in desperate need of transformation. The climate crisis is escalating at a scale that the human mind struggles to understand. War and mass violence permeate the planet, often fueled and funded by the American government, and experts warn that we have not been so close to nuclear annihilation since World War II. In a further echo of that dark era, authoritarian leaders are seizing power in both the Global South and the Global North. Here in the United States, Christian nationalists are building on what Republican leaders like Newt Gingrich and Ralph Reed did in the 1990s, although this time they have taken full command of one of our two major political parties. The leadership of the Democratic Party, meanwhile, regularly demonstrates a lack of moral urgency and political imagination, as well as a blue-blooded instinct for protecting the interests of the wealthy and well-off. Too many liberal politicians who are practiced at saying the "right" things spend the lion's share of their time and our tax dollars rearranging deck chairs on the *Titanic*, while the hull of our democracy splinters and floods.

The through line of these crises is a shameful reality that is only becoming more pronounced with each passing day: we are living in the most economically unequal time in modern history. The moral and cognitive dissonance of this reality can be difficult to fathom, as can the numbers. At a time when the value of the US economy is nearly $30 trillion and the wealth of the three richest Americans now exceeds $500 billion,[2] close to 40 million people live below the official poverty line and another 100 million people live in a steady state of economic insecurity—one pay cut, layoff, health emergency, debt collection, foreclosure, or eviction from catastrophe. These approximately 140 million people are disproportionately children and women of color, but every community and demographic is affected. According to the US Census Bureau, in 2023 this included 38.9 million Latinos, 22.5 million Black people, 8 million Asian people, 2.3 million Indigenous people, and nearly 61 million white people.[3]

Among highly developed nations, the United States lags behind in almost every important social and economic category. In this rich land, about 45 million people regularly experience hunger and food insecurity, over 80 million people are uninsured or underinsured, around 10 million people live without housing or experience chronic housing insecurity, and the American education system continues to score below average compared to other member-nations of the Organization for Economic Cooperation and Development.[4] Perhaps most damning, deaths by poverty are an American reality. A 2011 study from the Mailman School of Public Health at Columbia University found that seven hundred people died every day from poverty conditions.[5] Twelve years later, in 2023, researchers at the University of

California, Riverside found that poverty was the fourth leading cause of death in the US, after heart disease, smoking, and cancer (though it should be noted that these causes, as well as the ones that follow poverty in the study—including obesity, diabetes, homicide, overdose, and suicide—all have correlated relationships to poverty).[6] What we call "deaths of despair" are also accelerating, although the label can be misleading, considering that so many overdoses and suicides are not caused by some kind of amorphous social malaise but are the consequence of medical neglect and the lack of access to adequate care and mental health treatment, especially for the poor.

In the shadow of our nation's abundance, American poverty manifests itself in countless daily forms: hundreds of thousands of water taps shut off in Detroit, Michigan, and Jackson, Mississippi; children removed from their homes because their parents cannot afford the cost of basic utilities; tens of millions of people cut off of Medicaid; the impossible burdens of health-care deductibles and health insurance premiums; the devastation, displacement, and deaths caused by super storms and fires, which are disproportionately higher in poor communities. Poverty is reflected in the rise of children laboring in our nation's shadow economy; families dispossessed from their homes by the fossil-fuel industry; low-income voters targeted and barred from polls by voter suppression and racist gerrymandering; students racking up billions of dollars in debt; US-born people and immigrants working for poverty wages in restaurants, elder-care facilities, retail warehouses, and agricultural fields. Poverty looks like unhoused people dying on the streets and buried, unidentified, in common graves.

The reality of an economic system that produces needless deprivation alongside unprecedented abundance is not simply another item on the big list of important issues. The capitalist disorder of poverty amid plenty is a portal into understanding many of the major afflictions of our nation and our current moment—a crucible in which all of society's ills come together and are expressed. While the wealthy continue to reap the rewards of a system heavily stacked in their favor, it is poor people who most acutely suffer from the ravages of racism, sexism, homophobia, xenophobia, sickness, environmental disaster, policing, surveillance, incarceration, war, and more. The poor are not just another identity group. Their lives are the most visible sign of a society in dire straits and a warning about the direction in which many more people are hurtling if we don't immediately change our relationship to one another and to the earth itself.

I come by this view honestly. I was raised in Wisconsin, a state that has long been a testing ground for both radical progressivism and reactionary politics. My parents were acutely aware of both. My dad, Athan G. Theoharis, was the son of an undocumented Greek immigrant who ran a small diner out of the first floor of his home until it went bankrupt. After receiving a college scholarship from the University of Chicago at the age of fifteen and graduating with a PhD in history ten years later, my dad pursued a career as a historian and a civil liberties advocate, becoming one of the country's leading experts on the FBI. In his research, he used Freedom of Information Act requests to expose illegal subterfuge by J. Edgar Hoover and others, including evidence that they had targeted activists and organizers through counter-intelligence programs like COINTEL-PRO.* Building on his pioneering experience, he trained generations of truth-seeking researchers, journalists, and activists to navigate and decipher the labyrinthine sprawl of illicit government records.

Even as he tracked national political currents, my dad always emphasized the need to remain locally grounded. Growing up, I remember how angry he was at nearly everything then Republican governor

---

* Launched by the FBI in 1956, COINTELPRO (an abbreviation of "Counter Intelligence Program") illegally surveilled, infiltrated, and undermined dozens of political organizations, including the Black Panthers, the American Indian Movement, the United Farm Workers, and the Southern Christian Leadership Conference.

Tommy Thompson did, most notably his evisceration of Wisconsin's welfare system. But if my dad was often disappointed by the reality of politics, he always loved what democracy in its fullest expression could do for humanity, and he was proud of the democratic experimentation that punctuated the history of his hometown. As anyone who visited our family can attest, my dad relished the opportunity to give driving tours of Milwaukee, where he always paid special attention to our first-class public park system, a product of the city's rare history of progressive and socialist mayors.

By the time my dad retired in 2006, hard-right politicians and power brokers were again dragging Wisconsin toward a more sinister future. As the chair of the board of the Wisconsin ACLU, he worked to oppose the 2011 Wisconsin voter ID law, which maliciously required nearly all voters to have a driver's license, just one of the many racist and anti-poor methods of voter suppression that have reemerged across the country over the last couple decades. He also supported the infamous 2012 recall campaign against Governor Scott Walker, partially in response to Walker's austerity budget, which proposed to slash pensions and health benefits for public-sector workers and impose new statewide restrictions on the right to collective bargaining. The campaign unfolded over eighteen long, bitter months, with Walker, an evangelical Christian who later embraced Donald Trump, eventually holding onto the governorship. Mitt Romney, then on the presidential campaign trail, lauded Walker for his "sound fiscal policies" and promised that his victory would "echo beyond the borders of Wisconsin."[7]

Romney was right. Walker's win was an early sign of a growing anti-democratic strain within the Republican Party specifically and American politics more broadly, coupled with an ideology of economic austerity that has since siphoned billions of dollars to the largest corporations and the wealthiest Americans. Even in the early 2010s, when Trump was no more than a businessman in debt and a cartoonish TV show host, this economic ideology was masquerading as populism—just as it had in the 1990s, when Tommy Thompson's workfare policies, known as the "Wisconsin Model," were nationally exported to help end welfare as we knew it. (President George W. Bush rewarded Thompson for his efforts by nominating him as the secretary of Health and Human Services in 2001.)

If this worried my dad, it really pissed off my mom, Nancy Artinian Theoharis. The daughter of an Armenian genocide survivor and a lifelong member of the Presbyterian Church, she organized her life around the fight for human rights, inter-religious understanding, and the abolition of poverty, racism, and war. When I was growing up, my mom was a constant presence at both Sunday services and political gatherings, and she took me everywhere she went. In pre-school, I brought my Winnie the Pooh backpack stuffed with coloring books to church and community meetings with her. When I was in elementary school, she encouraged our family to help run the local volunteer office of the Mondale/Ferraro presidential campaign and plan a citywide benefit concert for nuclear disarmament. In middle school, I joined her in organizing an anti-racist day camp and meetings of the Milwaukee Committee for UNICEF, which she founded. In high school, she supported me when I led letter-writing campaigns for Amnesty International and when my friends and I rallied delegations of students to protest the first Iraq War.

My mom was a stubborn and unrelenting woman—good characteristics for an activist—and her tenacity was well-honed since her childhood. She contracted polio at the age of fourteen and as a teenager she had to learn how to walk again without assistance. Her life was forever impacted by the illness. So was mine. Growing up with a polio survivor, I learned firsthand about the deep social impacts of epidemics, disability, and inequality.

She often liked to joke that moms know everything. Beneath the smile, though, I think she believed it was true, and when it came to the justice that she insisted God requires us to champion, my mom knew a lot. She knew that charity alone cannot undo inequality, and that in one of the richest countries in the world, we have more than enough to meet everyone's needs. She knew that to fight for peace and equality in the US requires an understanding of American imperialism and a commitment to internationalism. She knew that all of life is sacred, no matter where a person is born and what they are born with. She knew—from her own Armenian heritage—that violent atrocities and genocides are made possible because of the complicity of people and nations with great power and wealth. She knew that there is a difference between engaged citizenship and nationalism and believed that this country could one day become the vibrant democracy it so often claims to be. (In fact, she met my boss and me in DC for the 1996 welfare march and took me on a tour of American museums and civil rights monuments to remind me that I shouldn't lose hope for the nation and that I had joined a long line of people who have struggled for justice.) And she knew that freedom fighters through the ages have drawn strength from the power of our religious traditions and the ancient promise of Jubilee. My mom's favorite Bible passage—the password for her computer, phone, and online accounts—was Micah 6:8: "And what does the Lord require of you? To act justly and to love mercy and to walk humbly with your God." For her, faith and activism were not separate, but synonymous.

Because of my parents' community work, as a child I met influential social justice leaders not just from Milwaukee but from places as far-flung as Russia, South Africa, El Salvador, and Palestine. When organizers, ministers, and human rights activists came to town for speaking events and fundraisers, we often hosted them. Some ended up sleeping on the pull-out couch in our family room. During those visits, our house hummed with animated discussions on everything from apartheid and occupation to war and nuclear freeze, and as I soaked up these conversations I began to recognize the interdependent bonds of humanity that connect us across great distances and fortified borders.

My family had the honor of hosting Archbishop Desmond Tutu on several occasions, both before the end of apartheid and after South Africa's Truth and Reconciliation Commission was formed in 1995.

After one of his earlier visits, he sent a small thank-you note that my mom framed and placed on the bookcase near our front door. This placement wasn't random. Every morning before school, I grabbed my glasses, which my father told me to leave on the bookcase so I wouldn't forget them, and caught a glimpse of the archbishop's handwriting. The framed note was meant as a daily, visual reminder: if I was to call myself a Christian—which I did, serving as a Sunday school teacher from the age of thirteen and as a deacon in my church at sixteen—my responsibility was to keep the social activism of Archbishop Tutu ever present in my mind and to make the spirit of Micah 6:8 real in my life. My mom insisted that the life of a Christian must be centered around the public ministry of welcoming and caring for immigrants and refugees, walking alongside those held captive by hate and bigotry, and lifting the load of poverty for all.

I like to say that the movement sent me to seminary. In the 1990s, un-housed organizers and welfare rights activists constantly encountered politicians and clergy who twisted Christian theology to denigrate the poor and provide cover for their racist beliefs and policies. In the lead-up to welfare reform, I began noticing the proliferation of perverse interpretations of obscure biblical passages like 2 Thessalo-nians 3—"If you do not work, you shall not eat"—in order to justify the dismantling of the welfare system and other public programs and social protections. And although this weaponization of the Bible originated among the far right, everyday Christians in mainline, Prot-estant congregations echoed more subtle, but still harmful, theological explanations of poverty. There was only minimal pushback, none of it especially energetic, which was all the more maddening to people like me who had always drawn sustenance from the Bible and who understood that many of these passages were being robbed of their original meanings. Indeed, 2 Thessalonians 3, when read in its histori-cal context, can actually be understood as a critique not of the laziness of the poor but of the *wealthy*, who idly accumulate their riches on the backs of the poor.

Despite this theological malpractice, many of us in the movement still felt deeply connected to our religious texts and traditions. In our encampments and the abandoned houses we took over, unhoused organizers often referred to biblical teachings, and prayer was the background hum of the movement. Some prayers were lively and communal, while others were quiet, individual pleas to God to deliver us from the evils of eviction and want. These early years of organizing among the poor made it clear to me that ending poverty depends on our ability to reimagine the moral values of our society. For Christians, this will require a serious reckoning within our own institutions and communities. Today the church is undergoing a historic crisis of identity and legitimacy, even as millions of people still hunger for spiritual meaning and connection. A new reformation of religious thought and action is necessary.

America's collective past has often pivoted on the abuse of scripture and faith by those with great power and wealth. The same is true today. But American history is also replete with examples of people from many religious backgrounds who have grounded their struggles for justice in the holy word and spirit of God. Like my mom, abolitionists, suffragists, labor organizers, students, civil rights leaders, and other representatives of poor and oppressed people have always insisted that divinity cannot be reduced to private matters of soul and salvation. Rather, they have demanded that the worship of God must be concerned with the building of a society in which all of life is cared for and treated with dignity. In every previous era, there were courageous people for whom protest and public action were a form of prayer, even as the religious leaders and institutions of their day hid behind sanctuary walls. Inseparable from my work as an anti-poverty organizer are my efforts as a pastor and theologian to follow in the prayerful footsteps of these ancestors; to reclaim their radical wisdom and breathe new life into the moral heart of our society.

My mentors in the movement understood the decisive role religion has always played in this country, and, as a student at Union Theological Seminary in New York City, I remained embedded in the network of poor people's organizations that I worked with and helped lead throughout the 1990s. In 2003, a group of seminarians and I founded the Poverty Initiative (reestablished in 2013 as the Kairos Center for Religions, Rights, and Social Justice). For over two decades, our goal has been to develop a national network of community and religious leaders committed to advancing the movement to end poverty, open to all, and led by the poor. In 2017, Kairos cofounded the Poor People's Campaign: A National Call for Moral Revival (PPC) with Bishop William Barber II and Repairers of the Breach. Today, we continue to co-anchor this campaign, alongside other efforts to organize and unite poor and dispossessed people.*

―――――――――

Over these many years, I have met countless people who have shaped and inspired me, and I consider myself incredibly fortunate to have such a vibrant community of family, friends, colleagues, and peers. It was through the movement to end poverty that I met my love and partner in life, Chris Caruso. Chris was one of Kathleen Sullivan's best friends in college and he worked with her and a small group of friends to lead Empty the Shelters. A first-generation college student from a working-class town in Connecticut, Chris was politicized as a teenager by the punk rock music scene and introduced to social theory by leaders in the National Union of the Homeless and other poor people's organizations. He was, and remains, a ravenous reader, organizer, educator, and strategist of enviable skill and versatility. We

―――――――――

* We use the formulation "poor and dispossessed" often in this book to describe the many millions of people in this country who have been impoverished and divested of their human rights, as well as of the power to determine the direction of their own lives.

forged a deep friendship years before we started a romantic relationship, but we eventually realized that what we shared wasn't simply respect and admiration but love. For the last thirty years, we have bowed
our heads together, put our hands to the plough, forged relationships
with some of the unsung heroes among the poor and dispossessed of
our day, and tried to plant as many seeds of justice as possible.

Two of those seeds are our beautiful, inquisitive children, who
are each still learning what the path of justice means for them. Our
daughter Sophia, whose name means divine wisdom, has never
doubted that anything less than the fulfillment of everyone's rights
is acceptable, although she sometimes questions why our family has
to go to so many protests, organizing meetings, and interfaith services.
Our son Luke, who is named for the gospel of the poor, has always
demanded that fairness be meted out in equal measure—for himself,
his sister, his classmates, and people the whole world over.

Included in my wider movement family is Noam Sandweiss-Back,
my coauthor. I first met Noam when he was a twenty-four-year-old
organizer living in New Orleans. In the fall of 2017, Kairos hired
him a few weeks before the launch of the Poor People's Campaign,
and the two of us have been working together ever since. Over the
years, we have discovered not just a political affinity, but a spiritual
kinship. Much like my own, his family has always blended faith and
the struggle for justice.

Noam's mom, Beth Sandweiss, was born in Detroit, into a family
only a generation removed from anti-Jewish Russian pogroms. His
dad, Aaron Back, was born on the other side of Lake Erie, in Buffalo,
into a big, observant Jewish family that toggled between the United
States and Jerusalem, where members of his family have lived since
the 1840s. Noam's parents met in Berkeley, California, in the late 1980s;
their first date was at a union hall, where his dad, then an aspiring
psychologist, was leading a training on the connection between oc-
cupational mental health and worker power, and their relationship
blossomed on picket lines and at antiwar marches to protest nuclear

proliferation and American interventionism in Latin America. In the mid-1980s, they moved to Jerusalem, after Aaron received a fellowship and a subsequent teaching position at a local university. What was originally meant to be a one-year stint turned into nearly a decade of life abroad.

While living in Jerusalem, Noam's parents grew increasingly troubled by the brutal subjugation of Palestinian people in both Israel and Palestine. With each new story of a Palestinian home being demolished by the Israeli army or an olive grove being plundered by Jewish settlers, they grew more firm in the understanding that peace and democracy could never exist so long as millions of people lived under the thumb of oppression. Along with a small group of other Jewish people, they began working in solidarity with Palestinians in the West Bank who were demanding freedom for themselves and their families. Aaron was on the founding staff of B'Tselem, still one of the most important human rights organizations in Israel, and Beth ran the Israeli desk of *Tikkun*, a Jewish American magazine started in 1985 to help revive the moral and spiritual dimensions of American progressivism. At the time, it was one of the only publications in the United States that regularly reported on the Israeli occupation and the violent dispossession of Palestinians.

Noam and his sister were both born in Jerusalem, and he was two years old when his family moved back to the United States. His dad continued his human rights work on Israel-Palestine, and the kitchen table in Noam's childhood home in New Jersey was often filled with organizers and peace activists who were passing through town. Meanwhile, his mom worked as a therapist, meditation teacher, and Jewish ritualist. Noam likes to say that although his mom is not a rabbi—as a teenager she briefly attended Jewish Theological Seminary before they began ordaining women—she has walked the rabbinical path.

When I met Noam, it was clear to me that he had metabolized the moral and political values of his family and was giving them new meaning through his own life. In his early twenties, Noam moved to New Orleans to participate in a year of Jewish public service. He ended up staying and working for a civil rights organization, investigating jails and prisons across Louisiana—which locks up more people per capita than almost any other place on earth.[8] He became immersed in a community of organizers, activists, and public interest lawyers who deepened the politicization process that his parents had begun during his childhood, helping him draw connections between Israel-Palestine and the United States, between the experience of poor and dispossessed people in his birthplace and his new home. Noam also began to better understand the ways that American militarism dispenses violence and drains vitally important resources not only abroad but domestically. Layered on top of these learnings was the illuminating experience of spending long days in Louisiana's decrepit carceral system, where poor people are often caged because they committed low-level crimes in order to survive or because they couldn't afford bail.

Working among the locked up, Noam wrestled with the byzantine mechanics of mass incarceration and the limitations of his own efforts. He believed in the cases he was building, but he also worried about the scale of their efficacy. These were cumbersome legal strategies that, on their own, could only ever tinker around the edges of poverty and systemic oppression. It often felt to Noam that he and his colleagues were standing at the mouth of a poisoned river, remediating what little they could, while the source of the poison remained upriver and out of sight. By the time we met, he was hungry to join a grassroots movement led by poor and dispossessed people themselves, not just lawyers and policy experts, with a larger vision of social transformation.

Noam has since emerged as an important leader in our work, with an expansive mind and a generous heart. Like the best organizers, he has a capacity to really be with people, to hear and see them, to make them feel known and valuable, and to lovingly push them beyond their comfort zones. He has worn a multitude of hats over the years, from setting up tables and taking notes in meetings to building new coalitions of grassroots organizations and planning the largest presidential candidates forum of the 2020 election season. I have taken special joy in watching him emerge as a faith leader in his own right, organizing other Jewish leaders in our midst, bringing Jewish learnings and rituals into our efforts, and enriching my own understanding of religious tradition and its continued relevance for our lives today.

Along the way, Noam and I have become writing partners, weaving threads of history, economics, theology, political strategy, and more in an attempt to make some sense of the world we are living in. The chapters in this book are an extension of that writing and a distillation of the organizing that the two of us and countless others are involved in and which precedes us. Many hands and minds are responsible for the ideas in this book. These pages are possible only because of the intelligence and insight of literally thousands of people—they are the result of decades of collective learning and struggle.

In this time of existential concern, when so many of us feel a deep sense of insecurity and are asking big questions about how we can change things for the better, it is important to learn from the people who have organized, *who are organizing*, in the many abandoned and forgotten corners of this country. Although the history books often tell a different story, many of this country's most significant, positive social changes have emerged from the bottom of society, with ripple effects that have ultimately yielded broad social benefits. This kind of progress is never linear or promised—it is demanded by those who, for their very survival, are first compelled to take transformative action. Today, poor people have the least to lose from unsettling the status quo and the most to gain from a shift in our national priorities toward a more equitable distribution of political and economic power. They are strategically placed to be a leading social force in our society, to spur into action not just their own communities but the millions more who have eked out just enough to maintain the false promise of stability and prosperity. The abolition of poverty depends on the courageous and visionary leadership of poor people themselves.

This book begins by interrogating some of the weightiest and most corrosive myths told about poverty, including the false assertion that it can never be eradicated and that the poor are helpless to do anything about it. Our answers to these, and other myths, are included in the early chapters. The rest of the book serves as our sustained rebuttal.

Over the last few years, Noam and I have poured over old pamphlets and documents, memories and mementos, to gather evidence that social transformation at the hands of the poor is an ever-present possibility and to summarize some of the most important ideas and principles that continue to animate the movement to end poverty. This is not a history book, but we spend considerable time reflecting on the hard-won experiences and lessons that have punctuated struggles of the poor in the past. Some of our reflections reach back decades, even centuries, and were passed down to us by mentors and leaders from earlier generations. Others come directly from the organizing that we have been involved in and witnessed all across the country.

We have a saying in our work: "Movements begin with the telling of untold stories." The movement to end poverty is thousands upon thousands of such stories—messy, incomplete, and full of thorny contradictions and daunting opposition. It is not by chance that the poor are the most politically disorganized section of society; their disorganization is fostered by an economy that relies on their cheap labor and an electoral system that often serves as a vehicle for the unequal accumulation of power and wealth at the expense of real democracy. It is also not by chance that throughout American history, the poor have been kept racially segregated to an extreme degree; not just geographically, but mentally and spiritually, within the fabricated hierarchy of white supremacy and racialized difference. When they have been able to unite across race to fight both systemic racism and economic exploitation, the poor have often discovered just how potent the power of their solidarity can be. The guardians of our established racial and economic order have time and again discovered the same, and their predictable response—division, hate, stoked fear, and violence—is proof of the threat they feel when poor and dispossessed people begin to organize and unite as an independent political force.

In the pages that follow, we tell just a few of the many stories that need to be told. We write of multiracial groups of unhoused people rising up from the streets and seizing empty, federally owned homes; of mothers on welfare shutting down entire city blocks and going toe to toe with some of the most powerful politicians in the country; of farmworkers busting modern-day slavery rings and winning living wages from multinational fast-food companies; of water defenders surviving the poisoning of their cities and clandestinely turning their water taps back on after the authorities shut them off and paved them over with cement; of coal miners, veterans, unemployed workers, students, artists, and others joining together in unusual and creative alliances to fight, sing, and pray their way toward freedom.

We offer this book with humility, with the hope that the stories, lessons, and ideas in these pages can provide a small sense of orientation amid the madness of these times. We hope that this book is a useful addition to the toolkit of moral audacity and radical imagination. We hope that it opens a window into the movement family to which we belong, which is always seeking new recruits who have the fires of love and justice burning in their hearts. This book is for all those who believe that the world does not have to be this way, that this is not as good as it gets, and that a future in which everyone thrives, not just barely survives, is possible and within reach.

YOU ONLY
GET WHAT
YOU'RE
ORGANIZED
TO TAKE

CHAPTER ONE

IS IT POSSIBLE TO END POVERTY?

I n the late spring of 1990, hundreds of unhoused people across the country broke the locks and chains off dozens of empty, federally owned houses and moved themselves in. Bedrooms and kitchens carpeted with layers of dust suddenly whirled with activity. Mattresses were carried in and bags of food were unpacked. Within hours, the new occupants made calls to the city's energy companies, requesting for the utilities to be turned on. When asked for their personal information, they gave the names and Social Security numbers of dead friends and relatives, a practice they called "borrowing from the ancestors." These leaders were disciplined and efficient. They were also kaleidoscopic: single moms living in their cars, veterans, students, low-wage or recently laid off workers, and people battling illness without healthcare. They were Black, Latino, Asian, Indigenous, and white, and although they came from radically different slices of society, the simple fact that bound them together was also the most important: they were poor, in need of housing, and fed up.

This wave of housing takeovers was led by the National Union of the Homeless (NUH), one among many carried out by the group during the late 1980s and early 1990s. Takeovers and encampments

were not unusual at the time, although they mostly occurred spontaneously, in isolated acts of necessity that flew under the public radar.
People without steady or reliable housing moved into the vacant
buildings that dotted their cityscapes, tenants refused to leave the
homes they were being evicted from or foreclosed upon, and others
cobbled together outdoor shelter in the neighborhoods where they
and their families lived. In their actions, the NUH reached deep into
this well of experience, adopting the ongoing survival strategies of
unhoused people and further politicizing them into a mass organizing drive of the poor.

There was a two-fold purpose to these takeovers. The first goal was
to meet the immediate needs of their members and secure temporary
refuge for as many of them as possible. But the NUH understood
they would never be able to occupy enough homes to house all their
members, let alone every unhoused person in the country. Only a reconstruction of society that put the needs of people over profit could
make that happen. So their second goal was to demonstrate their ability to take action together in response to a society that squandered its
abundance and treated the poor as if they were disposable.

An unacknowledged paradox plagued the country: there were
more empty houses than unhoused people, including millions sitting idly as pieds-à-terre, rental properties, and private investments,
as well as thousands that were owned and shuttered by the government through the Department of Housing and Urban Development
(HUD). Homelessness was a genuine problem, but it was misleading
to call it a housing crisis since the issue wasn't necessarily supply but
rather the ways that supply was being used, or, in this case, not being
used. A more accurate description of homelessness was as a crisis of
the inequitable distribution of resources, or, more plainly, as a crisis
of moral priorities and a failure of human imagination.

Despite naysaying arguments by politicians and a cottage industry of private homeless services, it was apparent to the NUH that
homelessness, and the poverty that produced it, were not inevitable

or unchangeable but human-made and solvable. But as they surveyed the wreckage of their neighborhoods, they understood that ending poverty would only happen if there was a political force strong enough to make such a demand and compel the nation into action. A force of that nature could, and in all likelihood must, originate from within their own communities, whose numbers were growing by the day amid worsening conditions. The NUH recognized that among poor and unhoused people rested a dormant power that, if ignited and sustained, could shift the political calculus of the entire nation.

First created after the Great Depression, the country's public housing system has always been a fraught and incomplete story. In the 1930s, amid an economic collapse that left at least two million people without homes, public housing represented a significant societal advance that lifted up people from the bottom of the economy. But from the beginning this system was chronically underfunded and built on the invasive surveillance, control, and racial segregation of its residents. In the 1970s and 1980s, it began to deteriorate amid major industrial transformations to the global economy that were accompanied by a sea change in domestic governance. The era of neoliberalism arrived with a fury, its sordid litany of new policies now well-known: deep tax cuts, deregulation of banking and financial markets, privatization of public utilities and services, and crushing anti-labor measures.

In the United States, after a decade of high inflation and unemployment, the government began cannibalizing its own best defenses against poverty. Little was off limits. In 1973, five years after the Fair Housing Act of 1968, which prohibited housing discrimination on the basis of identity and family status, Richard Nixon placed a moratorium on traditional public housing spending. This act was both a racist reaction to the progress of civil rights and an olive branch— one among many—extended to the bankers and CEOs whose appetites had been at least modestly constrained since the regulatory days of the New Deal. Nixon and his predecessors instead invested in a voucher system that funneled impoverished residents and public resources into the many far flung reaches of the for-profit rental market. From 1978 to 1983, during the presidencies of Jimmy Carter and Ronald Reagan, the HUD budget authority was reduced by nearly 80 percent.[1] Reagan also made severe cuts to the nation's public health infrastructure, including community mental health centers and psychiatric care facilities.

By the late 1980s, the last remnants of the once hopeful and always deficient public housing system were crumbling at precisely the moment that thousands of families were being forced onto the streets and into a new and growing network of privately owned and operated shelters (these families included both former public housing residents and renters and owners in the private market who could no longer afford their rents and mortgages). HUD only began collecting official data on homelessness in 2007, but government researchers estimate that the number of unhoused people on any given night grew from 250,000–350,000 in 1984 to 640,000–840,000 in 1996.[2] Millions more lived on the razor's edge of displacement. For much of American history, homelessness had been a temporary expression of severe economic crisis or a phenomenon confined to a few "skid rows" in major cities. It was now becoming a pervasive and permanent fixture of society. In the 1980s and 1990s, this reality was still so novel that computer companies didn't include the word *homelessness* in the spell-check dictionaries of their newly invented word processors.

The dramatic backdrop of this crisis was the triple threats of deindustrialization, globalization, and automation. For the nation's workers, the hollowing out and outsourcing of American industry, made even more intense by heavy attacks against organized labor, had enormous and alarming implications. Members of the NUH included people who had recently lost their manufacturing jobs and could no longer find steady work. They were also people with low-wage jobs who couldn't keep up with the growing costs of housing and other daily necessities. In these dire times, the position of the unhoused only foreshadowed the possible poverty and dislocation of millions of others. The NUH recognized this truth before most, as evidenced in one of their early slogans: "You Are Only One Paycheck Away from Homelessness!" The very name of the organization, the National Union of the Homeless, reflected an understanding of the connection between homelessness and the new political economy being shaped around them: as industrial work floundered and the labor unions of old were beginning to suffer and shrink, new unions of poor and dispossessed people were becoming increasingly necessary.

Homelessness has remained a chronic issue since the 1990s and housing insecurity as a whole has only worsened. Conservative estimates in 2023 suggested that between five and six hundred thousand people lived on our streets every night, the highest official numbers on record and likely still an underestimate since it is impossible to count every unhoused person.[3] When we factor in housing insecurity, these numbers multiply very quickly. There are now between eight and ten million people who are regularly at risk of homelessness—circulating in and out of our derelict shelter system, living with friends and family, and doubling or tripling up in whatever space is available to them, including crowded apartments and hotel rooms.[4]

Meanwhile, the nation's public housing stock has decreased by more than five hundred thousand units since the mid-1990s; federal legislation in 1996 eliminated one-for-one replacement, which required the government to make a new public housing unit available for every one eliminated.[5] The overall availability of affordable housing has also plummeted. According to a 2024 report from the National Low Income Housing Coalition, "In no state, metropolitan area, or county in the US can a full-time worker earning the federal minimum wage, or the prevailing state or local minimum wage, afford a modest two-bedroom rental home at fair market rate."[6] Alongside this crisis, there are about sixteen million houses that currently sit unoccupied across the country.[7] Despite our society's abundant capacity to meet

widespread human need, massive infusions of capital and public in-
centives continue to be funneled into the real estate industry, rather
than into public housing and rent caps, intensifying gentrification
and inequality.

On the island of Manhattan, ultra-luxury skyscrapers multiply
like metal weeds, a vertical invasion by a seemingly unstoppable
force. Along the southern end of Central Park, an outcropping of
tall, thin residential complexes make up what is unofficially known
as Billionaires' Row. The name is apt, considering that millionaires
and billionaires from the United States and elsewhere flock to the
developments to buy apartments at unimaginably high rates. In 2021,
the penthouse on the ninety-sixth floor of 432 Park Avenue was
listed at the astonishing price of $169 million.[8] Just as astonishing is
that these lavish, sky-high homes often sit empty, a vacancy perhaps
even more offensive than that of HUD houses. Rather than offer a
functional use, the empty residences of Billionaires' Row serve as
speculative investments for buyers who hope to one day resell them
for even higher prices, avoid taxes, or launder dirty money. For some
among the super-rich, flush with more money than they know what
to do with, an apartment on Billionaires' Row is simply an easy way
to park their wealth, more a financial strategy than a home.

The apartments on Billionaires' Row are the most extreme mani-
festation of an economic system that has become increasingly centered on the accumulation of wealth for a few and divorced from the
exigencies of life for the rest of us. The rapacious engine of capitalism
continues to transform housing—as well as other basic necessities
like healthcare and food—into an abstraction, taking its very real and
necessary material function and distorting it into a commodity to be
bundled and sold on the stock market for millions, even billions, of
dollars. Every time the NUH led a housing takeover, they temporarily
reversed this process, stripping away the commodification and turning
a vacant house "on the market" back into what it always should have
been: four walls and a roof for someone in need of shelter.

In the summer of 1988, the NUH launched the Take off the Boards campaign, their first major wave of housing takeovers. A year later, in October 1989, they organized the Exodus March, trekking hundreds of miles by foot from New England to Washington, DC, to participate in a hundred-thousand-person-strong Housing Now rally. The rally brought together dozens of housing organizations, including some large and more professionalized ones that claimed to speak for unhoused people without including them as decision-makers and leaders. The NUH demanded that Ron Casanova, their vice president, get to speak from the stage, insisting that because the group "had walked, they should talk." By then, they were brimming with well-earned confidence. The day before, the group had staged a highly visible protest outside of HUD's national office, forcing Jack Kemp, the famously pro-business secretary of HUD under George H. W. Bush, to sit down with them. During the meeting, they demanded that Kemp make ten thousand vacant HUD houses immediately available to the unhoused. Under pressure, he reluctantly agreed.

Shortly after the march, though, Kemp went back on his word, dropping the deal and cutting off communication with the NUH. They were disappointed and outraged, but not surprised. They had come to expect this kind of treatment from the government. Half a year later, in the spring of 1990, they made preparations to "reclaim" some of the ten thousand homes promised by Kemp, this time in eight urban strongholds: New York, Philadelphia, Chicago, Los Angeles, Minneapolis, Detroit, Tucson, and Oakland. They timed this takeover action for May 1, otherwise known as May Day or International Workers' Day. Members of the NUH saw themselves as continuing the time-worn tradition of struggle by the disinherited of the nation.

As the sun set in New York City on May 1, unhoused people, including Casanova, fanned out across lower Manhattan near Tompkins

Square Park, which had been an epicenter of homeless organizing for years. In the leadup to the night's activity, Casanova told a documentary crew what had brought them together: "We have one common goal and one thing we can't disagree with, which is the fact that we need houses. We need these buildings opened up for the people who are homeless and living in poverty. That is a uniting force that is able to bring all different types of people and organizations together to fight the one common enemy, instead of fighting each other."⁹ At the end of the night, Casanova stood silhouetted against a nondescript HUD apartment that had been bolted shut in the morning and was now occupied by the NUH. Wearing a black T-shirt emblazoned with the words "Up and Out of Poverty," he coolly explained to the same film crew: "The one thing I learned tonight is that it can be done, if people take the initiative of breaking into these houses. You've got to forget about it being against the law. I don't care. I'm dying in the streets. I think *that* should be against the law."¹⁰

Casanova's conclusion that night was so frustratingly obvious: rather than criminalize people for their poverty, poverty itself should be illegal, especially when evidence of the nation's untapped abundance was hiding, everywhere, in plain sight. The entire system of American law and policy was urgently in need of a moral overhaul. It was time, as in the gospels of old, for the tables of society to be turned over and systems reset.

Although the NUH couldn't do this alone, they did win a string of important victories in the late 1980s and early 1990s, including new policies that guaranteed twenty-four-hour shelter intake, access to public showers, and the right for the unhoused to vote.* They also won the formation of publicly funded housing programs run by their members in nearly a dozen cities. These victories were a barometer

---

* The NUH played an important role in advocating that unhoused people without a permanent address must be allowed to register to vote. NUH members often used the addresses of the shelters where they were living when registering to vote.

of the incipient power of the poor and a refutation of the dominant messages told every day about them: that they are stupid, lazy, helpless, and pitiable. These successes were also a corrective to the mistaken belief that poor people can at best only be a spark of spontaneous outrage and dissent, but never an organized force capable of wielding real and effective political power. The NUH proved this idea false. Led by some of the poorest people in the country, they built a highly sophisticated organization that became a political and spiritual home for thousands. In the process, they won over to their cause supporters from every walk of life and, for a time, captured the attention of the nation. Major news outlets covered their housing takeovers, and in 1987 *USA Today* named Chris Sprowal, the cofounder and president of the NUH, as a top-ten leader to watch.

At the heart of the NUH was a sweeping and visionary ethos, comprising three main principles. First, poor people can be agents of transformational change, not simply victims of a cruel history. Second, the power of the poor depends on their ability to unite across their differences, and this unity is a key to opening the way toward social transformation. Third, it is possible to abolish poverty. These guiding principles were crystalized in two of their slogans: "Homeless, Not Helpless" and "No Housing, No Peace." These deceptively simple phrases communicate an entire worldview and theory of change. In the first, we hear a fundamental, too-often obscured truth about the poor: their conditions do not define who they are nor do they limit their capacity to change both their own lives and the world around them. In the second slogan, their agency is named: there will be no peace and quiet until the demand for essential human needs is met.

There is another NUH slogan that has echoed through the years: "You Only Get What You're Organized to Take." This is a personal favorite because it expresses a core argument of this book. Poverty in this country will not end because of the goodwill of those who hold political power and wealth or through the charitable actions of well-meaning and sympathetic people alone. A change of such scale requires a protagonist with a more pressing and compelling agenda. Poverty will end when poor people refuse to allow it to exist; when they and their allies refuse to allow society to be complacent about the death and suffering caused by economic deprivation. Poverty will end when poor people become a united and organized force, not for one action, campaign, political moment, or election, but through a long-term human rights movement that can rally a critical mass of society to their cause and reorder the political and economic priorities of our nation. It is a simple and explosive idea.

THE MYTH OF SCARCITY

Social movements rise and fall on their ability to transform, through the power of collective action, previously unimaginable ideas into commonsense realities. We are not alone in believing that poverty can be abolished, and there is growing sentiment, especially among young people, that our nation's economic system is wildly out of sync and that big changes are both necessary and possible. Still, those of us who believe that poverty is a needless relic of the past are often derided in the press and polite society as naive or deluded. Critics and skeptics often reply with a tired, well-worn rebuttal: "Ending poverty sounds good, but be realistic. It has always existed." Other times people scold us for "pie-in-the-sky" thinking and explain, always with a knowing voice, that "there is not enough to go around." And perhaps the favorite criticism, disguised as a question, by many who oppose funding for anti-poverty programs is: "How are you going to pay for that?"

For most of us, the workings of our economy are fairly opaque and we are told it is best left to those who *really* understand it. When politicians, policy makers, and economists raise the specter of scarcity, they often speak in technocratic language that sounds smart and sensible. They talk in terms of balancing the budget, avoiding cumbersome debt, and limiting irresponsible spending. We are not economists, nor are we politicians or policy wonks, and this is not a book about the complex dynamics of capitalism and public policy. Noam and I are anti-poverty organizers and I am a preacher and a biblical scholar. But when it comes to the biggest questions about our economy, it is impossible for us to ignore how our moral vision as a society is constrained by an extremely limited economic vision.

We are reminded so often about the supposed scarcity of resources that it has become a seemingly unmovable fact of our public life, conditioning many of us to temper our boldest convictions into the weak and narrow frame of what we are told is "politically possible." When we step back, though, and take a wide view of the resources that are actually at our nation's disposal, is it clear that scarcity is a lie, a political invention, used to cover up vast reservoirs of capital and technology that could be marshaled to meet the needs of every person in this country and the world. We are not naive: unshackling this abundance is not a small or simple task. It will require major adjustments to the way we organize our public life, including tackling, head-on, the massive and widening wealth inequality at the base of our society. But we should at least be honest enough to acknowledge that when poverty is rationalized as an intractable issue, we are being offered a cynical, and inaccurate, view of the world.

Consider the early years of the COVID-19 pandemic, which marked the most unequal recession in modern American history, dwarfing the financial crisis of 2007–2008. When the virus first exploded in 2020, Jeff Bezos was the only American with a net worth of more than $100 billion. By the end of the year, he was joined by Mark Zuckerberg, Bill Gates, and Elon Musk. At Amazon, where the median pay in 2020 was about $30,000 a year, Bezos could have distributed the $71.4 billion he made that year to his own 810,000 employees and he still would have had more than $100 billion left.[11] And the money kept rolling in. Between 2020 and 2023, according to Oxfam USA, American billionaires increased their wealth by nearly one-third, totaling over $1 trillion.[12] Meanwhile, more than two-thirds of Americans in 2023 reported concern that if they lost their job they would be unable to afford their living expenses for more than one month.*[13]

This last point is especially damning, since the first and largest pandemic stimulus bill, Donald Trump's 2020 CARES Act, handed out billions of dollars' worth of benefits to the upper middle class, the rich, and corporations. Many of us only remember the $1,200 checks that low- and middle-income taxpayers received in the mail, but the bill also included provisions that favored the well-off, including higher corporate interest expense deductions, flexible corporate loss rules, increased charitable tax deductions, and historic tax breaks for the super-rich. Other parts of the CARES Act, like the Paycheck Protection Program (PPP), gave generously to large corporations. In 2022, the National Bureau of Economic Research found that more than 70 percent of the PPP funds that were meant to relieve the burden of lost work for everyday Americans were instead used by businesses to pay off their multinational investors, creditors, and suppliers.[14] Through these and other legislative actions, the pandemic became another opportunity for the wealthiest Americans to exploit a national crisis for their own gain—a new laboratory for disaster capitalism.

In 2020, while corporate coffers were filling back up with federal dollars, Feeding America, a network of over two hundred food banks, reported that more than sixty million people were seeking help from their affiliates and other charitable institutions, often standing for hours in crowded lines.[15] The absurdity of millions going hungry in the first year of the pandemic was accentuated by the fact that billions

---

* The unequal accumulation of wealth during the pandemic only intensified a process that was already well underway. Between 2013 and 2023, according to Oxfam USA, American billionaires got 86 percent richer, claiming $37 of every $100 of wealth created in our economy, while the bottom 50 percent of the country earned only $2 of that wealth. By 2024, there were an unprecedented 813 American billionaires and the list of Americans worth more than $100 billion had expanded to include ten people. This number will likely grow even higher in the coming years.

of dollars' worth of food was being burned and buried by big agricultural firms that could no longer get their products to market amid the breakdown of brittle, profit-driven supply chains.[16] Meanwhile, companies like Tyson Foods, the largest producer of chicken in the country, made record profits by jacking up their prices far beyond the rate of rising inflation.[17]

Perhaps the greatest myth told about wealth in this country is that it is self-made, the product of individual hard work rightfully earned and kept. But even a cursory glance at the balance sheets of the biggest companies shows that much of the wealth accrued at the top comes at the expense of those at the bottom. This dynamic plays out in times of both crisis and relative stability, not only through price gouging by corporations like Tyson, but through the suppression of wages and worker organizing, the increase in work hours with no raises, the construction of highly exploitative labor models, and government subsidies and bailouts. This unequal accumulation of wealth also comes from what could very well be the largest entitlement program in the country: our tax system.

Over the last seventy years, the tax rate of the top 0.01 percent decreased by over 83 percent as a share of their wealth.[18] This means that as the rich have gotten richer, they have paid a vanishingly small percentage of their wealth back into the economy. In the 1950s and 1960s, the top marginal tax rate—the amount of income paid in taxes for every dollar earned by the very rich—was close to 90 percent.[19] Today, it is 37 percent. These decades-long tax cuts have not only supercharged the accumulation of wealth by the already wealthy but hurt the rest of us by decreasing the amount of money available to the government and worsening national deficits. Falling public revenues have then been used by politicians as justification for opportunistic attacks on public spending, especially on social welfare programs that benefit the poor.[20]

And yet, one of the steadiest features of our economy is a permanent program of corporate welfare. At the state and federal level, alongside tax cuts, hundreds of billions of dollars in subsidies are handed out to the biggest companies every year. Before the pandemic, for example, taxpayers in multiple states paid Amazon a total of $3.7 billion in economic development subsidies, covering everything from new warehouses to a fashion studio in New York City.[21] In 2020, Amazon was valued at over $1 trillion, saturating the portfolios of its largest shareholders. And in a perverse sense, all of this wealth does trickle down, as Reaganomics argued—however, it trickles down not in broad societal benefit, but in generational inheritance. Between now and 2045, an estimated $21 trillion will circulate within the country's richest families, protected by the government through accommodating estate laws and IRS loopholes.[22] The foundational American myth of the self-made person crumbles under the dumbfounding weight of dynastic wealth.

———

Even just a small fraction of the untouched capital of America's billionaires could go a long way to solving endemic problems like homelessness, hunger, health and education inequity, and low wages. The equitable redistribution of abundantly available but hoarded resources in the private sector could also reinforce our public capacity to address poverty in its entirety. Today, nearly half of the *mandatory* federal budget—annual spending that does not rely on legislative appropriations and has historically been insulated from the most damaging political whims of the moment—goes to Social Security and Medicare. These popular public programs, which are now under assault by leading Republicans, are vitally important safeguards for the retired and elderly. Although they are far from perfect, their relative success is a suggestion of what robust social protections could offer all of us, independent of our age and our value as workers.

Meanwhile, the federal *discretionary* budget—money appropriated by Congress every year—offers damning evidence of our nation's distorted spending priorities. In 2023, researchers with the National

Priorities Project found that out of the $1.8 trillion federal discretion-
ary budget, $1.1 trillion was spent on militarized programs: on the Pen-
tagon and its ability to wage war, on the deportation and detention of
immigrants and refugees, and on the disproportionate imprisonment
and policing of racially oppressed people and the poor.[23]

The Pentagon budget is the keystone of a war economy that has
become an ever present, deadening force in our lives. That so many
of us do not question or even notice the militarization of our society
reflects how we fail to understand the issue of scarcity as a whole. The
Pentagon budget has grown every year for over a decade. In 2023, after
the United States pulled out of Afghanistan, the Biden administration still increased military spending to a record-high $816 billion for
just one year, more than half of the entire discretionary budget, and,
incredibly, even more than the Pentagon itself requested.[24] Especially
troubling is the fact that these resources are increasingly and inextricably tied up in the private defense industry and their profit models:
more than half of the Pentagon budget is now used to pay private
military contractors.[25]

American military spending, the highest in the world, is greater
than the next nine countries on the list combined.[26] This money is
used for a range of purposes: it sustains a tangled network of over 750
US military bases in eighty countries;[27] it finances new generations
of superfluous weapons systems; it pays for the Pentagon's ability to
wage multiple active military fronts across the world; and it advances
a nuclear weapons program that perpetuates dangerous nuclear proliferation and brinkmanship. To fuel all of this activity, the Pentagon has
become the largest institutional polluter in the world, the machinery
of war thus functioning as a prime catalyst of the climate crisis.[28]

In an age of historic partisan gridlock, the military is one of
the only true remaining bipartisan issues, evidenced in recent years
not only through its annual budget but through additional military
aid that Congress has appropriated for countries like Saudi Arabia,
Ukraine, and Israel. In 2023–24, the Israeli Defense Force dropped

thousands of American-made bombs on Gaza, leveling entire cities, directly killing tens of thousands of people—including entire family lines—and starving and displacing millions. In July 2024, public health experts conservatively estimated that in the final analysis the number of Gazan deaths attributable to the American-sponsored devastation could total in the hundreds of thousands.[29] In a very basic sense, this was a war on the poor, prosecuted by one very wealthy nation through the generous support of an even wealthier one. Given the twin conditions of global economic inequality and rising authoritarianism and political violence, we worry that Gaza, one of the poorest places on earth,[30] is not a deviation from the norm, but the future for poor and dispossessed people elsewhere.

In the US, the idea that the military is a pathway to economic security is core to our national narrative and remains a popular political talking point, especially among conservatives. This idea serves to justify both building up the military and cutting government social programs and protections. But it is not especially true that the military is a guaranteed route to long-term economic security. In 2021, entry-level enlistees in the Armed Forces made $45,000 a year, while the CEOs of the top five military contractors cumulatively earned $287 million.[31] In fact, while just a few men make money off war, many active-duty service members and veterans are so poor that they rely on food stamps and are eventually made homeless. And still, in a time of rising costs and low wages, when the remaining threads of the social safety net are being shredded and privatized, many young people see enlisting as one of their only options for economic mobility. There may not be a military draft in the US, but there is a poverty draft, which pushes thousands of people to sign up every year.

On the other side of the proverbial coin, less than two out of every five dollars of the 2023 federal discretionary budget was used to fund socially beneficial programs like public education, childcare, housing, disaster relief, debt cancellation, and environmental protections.[32] The

National Priorities Project reports that a fairly modest decrease in the Pentagon budget of $100 billion a year, when properly redirected, could increase our ability to fund public housing tenfold, send one in three kids to Head Start, and provide healthcare for 70 percent of uninsured adults.[33] An even larger reprioritization of spending could guarantee these and other anti-poverty measures for everyone who needs them and transform our war economy into a peace economy, structured around the preservation of life and the long-term health of our planet.

Our country's militarized spending is often justified through the rhetoric of security—securing our borders, securing our streets, securing democracy and freedom—but the overwhelming evidence of history is that war is motivated by the drive for power, profit, and resources. In the process, our nation becomes soul sick. The point is not just that our military spending diverts funds from programs that could uplift entire generations, but that war, in the most essential sense, devalues and obliterates human life, especially the lives of the poor, both at home and abroad. In this era of mass abandonment amid abundance, it is time we had an honest conversation about whose security, exactly, our resources are defending.

JUBILEE ECONOMICS

What might it actually look like to promote the long-term security of our society? As close readers of the Bible, we often return to the millennia old concept of Jubilee, that immortal trumpet blast of liberation, which has echoed down through the ages and taught us much about how to imagine a more sensible and humane economics for our own time.

In the books of Leviticus and Deuteronomy, the ancient Israelites establish a covenant with God in which every seven years "the land shall have a sabbath of sabbaths" and every fifty years there will be a year of Jubilee. Debt slaves are freed and people who had to sell their land in order to survive, or who took out interest-bearing loans and were foreclosed on, are restored to their homes. The land is left untouched by the tools of production and everyone is called to live off of its abundance. Without cultivated agriculture to fuel military activity, imperial war and plunder are brought to a standstill and, in an early form of environmental stewardship and preservation, the earth is finally able to regenerate from overwork. Through Jubilee, the land and all of creation are freed from the abuses of human hands and revert back to God for the benefit of all. In the Bible, this society-wide redistribution of resources is considered the most sacred of times. Among all human acts, Jubilee is the most important way that we can honor life.

Close to 1,500 years after the Jubilee codes were written down in the Torah, Jubilee reappears through the actions of Jesus and his disciples. In his first sermon, Jesus preaches: "The spirit of the Lord is upon me because the Lord has anointed me to bring good news to the poor; he has sent me to bind up the brokenhearted, to proclaim liberty to the captives and the opening of the prison to those who are bound; to proclaim the year of the Lord's favor" (Isaiah 61:1). When Jesus mentions "the year of the Lord's favor," he is explicitly referring to the economic practices of Jubilee.

Debt bondage was a key feature of the Roman economy and the empire as a whole was dangerously top-heavy, palatial estates existing beside widespread poverty and dispossession. In their revolt against the Roman Empire and its debt agents, Jesus and his disciples attempt to revive the commonsense economics of their ancestors, demanding not just a year of Jubilee but a lasting period in which economic exploitation is undone, hunger and homelessness are rectified, and the poor are made whole. In the eyes of Jesus and the movement he is leading, Jubilee is more than one policy or one moment in time—it is the full flowering of God's love and grace, not in heaven after death, but right here on earth, in the fertile dirt of the living.

At the beginning of the pandemic, as the engine of world industry ground to a halt and time itself was imbued with a weighted sense of immediacy, it was clear that this was a moment to revive the ancient call for Jubilee. In the early weeks of the global lockdown, Indian writer Arundhati Roy suggested that this sudden crisis, this enormous disruption of so-called normalcy, could be an opportunity to embrace new ways of relating to one another and the world around us.

> Historically, pandemics have forced humans to break with the past and imagine the world anew. This one is no different. It is a portal, a gateway, between one world and the next. We can choose to walk through it, dragging the carcasses of our prejudice and hatred, our avarice, our data banks and dead ideas, our dead rivers and smoky skies behind us. Or we can walk through lightly, with little luggage, ready to imagine another world. And ready to fight for it.[34]

For a brief moment, the pandemic portal offered a glimpse of what a world transformed by the justice of Jubilee could look like. In quieted cities across the globe, air pollution momentarily dissipated, opening up the skies and loosening the atmospheric stranglehold created by fossil fuel emissions. The worst and most lethal consequences of the virus were avoided in countries with communally oriented networks of care and more robust social safety nets. Here in the United States, where the same is untrue, the virus was allowed to spread along the historic fissures of our society, inflicting disproportionate damage in poor communities, including among low-wage workers who were hailed as "essential" even as they labored on the front lines of the pandemic and died in record numbers.[35] And yet, amid this preventable disaster, there were small but encouraging signs that a new, more life-affirming social contract might be in the making. Although most

of the economic gains in this period went to the wealthy and corporations, emergency federal policies signaled a fleeting, but noteworthy,
departure from the neoliberal consensus of the previous decades. These
policies offered powerful proof that it is possible to tackle poverty in
its many forms when the political will exists.

Under intense public pressure, the government temporarily embraced an embryonic and piecemeal form of Jubilee economics—
instituting moratoriums on evictions and student loan payments,
extending unemployment insurance and access to the Supplemental
Nutrition Assistance Program (SNAP), expanding and extending
the Child Tax Credit (CTC), issuing stimulus payments directly
to tens of millions of households, and expanding Medicaid and the
Children's Health Insurance Program (CHIP). As the virus grew
and mutated, enrollment in these last two programs swelled by the
millions, including in states that have historically been antagonistic
toward even the most basic public medical coverage, demonstrating
their widespread necessity and usefulness in the lives of everyday
people. None of these policy decisions dealt with the full extent of
need nationwide and, noted previously, they represented a drop in the
bucket of the resources that could have been mobilized. Still, they
made a significant and measurable impact.

The expanded CTC is a good example. First created in 1997, the
program was originally designed as one among many diminished
replacements to the old welfare system, tethering the distribution of
public resources to the work status of families through tax credits.
Historically, households with both small and large incomes were
eligible for the program, and while better-off families were generally allowed to take full advantage of the credit, poorer families
were often permitted access only to partial credit. Incredibly, the
poorest families were excluded from receiving any support at all.
Before the pandemic, the CTC was fettered by a baseline income,
meaning that families below the threshold, including those that

were too poor to pay taxes, were ineligible. The neoliberal logic of the original policy was that only people who worked should receive public support. The expanded CTC, created in March 2021 through Joe Biden's American Rescue Plan, transformed this calculus and made the tax credit "fully refundable," available to families below the income threshold independent of their work or tax status. For the first time poor families across the board began receiving modest and regular cash infusions.

The results were staggering. By December 2021, more than sixty-one million children benefited from the expanded CTC and four million children were lifted above the official poverty line.[36] This marked the single largest drop in official child poverty in American history, including a historic 25 percent decrease in poverty among Black children, narrowing the racial gap among poor children overall. A report co-commissioned by the Kairos Center for Religions, Rights, and Social Justice and coauthored by our colleague Shailly Gupta Barnes* found that the monthly payments of up to $300 significantly improved the ability of families to catch up on rent, afford food more regularly, cover childcare expenses, and attend to other daily needs. Survey data also suggested that the expanded CTC helped improve parental depression, stress, and anxiety that often accompany poverty and the suffering of one's children. After receiving the CTC, one parent in Boston reported: "I didn't have to worry about, you know, certain things too much. [The CTC] certainly helped with bills. I mean pretty much the same things that I . . . try to take care of now. It did provide like a little bit of a cushion. Plus, I was able to, I'll say, accumulate a little bit of a savings."[37]

---

* Gupta Barnes is the policy director of the Kairos Center and the Poor People's Campaign: A National Call for Moral Revival. She is one of the nation's leading grassroots anti-poverty experts and has authored many of our groundbreaking reports and policy agendas over the last decade.

How extraordinary, then, that rather than being embraced as the first sure-footed step through the pandemic portal, the expanded CTC was abandoned at the end of 2021 less than a year after it was created. The oppressive weight of our "dead ideas," to use Roy's formulation, crushed the possibility of Jubilee. Led by a block of united Republicans, as well as a few recalcitrant Democrats, Congress axed the fairly modest program, invoking the feeble myth of scarcity as justification even as billions of dollars were being siphoned off to the largest corporations and the military industrial complex. When asked about the expanded CTC, Congressman Kevin Brady, a Republican from Texas, claimed, "The country frankly doesn't have the time or the money for the partisan, expensive provisions such as the Child Tax Credit."[38] By 2023, many of the other emergency protections and investments suffered the same ignoble fate. Eviction moratoriums were allowed to expire, student debt servicers once again started knocking, and states, that were required to offer continuous Medicaid coverage at the beginning of the pandemic were allowed to cut recipients across the board and force people to reapply. By May 2024, over twenty-two million people were removed from Medicaid, undoing much of the progress made by the 2010 Affordable Care Act.[39]

The first years of the pandemic were an extended period of cognitive whiplash, offering a disorienting flurry of both hopeful and heartbreaking lessons. Jubilee, with its sweeping societal mandate, was never actually on the negotiating table, and yet for the first time tens of millions of people directly experienced, if only for a fleeting moment, what it might look like to "proclaim the year of the Lord's favor." The eviction and student loan moratoriums were a small but inspiring evocation of a world in which the profit motive is enervated of its power and every human being is housed and unburdened from the weight of predatory debt. Similarly, Medicaid protections and programs like the expanded CTC were an irrefutable reminder that at any point our society could simply choose to direct our abundance toward the meeting of human needs. Through these various measures we learned anew that the resources *are* at hand to resolve some of our thorniest economic and social problems. Despite protestations that we do not know what to do or how to do it, the solutions are straightforward enough: guarantee people housing, provide people with healthcare, ensure that people are paid fairly and have the money they need to feed and clothe their families.

This kind of bottom-up social investment is not only rational and morally sound but widely popular. In 2024, survey results from the polling organization Navigator found that nearly three in four Americans—across racial, geographic, and partisan lines—supported increased public funding for healthcare (76 percent), education (73 percent), housing (72 percent), childcare (72 percent), and crackdowns on tax evasion by corporations and the wealthy (70 percent).[40] In light of ample evidence that we do not have a scarcity of resources, knowledge, or popular support to abolish poverty, it has become even more chillingly clear that we do have a scarcity of political will to implement and sustain a true vision of Jubilee economics. On this side of the pandemic portal, the question is, What will it take to adjust course? What will it take to build the political will necessary to release our abundance in all of its astonishing and enlivening potential?

A NEW AND UNSETTLING FORCE

At the beginning of the last full year of his life, Rev. Dr. Martin Luther King Jr. traveled to Jamaica for a six-week writing retreat.* What emerged was his final book: *Where Do We Go From Here: Community or*

---

* King made it a practice to take regular writing breaks and sabbaticals in order to reflect on his work and hone his strategic thinking. Unfortunately, organizers are rarely afforded the opportunity to do the same today amid the bedlam of funding cycles, campaigns, and elections. This is to the detriment of our movements, whose leaders would greatly benefit from additional time not just for rest, but deeper reflection and study.

Chaos? On the heels of the Civil Rights Movement's biggest legislative victories, King was decidedly sober. For years, he had recognized
that beyond the legal scaffolding of Jim Crow and institutionalized
racism—areas in which the movement had made some significant
gains—American capitalism continued to keep millions of Black
people locked in poverty in the South and elsewhere, alongside many
others from different racial and ethnic backgrounds. King himself
was surprised to learn that poor white people outnumbered poor
Black people nationally. He counseled that the movement still had
to make an evolutionary leap from "civil rights to human rights" and
from "reform to revolution."[41]

King's diagnosis of the malady of poverty amid plenty, as articulated in his final book, reads as if it were written yesterday: "The
contemporary tendency in our society is to base our distribution on
scarcity, which has vanished, and to compress our abundance into
the overfed mouths of the upper classes until they gag with super-
fluity. If democracy is to have breadth of meaning, it is necessary to
adjust this inequity. It is not only moral, but it is also intelligent. We
are wasting and degrading human life by clinging to archaic thinking."[42] For King, poverty and inequality were not just problems for
the poor. As he saw it, they were existential threats to the health
of the nation and the possibility of a democratic society. He feared
that if poverty, and the interlocking evils of racism and militarism,
went unaddressed, the United States would spiral into a maelstrom
of "spiritual death," a phrase that feels hauntingly relevant today.[43]
He believed the dawning of a new era of movement building was
necessary, requiring a protracted commitment that would capitalize
on the successes of the previous decade and continue to demand
fundamental change.

Where Do We Go from Here was published in the summer of 1967.
By then, King had already begun laying the groundwork for his
next, and ultimately last, campaign. Many of his supporters, including liberal, middle-class white Northerners, clergy, journalists, and

established civil rights leaders had already begun to turn away as the focus shifted from codified racism in the South to the deformities of a national system that many of them were implicated in and benefited from. His strategic takeaway was that the lack of unity among the poor was the Achilles' heel of a society in need of restructuring. If poor people could come together into new political alliances, across the lines that historically divided them, they would be uniquely positioned to lead a broad and powerful human rights movement.

In November and December 1967, King delivered the Massey Lectures on CBC Radio, an annual Canadian broadcast heard across the world. On air, with thousands listening, he shared the essential idea animating his dreams:

> The dispossessed of this nation—the poor, both white and Negro— live in a cruelly unjust society. They must organize a revolution against the injustice, not against the lives of the persons who are their fellow citizens, but against the structures through which the society is refusing to take means which have been called for, and which are at hand, to lift the load of poverty. . . . There are millions of poor people in this country who have very little, or even nothing, to lose. If they can be helped to take action together, they will do so with a freedom and a power that will be a new and unsettling force in our complacent national life.[44]

A few months later, in March 1968, just weeks before King's assassination, more than sixty organizers gathered at the Southern Christian Leadership Conference office in Atlanta to discuss the prospect of a united campaign against poverty. Among them were representatives from the welfare rights movement (who for years had been calling for a similar campaign, a story told further in chapter 3), Chicano and Puerto Rican organizers, farmworkers, antiwar and student activists, Native American leaders, and poor white folks from Appalachia and beyond. There were also Christian and Jewish clergy, as well as leaders from organized labor. One third were women—an inadequate but still notable number for the time.

Once everyone settled in their seats, King surveyed the motley group and laid out his theory of the case with firm and measured excitement:

> We are assembled here together today with common problems. Bringing together ethnic groups that maybe have not been together in this type of meeting in the past—I know I haven't been in a meeting like this. And it has been one of my dreams that we would come together and realize our common problems. . . . Power for poor people will really mean having the ability, the togetherness, the assertiveness, and the aggressiveness to make the power structure of this nation say yes when they may be desirous to say no.[45]

King was articulating the need to do more than build just another coalition. What he was calling for was the need to awaken the sleeping giant of the poor, and in Atlanta he was attempting to weave together more tightly the dreams and destinies of the nation's most promising and powerful social movements. He would not survive to see this dream put into practice, nor would the nascent Poor People's Campaign survive much longer after his assassination. But other leaders did their best to carry the campaign forward. After King was killed on April 4 in Memphis while supporting a sanitation workers' strike, his wife, Coretta Scott King, traveled the country, insisting that the campaign must continue. Six weeks later, thousands of poor people flooded into Washington, DC. On May 12, Mother's Day, the National Welfare Rights Organization, led by poor mothers on welfare, organized the campaign's inaugural march alongside Mrs. King.

Afterward, thousands of people remained in the capitol, staging a peaceful occupation of the National Mall for six weeks between May and June 1968. Resurrection City was a mass, multiracial encampment of the poor that functioned like an autonomous city, with its own school, hospital, food stations, and cultural institutions. It began with grief-stricken but steely-eyed determination and ended in disaster, when the National Guard was called in to tear it down. After the residents of Resurrection City were violently evicted from the capitol on June 24, the words of Coretta Scott King, shared a few days earlier during the campaign's fifty-thousand-person strong "Solidarity Day Rally," echoed mournfully in the humid air:

> In this society, violence against poor people and minority groups is routine. I remind you that starving a child is violence. Suppressing a culture is violence. Neglecting school children is violence. Punishing a mother and her child is violence. Discrimination against a working man is violence. Ghetto housing is violence. Ignoring medical needs is violence. Contempt of poverty is violence. Even the lack of willpower to help humanity is a sick and sinister form of violence.[46]

In the years to come, the story of this revolutionary campaign was swept away from our public memory. But some among the poor kept the idea alive. I first learned about the 1968 Poor People's Campaign from unhoused organizers, some of whom were directly involved with Dr. King, while taking over a vacant house in Philadelphia in the mid-1990s. As we attempted to ignite a new multiracial movement of the poor, we studied the strategic principles that inspired the 1968 campaign, as well as its strengths and limitations, including the ways that it had fractured after King was killed. For the campaign to have reached its full potential for example, there would have needed to be not one but "many Martins" who shared the mantle of movement leadership and were positioned to carry its radical vision forward.

The 1968 Poor People's Campaign, like the National Union of the Homeless in the 1980s and 1990s, may have been imperfect, but it is a reminder that poor people have always been able to come together, against great odds, on the basis of their shared conditions and aspirations.* In every generation, poor people have risen up to defend their communities and advance the dream of a genuinely egalitarian society. Today these excavated histories carry with them an urgent and incendiary message from the past: if we came together, so can you.

People often ask us what our plan is to end poverty. Usually they want to know what our policy positions and prescriptions are, a line of inquiry we have plenty of thoughts on. But sometimes we prefer to first reorient the logic of the question, and for this King is a favorite resource. After being endlessly asked for an itemized list of plans and demands in the leadup to the Poor People's Campaign, he wrote in *Where Do We Go from Here*:

> When a people are mired in oppression, they realize deliverance when they have accumulated the power to enforce change. When they have amassed such strength, the writing of a program becomes almost an administrative detail. It is immaterial who presents the program. What is material is the presence of an ability to make events happen. . . . The call to prepare programs distracts us excessively from our basic and primary tasks. . . . We are, in fact, being counseled to put the cart before the horse. . . . Our nettlesome task is to discover how to organize our strength into compelling power so that government cannot elude our demands. We must develop, from strength, a situation in which government finds it wise and prudent to collaborate with us.[47]

---

* Just like the 1968 Poor People's Campaign, the National Union of the Homeless suffered from significant challenges, including the flood of drugs into their communities, especially crack cocaine, the co-optation of and their overdependence on a handful of leaders, and insufficient political education and consciousness raising among their base. Externally, the organization was also operating in a deeply reactionary political context amid stultifying economic change, including the inexorable march of gentrification. In 2019, unhoused organizers relaunched the National Union of the Homeless and are now organizing new chapters across the country. Every winter the Kairos Center collaborates with them on a season of educational sessions, religious gatherings, memorial services, and protests. We call it the Winter Offensive.

To end poverty, we certainly need our smartest and most creative ideas brought to the table. But we won't end poverty with the right analysis alone. We will end it out there, in the world. Today, there are millions of poor and dispossessed people across the country with little or nothing to lose. They are ready to become the new society's architects and builders, but only if they are brought into a movement that reflects their interests and is rooted in their collective leadership. As the tectonic plates of our society continue to shift in massively disruptive and unpredictable ways, we can no longer be content with a politics of pragmatism. We must be willing to expand our imaginations and embolden our agitation until we have amassed the kind of organized power King once envisioned—a power so compelling and substantial it can no longer be denied.

CHAPTER TWO

THE LIES WE'RE TOLD

"I don't find anywhere in the scripture," the congressman from Ohio argued in the chambers of the House Budget Committee, "where Jesus said it was Caesar's job to feed the poor and to clothe the widows and to take care of the orphans. He said it was the churches' responsibility. It is the community's responsibility. It is your neighbors' responsibility, it is your responsibility, as a neighbor, to do those things."[1]

It was a June morning in 2019 and the six members of the Poor People's Campaign: A National Call for Moral Revival (PPC) sitting behind the ornate table stared back in disbelief. It is always a little shocking to hear arguments that abdicate the government's responsibility to care for its citizens, but it was especially distressing that this was coming from a politician charged with developing the budget for one of the wealthiest countries in the world. Bishop William J. Barber II picked up the mic. "First of all," he said, "it is interesting that you all would define yourself as Caesar. That in itself is . . . right? I mean, we need to stop for a minute to even hear that." Self-identified Christian members of Congress likening themselves to Caesar? "And then the next thing is that you have to read the 2,000 scriptures in the Bible that talk about how society is supposed to treat the poor, the immigrant, the least of these . . . Jesus started his first sermon with good news to the *ptochos*. That is a Greek word which means those who have been made poor by economic systems."

It was the last day of our Poor People's Moral Action Congress, hosted at a small Catholic college in Washington, DC. A year earlier, we had relaunched the Poor People's Campaign on the fiftieth anniversary of the 1968 campaign. That morning, we were invited to a House of Representatives Budget Committee hearing titled "Poverty in America: Economic Realities of Struggling Families." We packed a bus full of people, while close to one thousand more watched the livestream in the college gymnasium.

As guests of the committee's chair, a Democrat from Kentucky, we were allowed six testifiers. These were Kenia Alcocer, a young undocumented Mexican mom fighting evictions and gentrification in Los Angeles; Savannah Kinsey, a twenty-one-year-old white lesbian woman from Johnstown, Pennsylvania, suffering from job loss, benefit cuts, and healthcare issues; Callie Greer, a Black mother of five from Alabama who had lost two children—her son to gun violence and her daughter to breast cancer; and Christopher Overfelt, a white air force veteran, substitute teacher, and farmer from Kansas. Joining them were Reverend Barber and myself, the cochairs of the PPC.

We arrived with a clear game plan. We weren't there to share sad stories or to beg for sympathy but to give voice to the needless suffering in our country and demonstrate the fighting spirit of poor people, including our testifiers, all of whom are organizers and community leaders. We had also come to broaden the country's understanding of who is poor and why they are poor, and to show Congress how different things could be. The day before we had released a report, *The Poor People's Moral Budget: Everybody Has the Right to Live*, which detailed the many troubling ways our public money is spent—funding for war, mass incarceration, deportations, fossil fuel subsidies, tax breaks for the wealthy—and how our society's abundance could be used to abolish poverty through key policy shifts. In the report we outlined how the public costs of poverty almost always outweigh the costs of eliminating poverty. For example, the Children's Defense Fund "estimated that the cost of lost productivity, worsened health, and increased crime rates that stem from child poverty total roughly $700 million per year or 3.5% of GDP," whereas "eliminating child poverty between the prenatal years and age 5 would increase lifetime earnings between $53,000 and $100,000 per child—a total lifetime benefit of $20 to $36 billion for all babies born in a given year."[2]

The title of our report reflected our belief that government budgets are never objective or apolitical. Every line item in every budget is more than just an administrative detail; it's a declaration of moral priorities. We had done the math and we were prepared to defend our case in the language of cold, hard numbers. But no amount of accounting could fully capture the fundamental point we had come to make: that behind the obfuscation of spending and saving, there are real lives—beautiful, complicated, invaluable lives—that are broken and cut short when they aren't prioritized in our nation's budget.

During her testimony, Callie Greer made this point crystal clear. Speaking through tears, she described how her daughter Venus Colley-Mims began complaining about a little knot in her breast in 2011. Colley-Mims, who was in her early thirties, was unemployed and in theory should have qualified for Medicaid. But she lived in Alabama, one of ten states that have still not expanded Medicaid coverage under the Affordable Care Act,[3] and without insurance she regularly sought treatment at the emergency room of their local hospital. At first, the doctors ignored her complaints, refusing to send her for a mammogram. One visit, though, the doctor noticed a terrible odor and asked, "What's that smell?" Colley-Mims replied, "It's my breast—it's rotting."[4] By then, it was too late. She had stage-four breast cancer, and although doctors pursued aggressive treatment, it ultimately spread to her lungs, liver, bones, and brain, quickly consuming her until she died a preventable death in 2013. Six years later, Greer stared straight at the budget committee members and succinctly explained: "Venus should not be dead. Willfull and deliberate policy violence killed Venus."[5]

The minority leader of the committee, a Republican from Arkansas, was unmoved by our presence, and his opening remarks were a litany of stale and untrue narratives about poverty. He argued against public funding for anti-poverty programs, pointing to the supposed failures of the War on Poverty in the 1960s, while glossing over its successes and its premature abandonment by the government. In place of public investments, he suggested a combination of tax cuts, deregulation, military service, and personal gumption. His claim: people earn their own success through hard work, not collective support.

To emphasize his point, he invited two Black pastors to testify. They denounced welfare, claiming that it creates a vicious cycle of dependency, and explained that their own escapes from poverty were thanks to perseverance, self-sufficiency, and the love of their church. It was disturbing to witness the willing part the pastors played in the minority leader's strategy—especially since their own stories actually *included* receiving life-saving public support through government jobs and housing programs. It was even more upsetting to see the way the minority leader used their faith and race as political insulation for his racist and reactionary ideas. After the pastors' testimonies, a string of Republican congressmen, forced to speak directly on the issue and no longer able to ignore or minimize poverty, admitted that they themselves came from districts riddled with economic need. They proudly explained that they understood poverty intimately and had achieved the American dream with elbow grease and through the grace of God. One representative even had the gall to herald Head Start as an effective example of private charity, completely ignoring the fact that the publicly funded early childhood development program was a cornerstone of the War on Poverty that he and others were now calling a failure.

The Democratic representatives were more sympathetic to our testimonies, but some of their comments revealed limited and unimaginative thinking about poverty and our nation's ability to overcome it. A few of them immediately zeroed in on specific and technical policy questions but were unable, or unwilling, to ask deeper ones about the root causes of poverty. They spent time promoting the policies they had supported in the past and celebrating what they had already done, but they largely sidestepped our call for bold and immediate action in the present. They struggled to envision doing anything other than tinkering around the edges. And almost all of the representatives in the Budget Committee, both Democrat and Republican, seemed to prefer hearing themselves talk about poverty rather than listening to and lifting up the stories and solutions put forward by poor people themselves.

As I listened to the lies and rhetorical evasions, I could feel my pulse acccelerating in exasperation. Over my clerical collar, I was wearing a stole with the words: "Jesus Was a Poor Man."* Leaning into the mic, I exclaimed:

> I just want to start by saying that I'm stunned that basically we've had unanimous acknowledgment that poverty is widespread across this country. We have pulled together a group of testifiers who are deeply and personally impacted by these problems. They are in the room. And people are not talking to them. . . . And then people are being blamed for the problems that this society has caused. . . . We need a real, serious conversation in this country, led by those that are most impacted. And I love this question about "does the Bible say anything about what nations, what Caesars, are supposed to do." Because Matthew 25 says, "I was hungry," to the nations, not to a church, not to a charity, not to an individual. I was hungry and what did your nation do?

---

* This stole was quilted by my friend and colleague Rev. Jessica Williams, inspired by one of my favorite banners from the 1968 Poor People's Campaign: "Don't Laugh Folks, Jesus Was a Poor Man." These words were written on the canopy of a mule train that carried dozens of poor people from Marks, Mississippi—where Dr. King first decided to call for the campaign—all the way to Washington, DC.

The congressional hearing was a master class in the distorted narratives we are told every day about poverty and the poor. In such a hyperpartisan context, the mental gymnastics and finger pointing were heightened for political effect. But beneath the posturing nearly every committee member fell back on well-worn myths about society and government, morality and religion, charity and personal responsibility, all of which reside at the center of our public life. "I have heard so many distortions today that it's actually hurting my ears," Bishop Barber concluded. "It is bothersome that in the 21st century we still have these weak, tired, old mythologies. . . . That people would stick with their partisan line and ignore the people who are really hurting." On the bus ride back to the Moral Action Congress, our testifiers, and the folks who came to support them, reflected on what they had heard. Sitting next to me was a young fast-food worker from Pennsylvania who was still in a state of stunned disbelief. She told me that if she was failing at her job, she would be fired. She then asked me how these representatives could admit there was poverty in their districts, be serving on the Budget Committee, and decide not to budget poverty elimination? "They're the ones who should be fired!" she concluded.

Our visit to the capitol was a maddening experience, but it was also illuminating. The congresspeople had inadvertently, and helpfully, packed dozens of political education classes into a couple hours. Over the course of the morning, it became increasingly clear that their opposition to and inaction on anti-poverty policymaking were founded on phony sociological theories, broken economic models, and misleading theological interpretations that distort the biblical texts they referenced. The myths about poverty that surfaced in the congressional hearing fell apart when they were held up against the undeniable truth of our members' testimonies.

If movements begin with the telling of untold stories, they only endure when we are able to free ourselves from the old, bitter narratives that enable the violent status quo of our society. The previous chapter took on the myth of scarcity and concluded that ending poverty is possible. In the pages that follow, we explore three more myths that, while far from exhaustive, further reveal the misinformation we are exposed to every day: (1) the myth that poverty is an accidental or minor problem; (2) the myth that poor people are "crazy, lazy, and stupid"; and (3) the myth that poverty is ordained by God.

All of us are caught up in a tangle of mythology about poverty, a misleading hydra of deception and misdirection. It is time we slay that many-headed monster.

MYTH #1: POVERTY IS AN ACCIDENTAL OR MINOR PROBLEM

If the political history of poverty were recorded on the Richter scale, one quiet decision in 1969, made in an unremarkable administrative building in Washington, DC, might rise to the level of earthshaking magnitude. On August 29 of that year, the Bureau of the Budget (the predecessor of the Office of Management and Budget) delivered a dry, unfussy memo to every federal government agency, instructing them to use a new formula for statistical measurements of poverty. The result was the creation of the official poverty measure (OPM), which has remained in place to this day, save a few minor adjustments here and there. The seeds of the 1969 memo were planted six years earlier, when Mollie Orshansky, a statistician at the Social Security Administration, authored a study on possible ways to measure poverty. Her math itself was fairly simple. To start, she rifled through a 1955 Department of Agriculture (USDA) survey which found that families generally spent about one-third of their income on food. Then, using a "low-cost" food plan published by the USDA, she estimated how much a low-income family of four would have to spend in order to meet their basic food needs. Finally, she multiplied that number by three and arrived at $3,165: one possible threshold for a poverty income.[6]

Orshansky's study arrived at an auspicious moment. At the time, John F. Kennedy was two years into his presidency, having run on promises to tackle poverty. After Kennedy's assassination in 1963, the new president, Lyndon B. Johnson, announced the War on Poverty, quickly passing the Economic Opportunity Act and creating the Office of Economic Opportunity (OEO) to oversee his administration's anti-poverty programs. But in order to determine who qualified for the programs and whether the programs were having their intended effect, the OEO needed a way to measure poverty. Orshansky's method worked nicely, especially since the OEO's mandate was focused not on the poor as a whole but primarily on what the OEO called the "hard-core poor."[7] Six years later, the US Census also picked up Orshansky's formula, and a year after that, the 1969 memo cemented what had originally been an experimental and partial measure into a permanent one that continues to influence how we understand poverty and the methods we use to address it.

Fast-forward five decades, adjust for a few small changes to the measurement, factor in the rate of inflation, and the poverty threshold in 2023 was $14,508 per year for one person and $30,000 for a family of four. According to the OPM, about thirty seven million people were considered poor.[8] These numbers should be enough to shock the conscience of a nation as wealthy as ours. But in reality, the limited measuring tools we use today contribute to a major myth about poverty in America: that it is an anomaly, an experience on the margins of our society. Connected are the common beliefs that poverty is an accident, an unfortunate byproduct of transient economic cycles, or something only specific communities experience, whether people of color in cities or white people in rural communities.

Mark Rank, a social scientist who has written extensively on poverty, puts it this way: "Those in poverty are seen as strangers to mainstream America . . . yet it turns out that the vast majority of Americans will experience at least one year below the poverty line. Poverty touches all races, all regions of the country, and all age groups. Very few of us are immune from the reach of poverty at some point."[9] Poverty is not a static phenomenon. A one-time snapshot of people living under the OPM fails to accurately capture the wide swath of the population that will at some point experience official poverty. In addition to the nearly forty million people who live below the poverty line, there are at least another hundred million people teetering just one emergency above it—and often falling below it, into official poverty, when that emergency arrives.[10] That said, even this fuller appreciation for the truth behind the official numbers fails to address a deeper problem: how we define poverty itself.

From the beginning, the OPM was grounded in an arbitrary and shallow understanding of human need. Orshansky's formula may have appeared pragmatic in its simplicity, but by focusing on access to food as a base line, it didn't take full account of other critical expenses. It was also, by Orshansky's own reckoning, based on an assessment of how much was too little versus how much might be enough for a person to meet all of their needs. Years later, she reflected critically on how her formula was entrenched into law: "The best that can be said of the measure is that at a time when it seemed useful, it was there."[11]

Since 1969, even as so much has changed, the OPM has remained untouched. Food prices, the basis for the OPM, have skyrocketed beyond the rate of inflation. A host of other essential expenses, like housing, utilities, prescription medicine, child care, and college tuition aren't part of the calculation and have been further privatized and commodified. Meanwhile, wage growth has essentially stagnated over the last four decades. Since 1973, wages for the majority of workers have risen by only 9 percent and have actually fallen for people making lower incomes.[12] Productivity, on the other hand, has grown almost exponentially. This means that workers are making comparatively less than their parents' generation, even as they produce more for the economy. CEOs have also taken bigger chunks out of their workers' paychecks over the last fifty years. The average CEO in 1965 made twenty-one times more than their workers; in 2022, they made

344 times more.[13] The federal minimum wage has also remained shamefully low, affecting not only those who receive it but millions more whose employers determine their pay based on the floor that the minimum wage creates. If the federal minimum wage had kept up with the pace of productivity and the demands of inflation, it would be over $20 an hour, rather than $7.25.[14]

This dramatic polarization of wages has occurred in an era of economic transformation that has often been very antagonistic to the poor and beneficial for the rich. Since the 1960s, our economy has been completely reshaped, altering the kinds of jobs most of us have and the ways we do them. Today, growing parts of our workforce have shifted from manufacturing to the service sector, and workers are increasingly nonunionized, low-waged, part-time, or contracted, often without job security and benefits like healthcare, paid sick leave, and retirement plans. These stark labor conditions are accompanied by spiraling debt. In 2024, Americans held nearly $18 trillion in personal debt, an unprecedented sum that includes mounting credit, medical, and student debt.[15] The American dream is no longer a house with a white picket fence—it is to be debt free, even if that means having zero dollars in the bank.[16]

As if this weren't enough, an even more momentous change is already unfolding. As we approach the quarter mark of the twenty-first century, we are stepping firmly into a new technological era characterized by unparalleled levels of digital power. The Fourth Industrial Revolution, as elite economists and think tanks call it, promises a technological transformation that, in the words of World Economic Forum founder Klaus Schwab, is occurring at a "scale, scope, and complexity" never before experienced.[17] This revolution includes the integration of artificial intelligence and other labor-replacing technology into vast fields of in-person and remote work and the de-skilling of our labor force from the point of production all the way to the market. The old industrial model of the American workforce is dying and, even in the most optimistic scenarios about new and emerging industries like renewable energy, it is not likely to be revived.

Residents of Detroit, once the Silicon Valley of auto manufacturing, understand this viscerally. At the turn of the twentieth century, the Ford River Rouge Plant was the largest and most productive factory in the world, with a hundred thousand workers and its own municipal services. Today the plant employs a fraction of that number—about six thousand people—but with a surge in robotic innovation it produces even more cars than it did in the heady days of the 1930s.[18] This technological shift is just a glimpse into the far-reaching changes that, as one veteran auto worker and union organizer warned us, are "coming to a city near you." The dangers posed to workers by the Fourth Industrial Revolution are especially frustrating because these remarkable technological advances could help abolish poverty and inaugurate an unprecedented era of human flourishing (imagine 3D-printed public housing, modernized public infrastructure, reimagined food and water systems, critical climate interventions, and medical breakthroughs that are accessible to every community in the country). But when these new technologies are instead designed and implemented to maximize profits and market control for a few companies, the risk of widening poverty and inequality looms very large.

The result of all of this? The OPM fails to show us the ways in which a massive number of people are moving in and out of economic crisis throughout their lifetimes, a trend that will likely only intensify without significant, society-wide intervention. The way we currently define poverty muddies our ability to recognize the depth of deprivation all around us, especially if we are to understand poverty as the inability of a person to consistently meet their daily needs. When we use a too-narrow definition of poverty, we immediately separate the unhoused person from the precariously positioned day laborer, artist, college student, delivery person, warehouse worker, or nurse, concealing the conditions they have in common and which a large percentage of the country knows firsthand. We risk falling prey to the false belief that poverty is an accidental or unavoidable feature of an otherwise "healthy" economy; health, in this case, evaluated not by the well-being of the majority of people but through measurements of productivity like GDP, which have much more to do with the well-being of corporations at the very top of the economy.

Today, the low-waged, laid-off, and locked-out cannot so easily be separated from people of every walk of life who are being economically downsized and dislocated. The position of the poor is not one to be ignored or pitied, as if there were just a small section of people who can be cordoned off from the rest of society. When we talk about the economically marginalized, it is easy to imagine small bands of people living in the shadows and along the edges of society. But the truth is that the marginalized now make up the near majority of the country.

MYTH #2: POOR PEOPLE ARE CRAZY, LAZY, AND STUPID

In the summer of 2000, the Republican Party held its national convention in Philadelphia, the official coronation of the Bush-Cheney ticket. On the first day of the convention, a coalition of anti-poverty and anti-racist groups organized a nonviolent march of twenty thousand people down Broad Street, one of the city's main thoroughfares. The needle of our protest was threaded carefully: we opposed Bush and Cheney not because they were Republicans but because they represented the next chapter in a multi-decade saga of hawkish foreign policy and trickle-down economics that hurt the poor at home and abroad and implicated both major parties.

Ten thousand journalists were on the ground for the convention. We knew this was a unique opportunity for us to capture the news cycle and show the world both the reality of American poverty and the growing movement to abolish it. The police had spent the previous few weeks surveilling and illegally infiltrating the meetings of dozens of grassroots organizations that were planning to protest the convention, and they used the lead-up to the event to further militarize the city. They armed themselves with military-grade weapons and riot gear and built an expansive web of street-camera infrastructure that set in motion a new era of surveillance for one of the poorest and Blackest big cities in the country.

In brave and artful political deployment, our most vulnerable and visible members and allies —families with children, disabled activists in wheelchairs, and military veterans—volunteered to lead the march. By placing themselves directly between the police and the main body of the march, and with thousands of cameras documenting every movement, they defused the police's ability to respond with force.* In the process, we pulled off what was at the time the largest march to end poverty since the 1968 Poor People's Campaign.

After the Supreme Court manufactured Bush and Cheney's victory in November, we decided to bring our protest to their inauguration. In the freezing days of late January 2001, we erected an encampment near the US Capitol. We were an unusually diverse bunch, including a large number of poor and unhoused Black, Brown, and white families. Along the inaugural parade route, we set up a makeshift tent city with tarps and signs, while Bush and Cheney supporters, most of them white and conspicuously wealthy, marched by. Adults well into their forties and fifties stopped and screamed at us, singling out our children with a barrage of expletives and demeaning insults. In a grotesque caricature of herself, one blonde woman clad in a fur coat and heels cursed at a seven-year-old child who was visibly poor.

Back in Philadelphia, I had heard it all before: "welfare queen," "deadbeat dad," "white trash," and far worse. It was another thing, though, to witness this aristocratic, proto-fascistic vitriol so close to the heart of political power. During their campaign, Cheney had

---

* We later learned that a documentary film made about the events, *The Battle for Broad*, was used by the New York Police Department as a training video in the lead-up to the 2004 Republican National Convention and for future events in which they would come into contact with protestors.

often served as the less-filtered foil to Bush's disingenuous theme of "compassionate conservatism." It seemed that his most ardent supporters were now pulling back the curtain even wider, showcasing their unbridled contempt for the poor. For me, at just twenty-four years old, this was a defining moment in the story of my still-emerging political consciousness, and I remember the creeping feeling that it was only the beginning of something far worse yet to come. Today, we can trace a twenty-year line connecting this moment in 2001 to the January 6 insurrection, those inauguration marchers to the deep-pocketed business owners who populate the command posts of the Make America Great Again (MAGA) movement. In a 2021 report, researchers at the Chicago Project on Security and Threats found that the majority of the January 6 rioters were not "distressed farmers from mortgaged lands or laid-off workers from idled factories," as some in the media lazily implied, "but white-collar professionals and business owners. Their ranks included CEOs, a cardiovascular specialist, lawyers, a design engineer, accountants, and the founder and president of a firm that tests satellites."[19]

The other thing I remember about that day in early 2001 is that it was our presence as a multiracial group of poor people that appeared to disturb Bush's supporters the most, and it was actually the white children among us who received their most devoted animus. My sense is that for the well-to-do marchers, these kids stirred up a deeply ingrained hatred of poor white people that has always been present among the white upper class in this country, as well as the fear that poor whites will someday break free from the toxic solidarity of white supremacy and discover how much they have in common with poor people of color. I think these kids were especially unwelcome because their presence clearly undermined the conveniently racist lie that poverty is the self-inflicted problem of Black and Brown people alone.

Now, more than two decades later, leading elements within the Republican Party have increasingly eschewed euphemisms and political correctness altogether, airing their anti-immigrant, anti-Black, and anti-poor prejudices in unapologetically broad and brazen terms. In 2020, Marjorie Taylor Greene, the far-right businesswoman and politician from Georgia, was recorded saying: "I know a ton of white people that are as lazy and sorry and probably worse than black people . . . and that has everything to do with their bad choices and their personal responsibility. That is not a skin-color issue."[20]

The 2001 inauguration was a damning window into the ways poverty is moralized and pathologized as the result of a person's decisions and identities. Within this worldview, people are poor at best because of their problematic behaviors and values and at worst because they are immoral and wicked. The myth that poor people are lazy, crazy, stupid, and even biologically inferior paints poverty as an inherited or learned trait among members of a parasitic "underclass" or a "culture" and "cycle" of poverty. For the rich and powerful, this myth is a favorite in their bag of tricks, a conceptual sleight-of-hand that diverts our attention away from their hoarding of wealth and justifies their exploitation of the poor.

When cultural explanations are used to explain poverty, the conclusion is that poor people need to be fixed, rather than the systems that produce their poverty. And although the most hateful manifestations of this myth may emerge from authoritarian wannabes and Christian nationalists, I regularly encounter softer and subtler versions of it among liberal and progressive audiences. These versions include the belief that poor people are unintelligent, feeble-minded, and powerless to change their own lives, let alone lead movements for social change. I have lost track of the number of times I have given a presentation about poverty at a liberal university or church, only to have someone come up to me afterward to say that poor people don't have the ability to lead, either because they are not sophisticated enough or because they are too busy and bogged down with their own lives. Others lament that if poor people had fewer kids, got a better education, and stopped using their SNAP benefits to buy needless things, they wouldn't suffer so much.

I am also regularly told by liberals that I shouldn't use the word *poor* because it is offensive—despite the fact that organized poor people have long claimed the word for themselves, refusing to cede it to the moralizing instincts of supposedly sympathetic audiences. Beneath this criticism, there is often a deeper subconscious one: that poverty is something to be ashamed of, rather than an objective economic condition that has shamefully been produced by this rich nation. In truth, this condescension presents some of the most consistent challenges in my work.

Years ago, the largest Methodist women's organization in the country held its national convention at the same venue in Philadelphia that hosted the 2000 Republican convention. One of my mentors, Willie Baptist, and I were invited to speak about anti-poverty organizing in the city. Before our talk, the lead communications specialist for the convention, a middle-aged white, liberal woman, asked to sit down with us. She wanted to set up media interviews with Baptist, who at the time was living and organizing among unhoused people, and she needed to learn more about him so she could determine the best angles to pitch. We had a brief conversation and shortly after Baptist began speaking we were surprised when she burst into tears. It quickly became clear to us that his story was having an intensely unsettling effect on her.

Baptist is a Black organizer and political educator who has lived in poverty his whole life and has worked for over fifty years to unite poor people and build the movement to end poverty. He was sixteen years old when the 1965 Watts Rebellion erupted in his neighborhood of Los Angeles, and he recalls that his political journey began the day he was forced onto his knees while a military-grade helicopter with a machine gun hovered overhead. Since then, he has worked with hundreds of grassroots groups, trade unions, and some of the most important poor people's organizations of the last half century, including the National Union of the Homeless, the National Welfare Rights Union, and the National Domestic Workers Alliance. Through these experiences, as well as his voracious appetite for learning, he has developed a masterful understanding of history, economics, and political strategy that he has shared as a mentor to thousands of organizers. Baptist is a humbly brilliant and generous man, and, from where I stand, he is one of our nation's unsung organic intellectuals, a leader from the ranks of the poor who has committed every fiber of his being to the abolition of poverty.

When the Methodist woman broke down crying, I believe she was experiencing a moment of profound cognitive dissonance. Baptist's sharp articulation and analysis was a radical refutation of the racist stereotypes we are usually offered about poor Black men—that they are either raggedy and helpless or out of control and dangerous. In a country with such a dense and complex history of racist and anti-poor propaganda, it is inevitable that all of us, even those of us who are poor, internalize judgmental and patronizing ideas about poverty. Most of the dominant institutions in our lives—the media, the education system, organized religion, the private sector, the government—condition us to see poor people as deserving of little more than sorriness or scorn. We are all on our own journey of unlearning and truth seeking, and for this woman I think it was the discordant shock of this discovery, of the distance between how society had allowed her to imagine unhoused Black men and who Baptist actually was, that left her stunned and teary-eyed.

Cultural explanations for poverty have been with us for a very long time. Dating back to the English Poor Laws that were exported to the American colonies, our society's default position has been to condemn the poor for their poverty and diagnose their deprivation as the result of personal failures. Before the modern welfare state, private charities and relief organizations, often connected to the church, were the primary source of aid for the poor. These organizations differentiated sharply between those they considered "deserving" and "undeserving." The deserving poor were the small minority of people who had permanent disabilities and could not care for themselves, including widows and orphans, while the undeserving poor were the majority of people who were supposedly to blame for their own homelessness, hunger, bad health, and other hardships. Even after the New Deal created a whole host of social programs and protections for the first time, many millions of "undeserving" people continued, at best, to be offered controlling and conditional government aid, with the goal not of permanently alleviating their poverty but of giving them just enough money to survive before pushing them back into the workforce, even when jobs were scarce and pay was low. Implemented during the Great Depression, these public interventions were also often discriminatory by design, throwing impoverished white people a lifeline while excluding many people of color entirely.

The backward idea of the undeserving poor found its modern expression in the mid-1960s, when American anthropologist Oscar Lewis famously proposed his "culture of poverty" theory in an attempt to explain the persistence of poverty in Mexico and the United States.[21] Lewis argued that among poor people this culture perpetuated feelings of inferiority and powerlessness, a lack of historical thinking, and a self-centered focus on their own troubles. His arguments were adopted by other social scientists, social workers, and government officials, including Daniel Patrick Moynihan, a sociologist and the assistant secretary of labor in the Johnson administration. Amid rising inflation, unemployment, and social unrest, especially among poor Black and Brown youth in hundreds of cities, Moynihan authored his watershed 1965 report, *The Negro Family: The Case for National Action*. In its ninety pages, he identified the "Negro family" as "the principle source of most of the aberrant, inadequate, or antisocial behavior that did not establish, but now serves to perpetuate, the cycle of poverty and deprivation."[22]

At a time when the economy was flagging and thousands were refusing to passively swallow their suffering, Moynihan argued that poor Black families were trapped in a "tangle of pathology." Republican administrations starting with Richard Nixon seized on this argument to cast poverty as a problem of the poor, rather than of society at large. By demonizing, pathologizing, and racializing the poor, those in power worked diligently to undermine claims about the responsibility of a government to ensure the well-being of its people. This, in turn, enabled the further chiseling away of a vision of society that might someday guarantee public goods like healthcare and housing. The goal of this newly emerging neoliberalism was not just to unshackle the private sector from interference by the government but to psychologically separate people from one another and compress their shared struggles into a private question of individual responsibility.

These culture of poverty arguments weren't limited to the Republican Party, and as debates about welfare heated up in the late 1980s and early 1990s, they seeped ever more across the aisle. In 1992, Bill Clinton campaigned on a promise to "end welfare as we have come to know it," armed with racist tales about the backwardness of the poor and their need to take personal responsibility for their lives. Four years later, he made good on his word, ushering in an intensely regressive and punitive era of policymaking through the Personal Responsibility and Work Opportunity Reconciliation Act (PRWORA). This legislation was some of the most "moralistic" in American history, impacting not only poor people of color but millions of poor white people as well. (Although the road to welfare reform was paved with racist propaganda, white women and their children have always been the largest recipients of public support.) Consider these words from the preamble: "(1) Marriage is the foundation of a successful society. (2) Marriage is an essential institution of a successful society which

promotes the interests of children. (3) Promotion of responsible fa-
therhood and motherhood is integral to successful child rearing and
the well-being of children."[23]

The PRWORA ended the federal right to welfare by taking funding power away from the federal government and moving it to the
states. It also added work requirements for aid, set limits on how long
someone could receive benefits, and created new laws that severely
punished people who did not comply with the new system. For example, the legislation included a provision that disallowed women
who were victims of domestic violence from receiving benefits unless they disclosed their abusers, often putting those women directly
in even greater danger and further chaining them to the very people
they needed to escape. In the place of our already beleaguered welfare
system, the era of mass incarceration, which began a couple decades
earlier, soon found its full expression. Low-wage workers and people
being pushed entirely out of the formal economy by deindustrialization, globalization, and automation were heavily fined, policed, and
criminalized for their poverty. Given the unbroken history of systemic
racism in this country, this explosion of incarceration disproportionately targeted poor communities of color, but, like the effects of welfare reform, it also reached deeply into poor white communities. Jails
and prisons emerged as a key method of social control over people
who were no longer considered necessary to the core functions of the
economy, as well as a method of economic development for impoverished towns and cities.

In 2018, Philip Alston, then the UN special rapporteur on extreme poverty and human rights, embarked on an investigatory tour
of American poverty. In his final report, he offered a scathing assessment of what he discovered: "Punishing and imprisoning the poor
is the distinctively American response to poverty in the twenty-first
century. . . . Even when imprisonment is not the preferred option,
the standard response to those facing economic hardship is to adopt

policies explicitly designed to make access to health care, sick leave, welfare and child benefits more difficult to access and the receipt of benefits more stigmatizing."*[24]

We saw this "standard response" play out in real time during the debates over Joe Biden's highly contested Build Back Better plan in 2020 and 2021. At the height of the COVID-19 pandemic, politicians on both sides of the aisle deployed arguments that stigmatized urgently needed public investments by vilifying the poor. Joe Manchin, the then powerful Democratic senator from West Virginia, argued against the plan because, he claimed, he could not "accept our economy, or basically our society, moving towards an entitlement mentality."[25] While torpedoing the legislation, he went so far as to suggest that families in his state would use money from the expanded Child Tax Credit to buy drugs and that work requirements, rather than more resources, would lift poor children out of poverty. At the time, *HuffPost* reported that he also privately told colleagues that "Americans would fraudulently use the proposed paid sick leave policy [in the plan], specifically saying people would feign being sick and go on hunting trips."[26] Consider Joe Manchin just one of many contemporary necromancers who have reanimated the corpse of the long-discredited idea of a culture of poverty.

MYTH #3: POVERTY IS ORDAINED BY GOD

When I began the ordination process in the Presbyterian Church, the denomination I was raised in, I received constant pushback from church leaders who disapproved of a ministry committed to the

---

* Alston has long supported using a human rights framework to assess American poverty, all the way back to the days when I was organizing in Philadelphia in the 1990s. In 2020, at the very beginning of the COVID-19 pandemic, he coauthored a CNN opinion piece with Bishop Barber and me about the unreported reality of poverty in this country. We gave the piece a hopeful, and in retrospect tragic, title: "The Pandemic Offers a Chance to Transform the US' Cruel Policies Toward Poor People."

abolition of poverty. Instead, they counseled that it would be better for me to become a pastor in a more traditional ministerial setting. During the first meeting with my ordination liaison, he suggested that if I continued talking about ending poverty I wouldn't be able to get ordained, reminding me that Jesus said, "The poor you will always have with you."* More than once, I was told my belief that poverty need not exist was at best a misunderstanding of the teachings of the gospel and at worst an act of disobedience to God. Over a twelve-year period in which I struggled to be ordained, I did a lot of soul searching about whether I wanted to stay with the church. Eventually, I decided that part of my call to ministry was to move my own community on the issue of poverty.

The theological pushback I experienced within my denomination is not especially unique in American Christianity. The well-known evangelical preacher Jim Wallis used to conduct a short Bible quiz with American audiences by asking: "What is the most famous biblical text about the poor?" He received the same answer almost every time: "The poor you will always have with you." People understand this passage in a multitude of ways, but perhaps its most common interpretations are these: (1) Poverty is the result of individual sin; (2) Jesus believed in the inevitable and unchangeable nature of poverty; and (3) Jesus is concerned solely with spiritual poverty and other matters of the soul, rather than the material problem of poverty.

These interpretations are pervasive in the writings of preachers and biblical scholars. Given the hegemonic nature of Christian values in our society, they are also commonplace in the minds of everyday

---

* In the Bible, to "ordain" means to set something apart for a specific purpose. Today, churches ordain clergy and lay leaders to ministries through a process that is specific to each denomination. The term "ordain" is also used theologically to describe how God appoints or decrees something into a certain order. In other words, the myth that poverty is ordained by God is a theological statement proclaiming that God wills some people to be poor to fulfill God's purposes on earth.

Christians and non-Christians alike. I cannot count how many times I've heard this passage quoted to justify inaction in the face of poverty. In fact, this has happened to me so often that I wrote an entire book dedicated to understanding its deeper meaning: *Always with Us: What Jesus Really Said About the Poor.*

Jesus's famous words are also regularly referenced by figures of both major parties. Barack Obama opened his remarks with them at Georgetown University's Poverty Summit in 2015, and a year earlier, Rick Perry, Texas governor before becoming secretary of energy under Donald Trump, said in a *Washington Post* interview, "Biblically, the poor are always going to be with us in some form or fashion."[27] In 2017, Roger Marshall, then a Republican congressman from Kansas before becoming a senator in 2021, wielded the verse as he decried the expansion of Medicaid in his state: "Just like Jesus said, 'the poor will always be with us.' . . . There is a group of people that just don't want health care and aren't going to take care of themselves." He continued: "Just like homeless people . . . I think morally, spiritually, socially, [some people] just don't want health care."[28]

When poverty is framed as a damnable and eternal part of the human condition—willed by God to fulfill God's purposes on earth—we are left with two dominant options for how to treat the poor: punishment or pity. As Marshall demonstrated during his battle to defeat Medicaid in Kansas, the punishment often comes with a heavy dose of religious paternalism. Marshall, a stalwart of the MAGA movement and a frequent flyer within Christian nationalist circles, once said, "[I] tried to read the Bible every day since I was 10 years of age, so a lot of the wisdom I've been given comes from reading the Bible."[29] Those many years of Bible study seem to have taught him a theology of avarice and fearmongering—a trickle-down theology—which he has imbued in his policymaking. Alongside attacks on Medicaid, Marshall and his ilk have used their considerable power within the Republican Party to advance a noxious combination of regressive Christian doctrine and free market, anti-poor governance (including voting against the expanded Child Tax Credit and in favor of massive tax cuts for the wealthy).

For many right-wing politicians, preachers, and parishioners, the engine of capitalism is not only the best Christian response to poverty but the final act of civilizing ourselves. Paul Froese, a professor of sociology and the director of Baylor Religion Surveys at the Baptist school in Texas, writes that "perhaps it is the fervent individualism of American Christianity which makes free market capitalism seem like a Divine mandate. Because evangelicals assert that you alone are responsible for your eternal salvation, it makes sense that the individual is also responsible for his or her economic salvation without government assistance, especially if God is the only assistance you really need."[30] Within this hyper-individualized worldview, pity for the poor is expressed through parsimonious acts of charity and private service, which are put forward as the only biblically sound response to poverty. The polling data on this belief system is compelling. A 2023 national survey from the Public Religion Research Institute found that about two-thirds of Americans who adhere to or are sympathetic to Christian nationalism, many of whom are evangelicals, believed that "when Jesus and the prophets talked about taking care of the poor, they were primarily talking about charitable acts by individuals" rather than about "our obligation to create a just society."[31] (It must be noted that not all evangelicals, who are a broad and diverse population, adhere to or are sympathetic to Christian nationalism.)

I saw this dynamic play out during the congressional hearing described at the beginning of the chapter, when a number of Christian congresspeople used religious references to rationalize the existence of poverty and prop up the charitable works of the church in lieu of public intervention. For someone less familiar with the arguments of these politicians, it might have been surprising to hear so many of them seek refuge under theological cover. But I have learned that with very little else to stand on, those in positions of reactionary power often fall back on weaponizing the Bible as their primary tactic. They do this because they believe they have a monopoly on morality and can distort the word of God with impunity.

———————

The irony is that trickle-down theology, like its sibling, trickle-down economics, often advances its free-market aspirations in the name of the poor. In 2015, the Institute for Faith, Work, and Economics, a Christian libertarian think tank, published a collection of essays titled *For the Least of These: A Biblical Answer to Poverty* (contributors include evangelical theologians, Christian economists, and a vice chairman of Goldman Sachs). In their introduction, the co-editors write:

> The Bible calls on us to care for the poor, demonstrating Christ's love as well as our own. All too often, however, Christians turn to the secular state as the answer for poverty rather than grasping their own responsibility and realizing that the best long-term solution is to enable people to use their gifts to serve others and to exchange goods and services through market trade. Government is impersonal and bureaucratic in the way it addresses poverty and, as such, often destroys rather than elevates the God-breathed dignity of the poor. By contrast, the local church and non-profit organizations are better positioned to adapt aid to the unique needs of the specific individuals because they are closer to those they are trying to help and are thus more knowledgeable and nimble in how they act.[32]

The editors walk a sophisticated line. The Bible, they remind us, instructs Christians to care for the poor, who are worthy of their love and the love of God. In fact, they seem to be suggesting that this worthiness, this "God-breathed dignity of the poor," is too good and important for matters of public policy. In their eyes, the "secular state" is cumbersome and detached, whereas the church and the nonprofit are right there on the ground, ready to serve. Ready, too, is the "market," a friendly venue in which to exchange goods and services, as if it were some kind of ancient bazaar from the Bible itself. In all of this the authors conspicuously gloss over the fact that the government is not an unchanging, monolithic force, but an always-contested terrain in which policy can be made more or less relevant to the lives of the poor. Missing, too, is any acknowledgment that widespread poverty and economic insecurity, which cannot possibly be addressed by charitable giving and nonprofit services alone, is directly connected to the unprecedented accumulation of wealth in the hands of a few.

The perspective these authors represent may be further to the right on the political spectrum, but elements of their thinking can also be found in more liberal, mainline Protestant communities. Liberal Christian congregations regularly engage in similar direct-service ministries as their conservative counterparts, offering charity for the poor as their primary form of public action despite proclaiming in words the need for larger societal repair. These so-called ministries of compassion and mercy are often divorced from ministries of advocacy and justice. The result is the advancement of a liberal version of trickle-down theology that on the surface appears more concerned with systemic change but still perpetuates paternalistic and individualistic ideas about the poor and maintains the social structures that produce poverty.*

Charity is usually an act of faith and goodwill, but too often its effect across ideological lines is to entrench a belief that the best we can do is help a few poor people with the problems immediately before them. For many liberal Christians, service work through their

---

* This perspective echoes the prosperity gospel of the Gilded Era. In 1889, Andrew Carnegie, titan of the steel industry, famously penned "The Gospel of Wealth," an article published by the *North American Review* that was steeped in moralizing paternalism. Carnegie suggested the answer to yawning wealth inequality was for the rich, who had nobly succeeded through hard work, to carefully give away their surplus resources, casting the poor as passive recipients of their benefactors' benevolence. Carnegie was in many ways the father of modern philanthropy.

church or community organization can also take on an apolitical posture, moving them away from the messy world of politics and toward
what can feel like a more unifying or wholesome experience. The era
of neoliberalism did more than just hollow out large sections of the
public sector—it conditioned generations of us to ignore or lose faith
in the government as a site for struggle and change. Instead, we have
been made increasingly dependent on private solutions to poverty
that extol acts of service and celebrate the wealthy for their humani-
tarianism, even as they reap the rewards of federal policymaking and
an economy rigged in their favor.

———

To regain a sense of moral direction amid the scarred theological
landscape of our society, it is helpful to return to the biblical line
that politicians love so much and Christian audiences know so well:
"The poor you will always have with you." What is striking about
this passage is that just like many others in the Bible, it is repeatedly
used to justify the existence of poverty *in spite* of its historical and
intertextual meaning.

In the biblical scene where Jesus speaks these words, he is visiting the home of a man with leprosy in a small town called Bethany
(translated from Hebrew as "house of the poor"). As he sits for a meal,
a poor, unnamed woman stands beside him and anoints him with an
expensive ointment usually reserved for kings and state-sanctioned
messiahs. Jesus is also anointed for his burial, for the woman recognizes that he is going to die at the hands of the Roman Empire and
wants to ensure that his body is sufficiently prepared. But when this
woman anoints Jesus, she is chided by his disciples. They accuse her
of destroying the valuable ointment and say that if they had instead
sold it, they could have earned money and donated it to the poor. This
perspective of the disciples follows the dominant economic thinking
of the Roman period, and their idea of earning money and giving

the proceeds to the poor mirrors how our own society often tries to address poverty: by doing charity work, by buying and selling and donating to the poor, but never questioning how poverty is created and why it exists at all.

In the version of this story told in the gospel according to John, it is Judas who criticizes the woman and the text reads that Judas offers this criticism not because he cares about the poor but because he is the treasurer and regularly steals from the coffers. Jesus recognizes Judas's motives and he does something interesting. He quiets the disciples and praises the woman for her alleged waste of the ointment. He says, "Leave her alone. It was intended that she should save this perfume for the day of my burial. For the poor you will always have with you, but you will not always have me" (John 12: 1-8).

A knowledge of the entire Bible is critical to understanding what Jesus is doing in this moment of high tension. With these words, he is deliberately referencing one of the old Jubilee passages from Deuteronomy in the Torah, which explains that it is precisely because those in power do not follow the laws of God and instead exploit their workers and hoard resources that "there will never cease to be some in need on the earth." Or, as Jesus later paraphrases, "The poor you will always have with you." When Jesus quotes this incisive line to his faithful Jewish disciples, there is no doubt they would understand his reference to Deuteronomy. In his reprimand, they would also recognize his reminder that rather than simply donating money to the poor, their sacred texts instruct them to organize their entire society around the policies of Jubilee. By instead praising the woman, Jesus cements the revolutionary nature of her simple act of care and devotion. In the face of the overwhelming power of Caesar and the Roman Empire, she bravely sanctifies a poor, unhoused man with an ointment supposedly fit only for kings. Through this small act of sublime courage, she affirms that the bottom-up movement they are building has just as legitimate a claim on the future as the empire itself and that after Jesus's assassination they will carry his vision for society forward.*

Whether or not you are religious or read the Bible, there is an important lesson to learn in excavating the truth of this popular passage. Not only is the Bible cynically used to defend or excuse the existence of poverty, but its chief references to poverty actually demand the exact opposite: a society in which people are treated fairly and economic exploitation is considered a sin of the highest order.

PLOWING THE FIELDS, PLANTING THE SEEDS

Leaders with the National Union of the Homeless used to say that before we can create a new society free of poverty, we need to create new human beings. We need to transform how our society understands the causes of poverty and the value of poor people as thinkers and agents of change. This country has a long and sordid history of ignoring and minimizing poverty, pathologizing the poor, blaming and shaming poor people for their own deprivation, and framing poverty as a judgment from God. During the House Budget Committee hearing in 2019, we saw just how poisonous this finger-pointing can be. But that hearing was also a call to action—a reminder that these myths are not reality and only serve the wealthy and powerful, while diminishing and atomizing the rest of us. For members of the Poor

---

* Students of mine sometimes ask why the woman remains unnamed. If she is so important, why deprive her of a name? But dig beneath the surface and we find that her namelessness has revolutionary implications. During Roman rule, charity and patronage functioned to bestow honor on, and more resources to, the wealthy people who gifted aid to the poor (the same is true today, when wealthy philanthropists often give money to furnish their reputations and receive tax breaks). Because she remains unnamed, the woman's generosity is removed from the normative process of top-down charitable giving. There is no college department, hospital wing, or church pew named after her. Her anointing of Jesus, and his reciprocal call for his followers to honor her memory, is not about personal reputation, but about advancing the struggle for human dignity.

People's Campaign, it was important to witness the intellectual eva-sions of the representatives and be reminded that these politicians were not smarter or better than us. In its own perverse way, the hear-ing was a gift: it affirmed for all of us that we could not wait for those in power to take action on the issues of poverty and the economic systems that produce it.

There is a saying in our work: "We have to plow the fields to plant the seeds." By "plowing the fields," we mean exposing the lies and myths told about poverty—discarding the cruel and vacuous ideas that hold us back to make room for new ones. By "planting the seeds," we mean creating the conditions in which the poor begin to recognize their own power and our society is finally freed to envision a world beyond poverty. In social movements, as in life, new human beings rarely, if ever, emerge from the seclusion of their own minds—they emerge through the illuminating experience of collective struggle. Entire communities of poor and dispossessed people learn that they are worthy and powerful not just by reading or talking about it but by seeing the evidence of their worthiness and power through their own actions. Once that happens, it is as if the lies and myths never existed at all. Suddenly, the truth is as plain as day, and anything feels possible.

CHAPTER THREE

UP AND OUT OF POVERTY NOW!

I n the winters of 1996 and 1997, the Kensington Welfare Rights
Union (KWRU) marked Christmas a little differently. Amid
the commercial cheer and the charity drives, unhoused organizers
launched a Homes for the Holidays campaign, moving themselves
and their families into dozens of abandoned, federally owned row
houses across North Philadelphia. When they took over a new house,
they hung a cardboard sign in the front window: "This house has been
reclaimed as part of the New Underground Railroad."

I spent significant time in these houses over the course of those
two winters, often sleeping over so that families weren't alone if federal marshals came to kick them out or local police came to hassle
them. Huddled together in temporary homes that could be raided at
any moment, the newly minted residents saw the truth of their lives
written on that flimsy cardboard. The members of KWRU recognized
that, just like their own housing takeovers, the Underground Railroad
once represented a survival struggle organized by the poorest and
most oppressed members of society. For these modern-day poverty
abolitionists, the main characters and central story of the movement

to end slavery were obvious: it was the enslaved Black workers and the extraordinary steps they took to collectively seize their own freedom.

KWRU was inspired by the revolutionary leadership of these hundreds of thousands of enslaved people. Yes, the abolitionists whose names endure all played an indispensable role in building the abolitionist movement, especially in agitating and polarizing the nation around the moral abomination of slavery. But in every popular movement there is a leading social force that, by virtue of its position in society and its place in the economic pecking order, is compelled to act first, not out of moral conviction but life-or-death necessity. This force is the urgent engine of a movement, and by moving into action it is able to awaken the indignation and imagination of others, in time winning wider circles of society to its cause.

During the first half of the nineteenth century, enslaved Black workers were such a force. Their mass exodus from slavery on the Underground Railroad and their very existence as fugitives unsettled the entire nation in the years leading up to the Civil War. Their willingness to escape at the risk of punishing violence, and the undeniable evidence of their abuse and torture, was an emphatic rebuttal to planter propaganda that the system of slavery was a benign institution. Once free, many of these formerly enslaved workers became abolitionist leaders themselves, organizing mass public awareness campaigns, writing articles and sermons, coordinating extralegal acts of resistance, and often re-entering the fray to lead others toward freedom.

As the planter class took more heavy-handed measures to maintain the slave system, including winning the Fugitive Slave Act and the *Dred Scott* decision in the 1850s, the courageous and disruptive actions of these enslaved workers convinced an increasing number of people across the country that slavery couldn't simply be tinkered with or contained. It had to be abolished everywhere. In *Black Reconstruction in America*, W. E. B. Du Bois underscores just how big a threat the Underground Railroad was to the slave system: "Not only was the fugitive slave important because of the actual loss involved, but for potentialities in the future. These free Negroes were furnishing a leadership for the mass of Black workers, and especially they were furnishing a text for the abolition idealists. Fugitive slaves . . . increased the number of abolitionists by thousands and spelled the doom of slavery."[1] Over the course of multiple decades, the Underground Railroad became an ideological training ground and a political vehicle for the building of a mass movement.

In Kensington, more than a century later, it was clear to us that abolition wouldn't have happened if not for the vision and initiative of thousands upon thousands of enslaved workers who did not wait to be freed but who seized freedom with their own hands—those whose names have largely been forgotten and who are often cast, even or especially in liberal memory, as broken or helpless victims in need of saving. During the Homes for the Holidays campaign, I saw history come to life, not through a book or a perfectly clean and linear narrative but through the bravery of KWRU's members. By drawing a connective thread between the Underground Railroad and our housing takeovers, we felt an enormous sense of power and of history in the making. When so-called "illegitimate" and "illegal" people are forced to do "illegitimate" and "illegal" things to survive, the legacy of struggle by similarly embattled people is a ballast against doubt and fear.

Viewed in isolation, the individual acts of fugitives in the antebellum South may have once seemed small or insignificant. But when we learned how those small sparks of dissent ignited into the wildfire of a mass movement, we began to believe the same was possible for us. This conviction fortified us as the cold weather deepened and the authorities caught wind of what we were doing.

KWRU was founded four years earlier, by six women, in the aftermath of another takeover—this time of an abandoned welfare office. These women—Black and white, young and old, some unhoused, some mothers, all welfare recipients—planned to place a ladder on the front of the office, climb up to the second story, and break in. Once inside, they would stay and turn the old office into a community center. This action was in part a practical decision since such a center would certainly benefit Kensington, the poorest neighborhood in the city. But it was also a political decision. It was April 1991, and the state's Democratic governor was preparing to make dramatic cuts to welfare. The women felt that they needed to protest with as much visibility as they could muster. Taking over a vacant welfare office in the middle of a desperately poor neighborhood, in broad daylight, seemed like it might do the trick.

The women—Cheri Honkala, Alexis Baptist, Sandy Brennan, Diane Coyett, Louis Mayberry, and Debra Witzman—organized their neighbors to march with them down to the office. When they got there, the police were already waiting. The women managed to hoist the ladder onto the building and one of them started climbing, but the police quickly grabbed her legs and pulled her back down to the concrete. Next a couple of officers seized the ladder and threw it into their van, causing an uproar from the crowd that had assembled around the office. Amid the commotion and confusion, someone unlocked a door leading into the office and beckoned the women.* They quietly snuck in.

By then, though, their plan had unraveled. The police followed and arrested them. The city prosecutor argued for lengthy prison

---

* Although these kinds of takeover actions often appear spontaneous, they require a great deal of planning and creativity. In this case, the women sent someone to the office earlier who managed to sneak in and stand at the ready to unlock the door. This level of coordination was common in the takeovers that I participated in throughout the 1990s.

sentences, charging them with breaking and entering and criminal conspiracy. The women feared they might not return home for years, but they deftly used their legal case as an opportunity to instead put the city and state on trial, demanding to know why welfare was being cut and buildings were allowed to sit empty even as people were forced to ricochet between shelters and the streets. The case gained significant media attention, and under the eye of public scrutiny the women were found not guilty. They walked out of the courtroom exonerated—and as the founding members of KWRU.

Kensington sits on the boundary between North Philadelphia and lower Northeast Philadelphia like a crudely drawn anvil. Today it is a poster child for gentrification; in the early 1990s, it was a microcosm of the changing demographics of the country. In a historically hypersegregated city, it was about one-third each white, Black, and Latino, with a growing number of immigrant communities from the former Soviet Union, the Middle East, Asia, and Africa. Once an important center of the textile industry, the neighborhood was pummeled by deindustrialization and by the 1990s the floor of the local economy had fully collaped and steady jobs were scarce. When I first started organizing with KWRU in the mid-1990s, the two main sources of income for residents were welfare and drugs, and 70 percent of the neighborhood was forced to do something illegal in order to survive.[2]

Many residents avoided the city's overflowing shelters since they were often dirtier and more dangerous than the streets. Some families and small groups of people squatted in abandoned homes and buildings, while others lived in their cars and pitched tents and set up encampments in empty lots and on street corners. In the midst of this hardship, the community was quietly performing epic feats of ingenuity, often collectivizing scarce resources to feed and house one another and protect themselves from an antagonistic police force and other city authorities. Like the National Union of the Homeless, which had never established a foothold in Kensington,

KWRU took the spontaneous survival strategies that poor and un-housed people were already using every day and adapted them into what we called "projects of survival." These were politicized forms of mutual aid that allowed us to meet some of our members' most immediate needs while we continued fighting for structural changes that could transform the conditions they were living in. The phrase "project of survival" was borrowed, in part, from the Black Panther Party, which in the 1960s and 1970s created "survival programs" like the Free Medical Clinic Program and the Free Breakfast Program. The Black Panthers saw these initiatives as one method to build a movement that could spark larger changes to the economic and racial social structure, and they infused all of their survival work with deep political education, highly visible protest, and sophisticated communications and cultural organizing.*

In 1968, J. Edgar Hoover, the director of the FBI, claimed: "The Black Panther Party, without question, represents the greatest threat to internal security in the country."[3] In truth, he wasn't all that worried about their guns, although he went to great lengths to paint them as violent and dangerous militants. But he was concerned that by giving away free breakfasts to tens of thousands of children the Black Panthers were becoming credible and trustworthy in the eyes of poor and dispossessed people, not just in Black communities but

---

* Our admiration for the Black Panthers was reflected in a 1999 organizing manual published by KWRU's Annie Smart Leadership Development Institute and titled *The Six Panther P's: Tools for the Poor Organizing the Poor in the Fight to End Poverty Now!* The authors, Willie Baptist and Phil Wider, identified six guiding principles from the Panthers that inspired our work: (1) programs, (2) protests, (3) projects of survival, (4) press work, (5) political education, and (6) plans, not personalities. (This last principle was offered as a loving critique. Baptist and Wider believed the Panthers, like many organizations at the time, relied too heavily on individual personalities over collective leadership and shared strategic plans.)

among other racial and ethnic groups as well.* In 1969, the head of
the national School Breakfast Program admitted that the Black Panthers were feeding more poor children than the State of California.[4]
That same year, amid intensive and illegal FBI operations to undermine the Black Panthers, Hoover sent a memo to agents across the
country: "The BCP (Breakfast for Children Program) promotes at
least tacit support for the BPP (Black Panther Party) among naïve
individuals. . . . Consequently, the BCP represents the best and most
influential activity going for the BPP and, as such, is potentially the
greatest threat to efforts by authorities to neutralize the BPP and
destroy what it stands for."[5]

KWRU learned from the Black Panthers. In the late fall of 1995,
at the onset of the Homes for the Holidays campaign, a cold front
swept through a large KWRU encampment known as Tent City,
in an abandoned lot where an old lace factory once stood. In need
of indoor shelter, we set our sights on a vacant church a few blocks
away. Earlier that year, the archdiocese of Philadelphia shuttered St.
Edward's Catholic Church, along with eight other churches, because
its congregants were poor and the drafty building was expensive to
maintain. After the sanctuary was closed, some of the congregants
continued coming back every Sunday to pray in a small park outside
the church. Eventually, dozens of residents from Tent City walked

---

* In Chicago, Fred Hampton, deputy chair of the national Black Panther Party
and chair of the Illinois chapter, famously organized the Rainbow Coalition,
forging new alliances with poor people's organizations across racial lines. Joining the Panthers were the Young Patriots, a group of poor white migrants from
Appalachia, and the Young Lords, which emerged from the city's Puerto Rican
community. The Rainbow Coalition was founded the same year as the 1968 Poor
People's Campaign, reflecting a shared understanding among disparate movement
leaders about the need for multiracial organizing among the poor. Hampton's
murder at the hands of the police and the FBI in 1969, much like the constant
public surveillance and abuse levied against King, also reflected the threat this
organizing posed to the power structure.

up the church steps and broke the locks on the front doors, igniting a highly publicized occupation that lasted through the winter.

On the walls of the church, we hung posters and banners, including one that asked, "Why do we worship a homeless man on Sunday and ignore one on Monday?" As winter engulfed the city, we fed and cared for one another within a fugitive congregation whose youngest resident was less than a year old and whose oldest was in his nineties. Our occupation ultimately pressured the archdiocese to re-prioritize its ministry within poor communities. It also electrified the local media and forced Philadelphians to pay attention to the rampant poverty that plagued the city but was normally swept under the rug.

Projects of survival like the St. Edward's takeover and the Homes for the Holidays campaign enabled KWRU to build trust within Kensington and support old and new leaders alike. With enough patience and skill, these projects also served as bases of operation for bigger and bolder organizing, connecting Kensington with other poor people outside the neighborhood. In the age of neoliberalism, KWRU recognized the need to build political alliances that could bridge the increasingly thin divide between employed and unemployed workers. In the late 1990s, KWRU became the first unemployed workers' organization in the country to join as an official affiliate of a labor union: District 1199C of the National Union of Hospital and Healthcare Employees AFSCME.

Thanks to KWRU, I gained new insight into how bottom-up change often begins. While media narratives regularly depict poor people as lazy, dangerous, or too over-burdened by their own problems to think about others, there is an immense spirit of cooperation and generosity among the poorest people in our society. Amid chaos and catastrophe, leaders within these communities will regularly take whatever life-saving actions are available to them, often working

together across wide differences of identity and risking everything to
support and defend their people. Indeed, the instinct of those in crisis
toward collective care is the generative ground from which powerful
social movements emerge.*

Helping me learn these and other lessons were seasoned organizers and movement elders with lifetimes of experience. Even as I ran
ragged around Kensington, they made sure I maintained a wider view
of what we were undertaking. They encouraged me to see our projects
of survival not only as communal acts of care but as radical forms of
nonviolent civil disobedience. In a society that criminalizes homelessness and valorizes property over people, taking over empty federally
owned houses, an abandoned industrial lot, and an old, empty church
was a direct challenge to the morally distorted order of the day. As a
young organizer, I found it undeniably powerful to situate our actions
within the long and noble tradition of nonviolent resistance among
the poor and dispossessed of this country. And the longer I worked
in Kensington, the more I began to see that our efforts were just one
bright star within a much larger and older constellation of organizing
and movement building.

KWRU was a local chapter of the National Welfare Rights Union,
founded in 1987 by a national group of mothers on welfare who opposed the passage of the Family Support Act, a Reagan-era policy
that laid the early groundwork for welfare reform. This group was

---

* Poor people in crisis, especially poor people of color, are often painted as violent
and lawless, even when their actions reveal the exact opposite. After Hurricane
Katrina in 2005, for example, the media falsely reported that poor Black residents
in New Orleans were thrown into a mob-like frenzy, looting and tearing the city
apart. While many people remained stranded on their roofs, hundreds of police
stopped their search-and-rescue operations and doubled back to the center of
the city to "protect" private and public property. The city's poor residents, on the
other hand, went to extraordinary lengths to care for one another, often risking
their lives to navigate the flooded streets in citizen-led rescue missions. For more,
read Rebecca Solnit's *A Paradise Built in Hell: The Extraordinary Communities That
Arise in Disasters* (New York: Viking Press, 2009).

itself the revival of a mid-twentieth-century organization called the National Welfare Rights Organization (NWRO), one of the largest poor people's organizations in American history. A number of the welfare rights leaders who mentored me in the 1990s were veterans of NWRO. They brought to my generation of organizing not only their wisdom and experience but also their unshakeable conviction that poor people have the capacity to provide political leadership within their own organizations and wider social movements.

In the late 1960s and early 1970s, NWRO built a mass organization of welfare recipients that wielded power at every level of government—a federation of local welfare rights groups that at its height had thirty thousand dues-paying members and a hundred chapters. Today the story of NWRO and its predecessors has largely been forgotten, but its impact is still abundantly evident in organized struggles of the poor. The many leaders of NWRO—mostly poor Black women—went on to directly influence an unbroken lineage of organizing, including the 1968 Poor People's Campaign, the welfare rights struggles of the 1990s, and the anti-poverty work that Noam and I are involved in today.

This political lineage offers compelling examples of an organizing model our mentor Willie Baptist calls "The Poor Organizing the Poor," or what the welfare rights movement called the "Johnnie Tillmon Model of Organizing," named after one of the legendary leaders of NWRO. The idea isn't terribly complicated, but it is radical in its simplicity. In this model, poor people are not just an oppressed identity group but a social force with untapped power. Because the poor have the least invested in the status quo and the most to gain from transformational change, they are uniquely positioned to rise up and rally others in society to fight for a better and more humane future—not around the usual horizontal axes of Democratic and Republican, liberal and conservative, left and right, but around the vertical axis of bottom and top. In order to harness this transformational potential, though, poor people must organize themselves into politically independent movements centered around their leadership and unity across difference.

Leadership, in this model, is not simply about platforming "directly impacted" people or people with "lived experience"—so often the parlance of social justice activism today—but about developing the shared political vision of entire communities of poor people through a regular and evolving process of on-the-ground organizing and education. Similarly, unity is not about bringing people together around lowest common denominator demands. Rather, it is a disciplined and farsighted unity that enables the poor to break through their isolation and the divisions that have been manufactured in their communities. It is the unity produced when poor people recognize the fundamental interests they have in common and begin to take action together to, as KWRU once put it, "kill the system before it kills them."

The Johnnie Tillmon model rarely appears in the literature on social change. We would wager this is not an accident. When the history of poor people's organizing is told, it is generally not poor people themselves who get to tell it. So it has been the responsibility of leaders in the movement to end poverty to document this model for themselves, trading notes with one another and passing them down generation by generation.

THE NATIONAL WELFARE RIGHTS ORGANIZATION

Johnnie Tillmon had her first brush with the California welfare system as she approached middle age. Born in 1926 to a Black sharecropping family in Arkansas, Tillmon began working at age seven and spent most of her childhood picking cotton. Years later, she explained to an oral historian that her parents "had to put me in the fields because . . . I was very mischievous."[6] At home, she learned how to cook, clean, and sew, but from an early age she had little interest in being a traditional homemaker. Instead, she dreamed of becoming a blues singer. During high school, as World War II transformed the country, Tillmon moved from the countryside to live with an aunt in Little

Rock, where she attended high school and worked the night shift at the local munitions factory. When the war ended, she dropped out of school and found a job at a nonsegregated laundromat, swapping stories with Black and white women alike. At twenty-two, Tillmon got married but soon divorced her husband after she learned that he was cheating on her. She continued working in the laundromat, and in her free time she was active in the PTA at her children's school and in the Women's Auxiliary of the local Methodist Church.

In 1959, Tillmon, now thirty-eight and a single mom of six children, decided to follow the beaten path that her brothers and tens of thousands of other Black Southerners had taken to the golden hills of California. As part of one of the last waves of the Great Migration, she and her kids settled in Nickerson Gardens, the largest public housing project in Los Angeles, in the neighborhood of Watts. In her new home, Tillmon again found work at a laundromat and became a shop steward of the local laundry and dye workers union, as well as a member of the Nickerson Gardens Planning Organization. In 1963, she fell ill with tonsillitis and was encouraged by the president of the planning organization to apply for welfare. At first she was hesitant, not because of the stigma associated with receiving public benefits but because of the horror stories she had heard from other women about the welfare system. Nearly a decade later, she explained, "before I was a welfare recipient I used to hear wild stories by women on welfare about the problems with the social workers, with the midnight raids, with the checks not coming on time. . . . Lots of people had such a hard time getting on welfare when they really needed it."[7]

Tillmon's worst fears were quickly confirmed. In order to receive what amounted to paltry stipends, she suffered a string of indignities, including regular home visits from caseworkers who stocked her refrigerator and made sure she was following a strict budget. They also checked to see if she was living with any unidentified men. At the time, "man in the house" rules in a number of states stipulated that families receiving welfare could not have men living with them, since men, the thinking at the time went, should be working rather than receiving public support. By then, Tillmon was a skilled organizer, with a practiced eye for recognizing larger patterns among the details of an individual life. As she continued receiving regular scrutiny and abuse from government workers, she saw with greater clarity how many women around her were enduring the same.

Tillmon realized that the only way to end this abuse would be to get the mothers on welfare organized. As Judith Shulevitz recounts in the *New York Review of Books*, she "sent notes to every woman in the housing project on welfare asking them that they come to the office to discuss their lease and benefits. Three hundred worried women showed up. First, Tillmon reassured them; then, she organized them."[8] Together, these women traveled from apartment to apartment, knocking on doors and speaking with other welfare recipients. Shortly after, they formed an organization called Aid to Needy Children-Mothers Anonymous (ANC), one of the first welfare rights organizations in the country. The swift rise of ANC was impressive, but it was not an isolated event. In the early to mid-1960s, similar welfare rights groups were spontaneously emerging in dozens of cities. Tillmon's story was mirrored by the leadership of other women, such as Dovie Thurman in Chicago, Beulah Sanders in New York City, Annie Smart in Baton Rouge, and Annie Chambers in Baltimore.

The welfare system was undergoing big changes at the time, including a significant rise in the number of people receiving public benefits. Although the national economy had expanded since World War II, widespread poverty and unemployment remained an open secret. By 1964, civil rights leaders became increasingly vocal in their demand for wages and jobs—not just in the South but across the country. The Johnson administration began rolling out the War on Poverty, the lynchpin of his Great Society program. It was, of course, a good thing that funding for welfare was increasing, but as the welfare rolls grew, more and more people began to experience the moral rot that undergirded the system. The welfare state was structured from the start to enforce work rather than solve poverty and it was designed to compel men and women to take any job at any pay, with any level of insecurity and abuse from their employers. Rather than receive benevolence from their government, welfare recipients received inadequate benefits and were constantly pummeled by racist, exclusionary, and moralizing policies.

This was the forge in which the early welfare rights organizations were hammered into shape. By the mid-1960s, these local groups suspected their power could be magnified if they banded together, especially since the changes they sought relied, in part, on the resources of the federal government. Veteran civil rights organizers like George Wiley also started paying attention to the women leading the welfare rights struggle. Wiley, a former leader with the Congress of Racial Equality, was beginning to understand that organizing around welfare was a strategic opening for a wider assault on poverty. In May 1966, a group of welfare recipients and activists, including Wiley, met at a conference in Chicago. They decided to hold a nationally coordinated action a month later, on the same day that a welfare rights group in Ohio was planning a 150-mile march from Cleveland to the capitol in Columbus. That day, five thousand welfare recipients and their supporters marched across Ohio in the "Walk for Decent Welfare," and thousands more demonstrated in dozens of other cities. It was the first action of what soon became the National Welfare Rights Organization.

<hr>

NWRO's welfare mothers—as they called themselves—believed that the ultimate prize was poor people's power, and they emphasized the need for joint leadership among poor Black, Latino, Indigenous, and white women. This was the strategic backbone of their movement. As they saw it, poverty was a fundamental issue for Black people, but it was also the critical link that connected them with millions of others. Wiley was well-known for reminding folks that the dirty secret of American poverty was that "the majority of Black people are poor, but the majority of [the] poor are white."[9] This dynamic also played out in the welfare system, which, as we write in chapter 2, was becoming increasingly racialized in the American imagination and undermined with racist stereotypes even though the majority of welfare recipients have always been white women and their children. For Tillmon, the first chairperson of NWRO and later its executive director, poor people's power was a new kind of racial integration that centered on the lives of those most impacted by poverty and fought for the unity of people at the very bottom of the economy. NWRO adopted as their motto "linking up the struggles" and began using an image of a chain link, which also resembled the infinity sign, as their logo.

Guida West, an activist supporter of NWRO and later its leading historian, writes about Tillmon in her book *The National Welfare Rights Organization: The Social Protest of Poor Women*:

> She repeatedly pointed out the uniqueness of NWRO, noting that its integrated structure was a "fairly unusual thing" for poor people and disconcerting to the "power structure." She emphasized "that NWRO is not a black organization, not a white organization . . . but a poor people's organization." She noted that "in some instances the poor whites have stopped fighting the poor blacks," and this new solidarity among the poor "kind of shakes people" in the power structure. She pointed out that "white women in Kentucky" were uniting with "black women, talking about working for a common goal." Tillmon emphasized that this was an event that had never happened before.[10]

Still, because NWRO focused its energies primarily in urban areas, where there were a high number of Black women on welfare, and because many of these women had been politicized through the Black Freedom Struggle, NWRO became a movement of and for mostly poor Black women. For these women, it was a vehicle to break their isolation, pool their strength in order to access urgently needed resources, and develop a collective spirit of "motherpower."[11] NWRO regularly led marches and demonstrations and held picket lines and sit-ins at welfare offices. In 1971 in Nevada, where the governor was cutting benefits, the local NWRO chapter organized a thousand women to storm the casino hotel Caesars Palace and shut down the main drag in Las Vegas for weeks. Eventually, a federal judge reinstated the benefits.[12] All of this activity and more doubtlessly played a role in encouraging thousands of families across the country to unapologetically demand fair treatment within the welfare system. The efforts of NWRO also helped improve what became the Supplemental Nutrition Assistance Program (SNAP) and inspired the creation of the Special Supplemental Nutrition Program for Women, Infants, and Children (WIC).[13]

Among NWRO's members there were many churchgoers, and the organization relied on donations from individual churches. But the welfare mothers were clear that a deeper level of support should come from Christians who believed in the gospel preached by Jesus. NWRO demanded that the church marshal its vast resources to aid in the fight against poverty. In a 1972 speech to the National Council of Churches, Beulah Sanders, a leader with the Citywide Coordinating Committee of Welfare Groups in New York City and vice president of NWRO, spoke candidly:

> I represent all of those poor people who are on welfare and many who are not . . . people who believe in the Christian way of life . . . people whose nickels and dimes and quarters have built the Christian churches of America. Because we believe in Christianity, we have continued to support the Christian churches. And I am saying to you here and now that we fully expect the Christian churches to support us. . . . We call upon you . . . to join us in the National

Welfare Rights Organization. We ask for your moral, personal, and financial support in this battle for bread, dignity, and justice for all of our people. If we fail in our struggle, Christianity will have failed.[14]

Sanders's words, addressed to some of the nation's most influential Christian leaders, were an extraordinary theological intervention that placed the welfare mothers at the moral center of society. A Christianity that does not defend poor people, Sanders was saying, could no longer claim to be Christianity at all.

The leaders of NWRO were just as exacting with fellow organizers and movement allies as they were with the church, unwavering in their commitment that they be treated as equal partners in strategic discussions and decisions. But they also knew that they needed to expand their ranks, and they remained open to new alliances that could foster the broader unity of the poor. The 1968 Poor People's Campaign is a good example. In February of that year, Dr. King and his team were immersed in preparations for the campaign and, two months before his assassination, he made his way to Chicago to meet with NWRO for the first time. The welfare mothers had come not to passively listen but to dialogue with King about joining the Poor People's Campaign. The idea itself was not new to them. They had been calling for a similar campaign for a few years and they were cautious about newcomers sweeping in and taking over without an appreciation for the organizing they were leading or an understanding of the demands they and other poor people were already fighting for. One of King's lieutenants, Al Sampson, later explained, "The women's concern was that they had a major constituency organization. They had created it with their blood, sweat, and tears, and it was something magnificent to them. Not to be recognized was an attack on their very being. And to have it taken away was unthinkable."[15]

The meeting was set at the downtown Chicago YMCA. Waiting for King upstairs were the thirty members of NWRO's national steering committee, seated around a large rectangular table in what Sampson described as a "grand piece of psychological warfare."[16] After every woman introduced herself, King laid out his vision and urged them to join the Poor People's Campaign. This was the moment NWRO had been waiting for. Etta Horn, a leader from Washington, DC, turned to King and asked about his position on the recent passage of a specific piece of anti-welfare legislation in Congress. He appeared puzzled. Johnnie Tillmon, sitting next to King with her granddaughter on her lap, stepped in: "You know, Dr. King, if you don't know about these questions, you should just say you don't know, and then we could go on with this meeting."[17]

"You're right, Mrs. Tillmon," Dr. King replied. "We don't know anything about welfare. We are here to learn." His admission reassured them, and NWRO officially joined the 1968 Poor People's Campaign as a leading organizational sponsor. After King's assassination, the welfare mothers continued to hold a prominent role within the campaign, helping shape its demands and lead its opening march on Mother's Day alongside Coretta Scott King. Annie Chambers, the legendary welfare rights leader from Baltimore, was pregnant in the weeks leading up to the march. She later recounted to me that after giving birth she dropped her newborn off with her dad, resolute in her conviction that she had to be in DC when the Poor People's Campaign pitched its tents on the national mall.

The welfare mothers were organizers, caretakers, strategists, intellectuals, and ethicists of the highest order. They were also feminists of an entirely new mold. At a time when many women were fighting for equality within the workplace, they championed "welfare as a right," challenging the notion that the value of a human is tied to their ability to work within the marketplace and raising fundamental questions about how a society cares for its people. In the same speech to the National Council of Churches, Sanders provocatively asked the audience, "Is it fair to call a woman lazy who stays at home, cooks, washes, irons, cleans house, teaches her kids how to do things, and helps them

with their homework? If she does the same work for somebody else
for two dollars or less an hour is she really a better woman?"[18]

NWRO brought a new face to the feminist movement, pushing
people to think more expansively about what gender liberation would
require. In a groundbreaking essay for *Ms.* magazine in 1972, Tillmon
described a reality that is still all too resonant today:

> I'm a woman. I'm a Black woman. I'm a poor woman. I'm a fat
> woman. I'm a middle-aged woman. And I'm on welfare. In the
> country, if you're any one of those things you count less as a human
> being. If you're all those things, you don't count at all. Except as a
> statistic. . . . Welfare is a women's issue. For a lot of middle-class
> women in this country, Women's Liberation is a matter of concern.
> For women on welfare, it's a matter of survival.[19]

Later in the same essay, Tillmon wrote that the women of NWRO
were the "frontline troops of women's freedom. Both because we
have so few illusions and because our issues are so important to all
women—the right to a living wage for women's work, the right to
life itself." In addition to demanding living wages, higher welfare
benefits, and an end to abusive policies, NWRO became early supporters of a guaranteed, adequate income, or what is now often called
a universal basic income. They believed that such an income, open and
available to everyone, could undercut poverty's worst effects and raise
the floor of the economy as a whole. This pioneering policy proposal
pushed the entirety of society to take seriously what had once been
a marginal idea, and even their most avid detractors were forced to
play ball, despite the fact that they weren't actually supportive of
the women's demands. In 1969, for example, the Nixon administration ostensibly proposed a guaranteed income. The welfare mothers
weren't fooled. They found themselves in fierce opposition to the plan
because its restrictive nature, low-benefit levels, work requirements,
and Nixon's intention to simultaneously terminate Aid to Families

with Dependent Children all meant that it actually amounted to a further attack on the poor. Even as they continued to champion a guaranteed, adequate income that was additive to a more comprehensive anti-poverty agenda, they succeeded in defeating Nixon's Family Assistance Plan—a testament to their political savvy and to the power they had built.

Even during the heyday of NWRO, there was an important and largely unresolved debate among its leaders about the agency of the poor and their model of organizing. In 1966, George Wiley met Frances Fox Piven and Richard Cloward, two social scientists at the Columbia School of Social Work. They went on to play a leadership role within NWRO and write some of the authoritative texts on the welfare system and organizing among the poor, including *Regulating the Poor* and *Poor People's Movements: How They Succeed and Why They Fail*. During the days of NWRO, they felt strongly that the welfare mothers should focus on being a disruptive force in society rather than building a mass membership organization and attemping to meet the daily needs of their members. Piven and Cloward questioned the "dubious premise that poor people can develop political power through permanent membership organizations"[20] and worried that an attention to organizing, leadership development, and political education got in the way of mobilizing the discontent of the poor. In their 1966 paper "Organizing the Poor: How It Can Be Done," they argued that welfare recipients should instead dedicate their activity to "flooding the welfare rolls" to the point that the system was overwhelmed, thus allowing them to secure whatever concessions, big or small, they could win from the government.[21] Theirs was a tactical position that failed to anticipate the punishing state repression that poor people's movements faced in the late 1960s and 1970s.

In his 2011 book, *Pedagogy of the Poor*, Willie Baptist, who has worked alongside leaders of the welfare rights movement for decades,

reflects on the differing strategic outlook of the welfare mothers and
Piven and Cloward:

> On the one side, you had the welfare recipients who were arguing
> that they themselves should assume leadership of this process—
> determining the allocation of money, target, tactics, and so on.
> They argued that those decisions should come from the women
> who were facing the problems and were directly affected. . . . On
> the other side, Cloward and Piven argued that the poor were too
> poor to organize. Poor people's organizations could never get the
> clout necessary to offer economic benefits for their members, like
> the unions. To devote their energies and meager resources for or-
> ganizing efforts was to forfeit energies that should have gone into
> disruption. In my reading of them, Cloward and Piven relegated the
> poor, for the most part, to the role and function of disrupters, while
> the leadership of that process would be passed on to the middle-
> class intellectuals through which the interests of the upper-class
> and their two party system would dominate.[22]

This internal debate was never resolved and continued to play out
within NWRO until its decline in the early to mid-1970s. But perhaps
the most insurmountable challenges for the organization were the
counterreaction to gains won through the Black Freedom Struggle in
the 1960s and the country's turn, in the 1970s, toward neoliberalism.
As high inflation and unemployment weakened the economy, the
Nixon administration began to implement the three-headed hound of
"decentralization," "workfare," and "individualism." Guida West writes
that all three principles were aimed at shifting the role of government in the lives of its citizens: (1) Decentralization involved taking
decision-making power out of the hands of the federal government
and placing it into the hands of local and state government or private
business. (2) Workfare involved new schemes to force people to "pay

off" their benefits through low-wage or no-wage work, a precursor to the work requirements that now riddle our welfare system. (3) Individualism was a narrative campaign that trumpeted the mythical idea of the rugged individual who doesn't—and shouldn't—need a community or the government to support them.[23]

Despite this reactionary turn of American politics, the welfare mothers of NWRO left a lasting, if underappreciated, mark on the life of our nation. Their position at the very bottom of the economy was painful, but it also offered them a potent clarity about themselves and society. Struggling every day to get by, they were clear about what they were up against and equally clear that their survival depended on their ability to organize their communities across lines of historic division. NWRO's fusion of an economic, racial, and gender analysis was years ahead of its time, and their policy demands were prescient, anticipating the needs of wider sections of the workforce as deindustrialization worsened and neoliberalism set in. Most importantly, NWRO backed up their visionary analysis with robust organization, proving to themselves, the world, and future generations that poor people are often best positioned to recognize the direction our society needs to travel in order to resolve its biggest problems—and that they are capable of leading the fight to make the solutions to these problems a reality.

Many of NWRO's mothers never stopped fighting. Annie Chambers, the leader from Baltimore, has long been an important political mentor to me, as well as a seemingly bottomless source of unconventional organizing tactics. She has mothered thirty-nine kids (through birth and adoption), fostered many more, and her house has been a center of mutual aid and solidarity in Baltimore through the decades. One of my favorite stories from Chambers is drawn from a time the governor of Maryland was threatening cuts in the lead-up to welfare reform in the 1990s. She invited him and the local media to visit her and see how people on welfare lived. She fed the governor dinner and he commented that although welfare benefits were modest, poor people were able to survive on them. It was at this moment that Chambers brought out empty Alpo cans; she had served the governor dog food. In front of the news cameras, she proceeded to explain that this was how poor people were faring in Maryland, even before the governor's proposed welfare cuts—they were sometimes forced to live and eat like dogs to survive. Needless to say, the welfare rights movement was a force to be reckoned with.

UP AND OUT OF POVERTY NOW!

When the welfare mothers of NWRO first came together in the 1960s, the welfare state was a growing part of the nation's domestic economic policy. Two decades later, welfare, which had always been wholly inadequate, was under existential assault. In the early 1990s, the National Welfare Rights Union, the organizational successor of NWRO, released a strategy paper explaining that they were fighting for far more than a humane welfare system. What they were really fighting for was a world in which the welfare system was unnecessary and no longer used to manage poverty and control the poor. In the paper, titled "Which Way Welfare Rights? New Situation, New Strategy," a quote from Annie Smart, a veteran leader of NWRO and the third president of the National Welfare Rights Union, flipped the issue of survival on its head with one simple and piercing question:

Can America survive without poverty? If the answer is no, then in order for America to survive it must have some type of public benefits in order to regulate the victims of poverty, the permanent army of the unemployed. If the answer is yes, then everybody will have to be brought UP AND OUT OF POVERTY NOW! . . . We are not fighting for a trickle-down economy, but for society to work in our interests: to end homelessness, to provide health care and free quality education for all, and to end hunger.[24]

In the decades that followed the NWRO, veterans of the organization and other grassroots leaders endeavored to preserve and fine-tune the theory of change that the welfare mothers had fought for. In "Which Way Welfare Rights?," the National Welfare Rights Union identified three strategic principles of the Johnnie Tillmon organizing model: "(1) the organized poor must assume strong leadership within the movement, (2) the movement must be able to operate as a politically and financially independent force, and (3) the leaders of the movement must attend to the daily needs of their communities by building strong and visionary projects of survival." Years later, Marian Kramer, one of my first mentors and another president of the National Welfare Rights Union, summarized the Johnnie Tillmon model this way:

> In the Tillmon model, it's not winning benefits just for this or that person. We might get a little social security to be able to pay for all the bills they sent you, and you might have a little left. But we want a society where we can enjoy life. We want that for all. But that's not going to come from these nuts in DC talking about how we've put too much money in poor communities. They don't give a damn about us. Poor people, we always have a tendency to beat ourselves down and say we can't do things. But we know how to put a menu together, to take care of our families and all the children in the neighborhood. We don't have the money that the rich folks have to do these things for them. The Tillmon model uses these as leadership skills to help the poor organize around the demand that everybody should have what they need.[25]

In the Kensington Welfare Rights Union, one of the strongest chapters of the National Welfare Rights Union during the 1990s, we did our best to put this model into action. People came to KWRU first out of necessity, but they stuck around because we had something larger to offer them. In our encampments and during our takeovers, we worked to secure not only housing, clothing, and food for our members but also a deepening of their leadership and political consciousness. Just like Johnnie Tillmon, we were uncompromising in our belief that the residents of Kensington could think and act for themselves. But we knew this would happen only if we approached every setback and crisis as an opportunity to politicize our community and help them understand the deeper roots of the problems they were facing.

By the mid-1990s, our street-level organizing was making waves across Philadelphia, and city authorities nervously took notice. From the beginning, uniformed and undercover officers with the Civil Affairs Unit of the Philadelphia Police Department constantly surveilled and harassed our members. Meanwhile, welfare agents with the Department of Human Services investigated some of KWRU's mothers, scrutinizing their benefits and their living situations. A number of our members who were unhoused or didn't have running water in their homes had their children taken away and were told that they had as little as ten days to find stable housing—at a time when public housing and welfare were being gutted and gentrification had all but ensured there was no affordable housing to be found. More than once, a KWRU mother never got her children back. We were doing good work, but there is no need to view it through rose-tinted glasses. Organizing in Kensington was incredibly difficult given the terrorizing pushback we were up against, levied most harshly against the poor women of color in our ranks.

By the time I joined KWRU, welfare cuts were already creeping across the nation at the state and federal levels. In May 1996, Pennsylvania's Republican governor, Tom Ridge, who later served as the first secretary of Homeland Security after 9/11, signed into law a sweeping anti-welfare bill. This legislation introduced punishing work requirements and slashed healthcare for 250,000 across the state.[26]

Three months later, Clinton signed the Personal Responsibility and Work Opportunity Reconciliation Act into law. In Kensington, these latest attacks only added fuel to the fire of economic depression that our members were already battling. For every family we could house, countless more were being thrown into homelessness around us. At the time, it was tempting to hunker down and try to preserve what little we had, but the survival of our friends and families depended on more. We knew that we needed to broaden our reach beyond the boarded-up homes and pothole-laden streets of Kensington.

Over the next couple years, we led actions and marches both inside and outside the neighborhood, including a hundred-mile trek from the Liberty Bell in Philadelphia to the United Nations building in New York City called the "March for Our Lives." Still, more was needed, and in the winter of 1998, the policymaking council of KWRU, made up of poor and unhoused residents from Kensington, voted to launch a national organizing drive: the "New Freedom Bus Tour: Freedom from Unemployment, Hunger, and Homelessness." The decision was a big one, considering that we had scarce funds and the people voting desperately needed money to house and feed themselves and their families. But the decision reflected our growing clarity that conditions in Kensington would fundamentally change only through a national movement to end poverty, led by the poor.

As we prepared for the bus tour, we drew on whatever connections and relationships we had. In the mountains of eastern Tennessee, we held a national gathering called the "North-South Dialogue" at the Highlander Research and Education Center (once called the Highlander Folk School), the historic training ground for the industrial labor movement and the Civil Rights Movement. Afterward, we planned a route that would allow us to visit dozens of communities doing similar survival organizing.

We hit the road in the summer of 1998 in a rented Coach USA bus that swallowed up most of our already skeletal budget. Onboard were unhoused people, welfare recipients, low-wage workers, students, journalists, and filmmakers.* The tour began one month after I graduated from college and it was a major turning point in my life. As we made our way along interstate highways and back roads, I began to see the country, and the fight to end poverty, in an entirely new light.

As we swung through the South, we stopped in Columbia, Mississippi, a mostly poor, Black town built on a bluff atop a small river. In 1977, an explosion at a local chemical factory rocked the town, and a few years later a federal investigation revealed massive corporate malfeasance.[27] The chemical company had contaminated the local soil and pond water, and, after the explosion, it dumped hundreds of chemical-filled barrels near Columbia's water supply. This waste included toxins believed to be associated with Agent Orange, the lethal herbicide mixture used by the US military during the Vietnam War. The Environmental Protection Agency identified the factory as a Superfund site, a classification given to areas in need of environmental remediation due to corporate pollution. In the years that followed, the government claimed that the area was being sufficiently cleaned up, but during our visit a community leader named Evangelist Charlotte Keys, a deeply religious woman who carried a huge, dog-eared Bible wherever she went, showed us the truth.

Two decades after the explosion, the community was suffering from unusually high rates of cancer. As we walked through the town—the hundred-degree air thick with a synthetic stench—she pointed out which households were sick. In one house, two people had died from

---

* My partner, Chris, set up an interactive web page so that people across the country could follow the tour in real time. During the early days of the internet, he was something of a tech wizard and has since trained thousands of grassroots organizers how to harness digital power for social change. During the bus tour, thousands of people tuned in online.

the same cancer; right around the corner, five people from multiple generations of one family were sick. Many of these residents were living in federally funded houses for the elderly and disabled. The community had become a sacrifice zone for profit and war.

That visit to Columbia crystalized my understanding of how we will—and how we will not—end poverty in this country. Bearing witness to a form of corporate corruption and government complicity that was blatantly killing people, I began to grasp that it is not enough to simply break people's ignorance on the topic or appeal to their better angels. Poverty is not a bleeding-heart liberal issue that can be solved through guilt trips or good messaging. In Columbia, on federal land sick with poison and host to cancer, I understood, in a new way, how deeply poverty is baked into the heart of our profit-driven economy. Brave people like Evangelist Keys were doing whatever they could to raise awareness. Six years earlier, in 1992, she founded a group called Jesus People Against Pollution after, as she told me during the tour, she received a divine vision from God to investigate the town's water quality. But the community was still dying because of two simple facts: their lives were considered expendable and they were not powerful enough to fight back on their own. To disentangle themselves from a reality defined by disease and loss, they needed to confront the death-dealing power they were up against with even greater, life-affirming power.

Columbia was a wake-up call. In other communities, I saw the glimmer of what might be possible when poor people come together across their differences to demand everything they need and deserve. In the small rustbelt city of Lorain, Ohio—a multiracial union town with a long history of labor organizing and just miles from Oberlin, Ohio, once an important stop on the Underground Railroad—the local authorities publicly acknowledged how bad things were and how little they could do on their own. We held an Economic Human Rights Tribunal there, with members of the fire department and local police force selected as commissioners. Rather than distance themselves from poverty or beat up on the poor, the commissioners found the federal government guilty of human rights abuses. They recognized that their entire city had been impoverished by the nation's corporate elite. In Lorain, it was clear just how hungry a broad cross-section of people were for transformative change and how many unlikely allies were out there, ready to fight for it.

CHAPTER FOUR

THE RIGHT TO NOT BE POOR

The chapel at Union Theological Seminary in Harlem reverberated with laughter and song, eleven languages swirling together in a brilliant chorus of voices. It was the night before Halloween, 1999 and hundreds of us had crowded into the chapel, bleary-eyed but in good spirits. For the last thirty days, we had marched north from Washington, DC, to New York City, pitching tents alongside highways and in the parking lots of friendly churches and union halls. Among us were unhoused people from Philadelphia, laid-off autoworkers from Detroit, tomato pickers from central Florida, unemployed organizers from Quebec, Indigenous activists from the southern tip of Mexico, coca growers from Bolivia, and landless workers from Brazil. We called ourselves the March of the Americas.

It had been sixteen months since the New Freedom Bus Tour. In that time, the Kensington Welfare Rights Union decided to take everything we had learned in Kensington to launch the Poor People's Economic Human Rights Campaign (PPEHRC). Dozens of other poor people's organizations joined us as cosponsors, including many of those we met during the bus tour. The campaign's name was a direct callback to the 1968 Poor People's Campaign, but it also reflected a new strategic focus. Welfare reform and other neoliberal policies had forced the movement to end poverty into a desperately defensive posture and many grassroots organizers and community leaders were left feeling unmoored and rudderless. At KWRU, we knew that in order to survive we needed to find a new source of strength to anchor our struggle. We looked backward to history and outward to the rest of the world. What we discovered was the transformative power of human rights and of economic rights in particular.

Of course, we weren't unfamiliar with the idea of human rights, but it had often felt distant to many of us, academic or legalistic. In the news, we heard about human rights mainly in relation to faraway conflicts and the corruption of foreign governments. We were accustomed to thinking of human rights as a humanitarian tool used to alleviate the ravages of war or temper dictators, not as something relevant to our lives in the United States. Veterans of the welfare rights movement, like Marian Kramer of Michigan and Dottie Stevens of Massachusetts, argued otherwise.* They believed that while the concept of human rights often became narrow and toothless in the hands of governments, it had the potential to be an expansive, unifying force in the hands of poor and dispossessed people. The power of human rights rested in their transcendent moral clarity: that every person is endowed at birth with fundamental freedoms and protections, no matter who they are or where they are born.

So we at KWRU did our homework. We studied the history of the early movement for human rights, culminating in the ratification

---

* Kramer's story is shared further in this chapter. Stevens, a poor white mom from Boston and president of the Massachusetts Welfare Rights Union, ran for governor in 1990 on an "elect the victims of poverty" platform (see her May 10, 2014, obituary in the *Boston Globe* for more details). She said that she joined the welfare rights movement because many leaders were people of faith and she wanted to be on the side of God. She was the first welfare rights leader to adopt a human rights framework for poverty and welfare issues.

of the Universal Declaration of Human Rights (UDHR) by the United Nations in 1948. The UDHR was the product of tense political deliberations, not just moral ones, and the breadth of its vision was limited by the geopolitical jockeying of the world's superpowers at the dawn of the Cold War. Western countries, led by the United States, held the most power and leverage during the document's drafting, grounding it in individualistic and capitalistic principles. Still, the document—which includes a wide range of civil, political, economic, social, and cultural rights—represented a foundational benchmark in the evolving story of human rights. In a US context, it was especially resonant since its authors drew heavily from the moral principles of the Declaration of Independence and other founding documents that social movement leaders have appealed to for generations.

Amid the fallout of early twentieth-century fascism, political and civil rights, such as universal suffrage and equal protection, were considered of utmost importance by many. But some felt more was needed. In the *Evolution of International Human Rights: Visions Seen*, historian Paul Gordon Lauren writes that as the drafters the UDHR assessed the wreckage of the previous few decades, they

> came to regard the economic and social hardship suffered during the course of the Depression as contributing greatly to the rise of fascist regimes, the emergence of severe global competition, and ultimately to the outbreak of war itself. . . . They believed that poverty, misery, unemployment, and depressed standards of living anywhere in an age of a global economy and a technological shrinking of the world bred instability elsewhere and thereby threatened peace.[1]

Their response was to enshrine not only political and civil rights into the UDHR but also economic, social, and cultural rights. These included the right to health, food, clothing, housing, education, medical care, and a healthy environment; the right to equal and fair pay; the right to Social Security in the case of unemployment, sickness, disability, and old age; the right to rest and to not be overworked; and the right to form and join unions.

In the UDHR, human rights are given meaning through three key principles: they are inalienable, universal, and indivisible from one another. Given our experience in Kensington, these principles were especially salient for our organizing. If human rights, including economic rights, are universal and indivisible—if no single right can be realized without all of them being realized—then this was a simple and potent framework through which very different groups of people could find common cause across the many issues that shaped their lives. Just as compelling was the inalienable nature of human rights. In Kensington, we often encountered people who had been so dehumanized that they had come to believe in their own unworthiness as humans. Many of the members of KWRU were religious, and we often spoke about the sacredness of all life as we built tent encampments and took over vacant homes. In the framework of human rights, we found the perfect complement, one that was backed up by the consensus of the global community. The belief that we all have absolute, nonnegotiable rights simply because we are alive is an incredible act of faith, whether or not one is religious, and it is a stirring rebuttal to the experience of millions of people in this country, and billions across the world, whose basic needs are routinely ignored and abused.

Human rights have always been deeply contested in the United States. From the start, economic rights have either been excluded entirely from the framework or cast as impractical and unenforceable. This is in no small part because they are positive rights, demanding proactive action by the government within the economy, rather than negative rights, which, like religious liberty, demand freedom from unjust interference. Negative rights can be thought of as the right to be left alone, without abuse or persecution, while positive rights depend on collective action, with the goal of making all of our lives better. Positive rights also demand more public investments than negative rights, which make them difficult to implement given the limited space they inhabit in our nation's political imagination. To enforce economic rights in their totality would require our government to regulate the private sector, redistribute wealth from the top to the bottom, and more strongly protect the interests of the poor.

Even when economic rights are articulated by the government, their exercise is typically confined and recontextualized in strictly legal terms. The right to housing, for example, has been narrowed to become the right to due process in eviction hearings; the right to health or food has become the right to access certain welfare benefits, determined by a person's employment and income status. Since the hopeful days of the UDHR, economic rights have been stripped of their most transformative implications and chopped up into limited privileges for limited populations—they have become "opportunities" for us to compete within the profit-driven market for the necessities of life, rather than inalienable, universal, and indivisible guarantees. A full embrace of the human rights tradition, on the other hand, would require us to question whether profits should be allowed to take precedence over our rights to food, shelter, healthcare, and more.

Within this dynamic, economic rights have increasingly disappeared from our public discourse, so that many Americans now think only in terms of civil and political rights. But civil and political rights have also suffered, and over the last decade they have been steadily diminished into empty statements of national unity, while racial justice, Indigenous rights, immigrant rights, women's rights, LGBTQ+ rights, and more—all championed by powerful social movements of the past and present—are pilloried at a furious pace. We have also seen a massive spike in legal and political attacks on our election process, including voter suppression, racist gerrymandering, the influence of dark money, and election denial. What's more, our democracy itself is impoverished, not just in terms of formal legal processes but in terms of the inability of nearly half of the country to regularly meet their daily needs and have a say in the policies that determine their lives.

The result? We find ourselves in a situation in which we are forced to choose whose rights—and which rights of those people—can be realized. When human rights are divided, abridged, and ignored, our movements become scattered and we are reduced to fighting one another for slivers of the good life.

In the 1990s, a new generation of human rights advocates and organizers revived the fight for economic rights, both in the United States and internationally. KWRU and PPEHRC were on the frontlines of that fight. We argued that welfare reform—the stripping away of life-saving resources for tens of millions of people—was not only a callous policy decision but a massive abuse of human rights. For one, it violated the "prohibition on retrogression," which in human rights law forbids the rescinding of rights once they have been extended. It also violated the "maximum available resources" provision, which requires governments to allocate all the resources at their disposal to advance the human rights of their citizens. In one of the wealthiest countries in the world, cutting off some of the poorest people from what already amounted to paltry food and housing programs was clearly a fundamental attack on what it means to be human in the modern world.

At the same time as welfare reform, the Clinton administration was preparing to repeal the Glass-Steagall Act of 1933, a move that deregulated commercial and investment banks and remains a major source of global economic destabilization. The government was also hard at work putting the North American Free Trade Agreement (NAFTA) into motion, a free-trade zone created in 1994 between Canada, the United States, and Mexico. With the formation of NAFTA, large corporations were quickly granted unprecedented intellectual property protections* and free rein to dominate local markets, uproot jobs, and dispossess millions of people across North America. (NAFTA and the other free-trade agreements that followed helped destabilize economies across Latin American and remain a primary reason so many people are forced to migrate to the US.) Within the dark shadow of this multilateral agreement—which only accelerated the economic disinvestment already plaguing Kensington—we began to understand just how intimately bound up our fight against poverty and for human rights was with people not just across the country but the world.

When KWRU launched the Poor People's Economic Human Rights Campaign in 1999, we decided that our first action needed to make these connections explicit, so we invited poor people's movements throughout the Western Hemisphere to join us in October for our month-long march from Washington, DC, to the United Nations in New York City. We began at the headquarters of the Inter-American Commission on Human Rights where we filed a petition indicting the US for economic human rights violations because of welfare reform and NAFTA. Although this was largely a symbolic gesture, it was important. Here we were, an international coalition of poor people's movements, filing a sound legal case against the

---

* Economic rights, meant to uplift life, are often perversely twisted to protect intellectual property rights. At the end of 2020, as the world awaited the arrival of multiple COVID-19 vaccines, India and South Africa made an urgent proposal to the World Trade Organization. They requested that it temporarily suspend intellectual property rights to ensure that all nations could access and produce vaccines and other medical technologies like ventilators, masks, and protective gear. Dozens of other countries came forward to support the proposal, but a few powerful countries like the United States, the United Kingdom, and members of the European Union rejected and ultimately quashed it to protect the patents of pharmaceutical companies. For more on this, read this article I wrote in 2021: "Whose Rights Matter in Pandemic America?" Tom Dispatch, https://tomdispatch.com /whose-rights-matter-in-pandemic-america/.

American government for its grim human rights record both at home and abroad. It was a David and Goliath moment.

From DC we marched north, up through the city's lush suburbs and into rural Maryland, through conservative areas that had long been written off by liberals and progressives and were notorious for white supremacist activity. I was a lead organizer of the march, and Willie Baptist and I were responsible for mapping out the route. As we scouted ahead, we learned that a group of antiwar activists had recently attempted to march through a nearby town to protest American sanctions in Iraq. Their march hadn't progressed very far before locals started pelting them with tomatoes. When we spoke with these activists, they advised us to steer clear of the town, but we told them we had made promises to local organizers that we would march through. Still, we prepared for the worst.

We were delighted when our arrival was received not with venom but near total acceptance. Folks in this white working-class town welcomed us and expressed their strong support for the slogans on our banners and signs, which said things like "Healthcare for All" and "Housing Is a Human Right." They told us about the low wages and the lack of workers' rights devouring their community, about their healthcare crises and crumbling homes, and they encouraged us to keep fighting. Our collective experience working in places like this taught us that people typically join movements when they see them-selves, their own dilemmas and dreams, reflected back to them. Many of us were peace activists, and we suspected that these folks might be receptive to discussing the human rights violations of NAFTA and even of the sanctions that were starving millions of Iraqi civilians, including hundreds of thousands of children. But we also knew that was most likely to happen if we connected the dots between what our government was doing abroad and what it was failing to do here in this town: to uphold the human rights of its residents. We understood that the same politicians who were supporting sanctions against Iraqi children* were denying the economic rights of millions of Americans. Our belief was that if we challenged the government where it was weak on issues like healthcare and housing, it would go a long way to shifting the political priorities of the nation toward human rights and peace for all.

For the next three weeks, we marched ten to twenty miles a day, punctuated by regular cultural events and concerts with artists and musicians including Ani DiFranco, Dar Williams, Steve Earle, Jackson Browne, and Wyclef Jean, as well as local hip-hop, folk, gospel, and country artists. In the late afternoons and evenings, we stopped to make camp and learn from one another. When grassroots organizers gather together in numbers, their conversations are often mediated by foundations and large NGOs, and although the intentions of funders are usually genuine, the presence of money tends to have a warping effect on the ability of people to speak honestly with one another. During the march, we had a unique opportunity to have an extended and direct encounter between some of the most important poor people's movements in the Western Hemisphere. We called ourselves the University of the Poor, a traveling school, and our discussions had a lasting impact on all of us, shaping our movements for years to come.

For those of us from the US, it was remarkable to meet organizers who were waging, even winning, similar struggles in other countries. Community leaders from Cochabamba, Bolivia, for example, taught us about their ongoing fight against the privatization of water in their city—efforts that were reversed the next year, in 2000, after massive street protests triggered the first water wars of the twenty-first

---

* During a 1996 interview on *60 Minutes*, a journalist asked then US ambassador to the United Nations Madeleine Albright, "We have heard that half a million children have died. I mean, that is more children than died in Hiroshima . . . and, you know, is the price worth it?" Albright famously replied: "I think that is a very hard choice, but the price, we think, the price is worth it."

century. Organizers from Highland Park and Detroit, Michigan, listened carefully and referred back to these conversations when their own water began to get shut off and privatized just a few years later. For the folks from Latin America, the march was also eye-opening. Many were visiting the US for the first time and were stunned by the poverty they saw, so different from the glitzy image of a country whose streets are supposedly paved with gold. When we asked these international organizers how we could support their movements, including their fight against American interventionism, they replied that the best way to help was to build power among the poor right here in the "belly of the beast."*

After weeks of marching, bedraggled but brimming with new conversations and comrades, we arrived in New York City. We piled into James Memorial Chapel at Union Theological Seminary, where waiting students, faculty, and staff had cooked us a meal and organized a Halloween party for our kids. That afternoon we hosted a public dialogue on the human rights violations of welfare reform and NAFTA. By then we were practiced at bridging the linguistic divide, and the event was simultaneously translated into eleven languages, including American Sign Language.

I was a delirious blend of exhausted and exhilarated. Looking around the chapel with pride, I understood that the immediate victory of this march was not going to be the policy changes we were demanding but the relationships and political consciousness we were bringing home. At the time, elite historians and political scientists brazenly claimed that the political evolution of history had reached its final and most advanced stage: the end of history. But we were living proof that, on the precipice of a new millennium, history was

---

* Some of the organizers with us went on to teach tactics to the anti-globalization protestors who took on the World Trade Organization a few months later in the now famous 1999 Battle of Seattle.

far from over. Through the March of the Americas, we had asserted
the undaunted agency of the world's poor and helped usher in the
grassroots struggle for human rights in the twenty-first century.

During the battle over welfare reform, the movement had a common
slogan: "They say cut back, we say fight back!" It was a good rallying cry, but it exemplifies how much time we spent on the back foot,
defensively responding to attacks on our communities as our political horizons narrowed. When welfare was cut, we tried to regain the
ground that was lost. When those in power attacked healthcare or
protections for women's rights or labor rights, we rallied with each
community that was under assault, attempting to lessen the blow and
soften their isolation. But the losses kept coming. At the end of the
1990s, our turn toward human rights finally provided us with clear
and universal demands that shifted our struggles from a reactive and
defensive position to an offensive one. In KWRU and PPEHRC,
for example, our fight *against* welfare reform became our fight *for*
the universal rights to food, water, clothing, housing, health care, and
good jobs. By bringing together dozens of different poor people's organizations, we also demonstrated that our power rested not in any
one issue but in the multiplicity of our demands and communities
coming together. Successful movements never just curse the darkness;
they offer new ways of illuminating the future.

Economic rights, which we could call the "right to not be poor,"
suggest a vision of the world free from want, especially in a time of
plenty. Over seventy-five years after its ratification, the UDHR should
not be understood as a conclusive text but as a useful road map to be
expanded upon as the changing times help us fill in the blank spots.
Human rights today are formally expressed through fairly weak laws,
treaties, and judicial processes. But when the emancipatory vision
of human rights is liberated from the elite strata of politicians and

lawyers and brought directly into the places and spaces of poor and dispossessed people, it becomes a transformed and transformative force. When a tenants' union on rent strike demands that housing is a human right, or when a community group fighting a rural hospital closure demands that healthcare is a human right, they are making broad moral claims about our individual and collective lives that must then be debated in the public square.

The fight for human rights also has the power to connect and expand struggles of the poor that are too often siloed from one another, both in the US and internationally. This became clear to me on the March of the Americas, which solidified my understanding that although the circumstances of the march's participants varied wildly, more united us than separated us. This perspective grounded the work of the Poor People's Economic Human Rights Campaign during the 2000s. For nearly ten years, hundreds of community leaders came together through PPEHRC to share strategies on how to organize around various economic rights issues. We also collaborated on regional and national actions, like the 2000 Republican National Convention demonstration described in chapter 2. Through these relationships, I continued to learn about the long and fraught history of human rights in the US, and its radical potential for the future.

THE ELUSIVE PRIZE OF ECONOMIC RIGHTS

The end of World War II answered one set of burning questions for the world's power brokers and opened up a Pandora's box of new ones. How would peace and stability be forged after so much death and destruction? Who would rise to the top of the global pecking order now that the old European imperial powers were in shambles? From the perspective of the US elite, the answers were clear: this was the dawn of the "American Century," and it would be American values and dollars that would broker a new world order. Amid this postwar bravado, top leaders in the US government saw the formation of the United Nations, including its framework of human rights, as an important, if complicated, vehicle to legitimize its moral leadership on the world stage.

Back in the United States, human rights became the lingua franca of both the elite and the oppressed, including some of the largest Black-led organizations in the country. The previous decades had seen brutal racial discrimination and white supremacist violence, including mass lynchings, and little seemed to be changing. Alongside these intolerable horrors, there was the reality of rampant poverty in Black communities. Many young Black organizers were soldiers who returned home to segregation and deprivation after fighting alongside white men in Europe. This stark experience only deepened their understanding of the hypocrisies of American democracy, which claimed to be a force for freedom in the world, only to deny basic freedoms to its own citizens.

During the mid-to-late 1940s, many Black-led organizations, including the NAACP, worked vigorously to secure human rights as the new standard for American policymaking. In 1947, a year before the ratification of the UDHR, W. E. B. Du Bois supervised the delivery of the first people's petition to the newly formed United Nations. The ninety-six-page document, titled *An Appeal to the World*, took the United States to task for its human rights violations against Black Americans on everything from voting rights to education, healthcare, and wages. For many in the White House and Congress, this upsurge in homegrown human rights organizing was a bridge too far.

In 1944, a year before his death, President Franklin D. Roosevelt called for a Second Bill of Rights, or an Economic Bill of Rights, but the idea of marrying civil and political rights with economic rights was the target of fierce and ongoing opposition from Southern segregationists and others. A few years later, even liberal political actors like Roosevelt's wife, Eleanor, hailed as a friend of racial equality and one of the American architects of the UDHR, was reticent about how far to go on economic rights. In *Eyes Off the Prize: The United Nations and the African American Struggle for Human Rights, 1944–1955*, historian Carol Anderson writes that during the drafting of the UDHR

> Eleanor Roosevelt made the political distinction between the revered political and legal rights emanating from Western thought, such as the right to free speech, and the untried, untested, and unwashed economic and social rights that seemed so dear to the Soviets and other communists. Truman and his advisors agreed and tried desperately to reign in or at least neutralize the UN's rights initiatives and to supplant the international community's expansive definition of human rights with one that included only a small number of political and legal rights.[2]

Over the next decade, as the Cold War began to heat up, human rights were further denigrated by leading American politicians. Anderson continues: "During the McCarthy era, human rights and the United Nations became synonymous with the Kremlin and the Soviet-led subversion of American democracy." As Red Scare hysteria swept across the country, both Democrats and Republicans "denounced rights, such as housing and health care, as foreign to all liberty-loving Americans and inspired by the scourge of Marxist dogma." Social movements for racial and economic justice suffered from this ideological assault. But, although the government refused to engage on the terrain of human rights, organizers continued fighting for them. In 1965, Bayard Rustin, A. Philip Randolph, Dr. King, and a number of other allies who had taken part in the 1963 March on Washington for Jobs and Freedom published *A Freedom Budget for All Americans*. The budget was explicitly written within the frame of human rights and called for massive public investments to tackle American poverty wherever it existed. A few years later, this document served as inspiration for the policy platform of the 1968 Poor People's Campaign, including its revived demand for an Economic Bill of Rights.

Near the end of his life, King reflected on the fact that up until then the government had only been willing to advance civil and political rights, and even those within significant limits. The government had evaded the movement's broader social and economic demands. In *Where Do We Go from Here*, he wrote that the movement, and the country as a whole, had arrived at a decisive crossroads:

> So far, we have had constitutional backing for most of the demands for change, and this has made our work easier, since we could be sure of legal support from the federal courts. Now we are approaching areas where the voice of the Constitution is not clear. We have left the realm of constitutional rights and we are entering the area of human rights. The Constitution assured the right to vote, but there is no such assurance of the right to adequate housing, or the right to an adequate income. And yet, in a nation which has a gross national product of 750 billion dollars a year [$27 trillion in 2023], it is morally right to insist that every person have a decent house, an adequate education, and enough money to provide basic necessities for one's family. Achievement of these goals will be a lot more difficult and require much more discipline, understanding, organization, and sacrifice.[3]

King's commentary on human rights was tragically prescient. In the 1970s, social movements both in the US and elsewhere suffered under the weight of increased state repression and the inauspicious arrival of neoliberalism. Meanwhile, major self-identified human rights leaders in the US, including King, Malcolm X, and Fred Hampton, were assassinated by the end of the 1960s. All of them were being investigated and targeted by the state at the time of their deaths.

The next decade saw the birth of the international human rights movement as it is more commonly understood, anchored by a community of intergovernmental agencies and NGOs, mostly in the Global North. Many of these groups started small and scrappy and later grew in prominence and professional polish. Organizations like Amnesty International, which was founded in 1961 and expanded massively in the 1970s and 1980s, worked on a host of civil and political issues like freedom of speech, torture, and the death penalty. They won important victories, and by capturing the attention of tens of millions around the world, they further popularized the idea of human rights. But although these organizations were international in scope, they remained rooted in Europe and North America, moving their work along the grooves and fissures created by Western colonialism and imperialism. Their vision of human rights was also conditioned and constrained by Western values. Economic rights were largely left off the table and the more radical initiatives of these groups to expand civil and political rights, even within Western countries, were met with fierce opposition and elite cooptation.

A colleague of mine, Larry Cox, spent most of his career working for some of the world's largest human rights organizations, including Amnesty International and the Rainforest Foundation. Cox was raised by a poor, white, single mom in small-town Ohio, and he once told me that as a boy he watched Dr. King on TV and felt that this Black leader was also fighting for the rights of his community. In the 1990s, Cox was a program officer at the Ford Foundation—with a focus on human rights in the United States—and was one of the only funders of KWRU at a time when no one in philanthropy would take our calls. After a stint as the executive director of Amnesty International USA in the 2000s, he returned to Union Theological Seminary to finish a degree he once started, and in 2013 he cofounded the Kairos Center for Religions, Rights, and Social Justice with me.

Just before he retired in 2018, Cox was the keynote speaker at a symposium on human rights and religion at Yale University. He reflected on the achievements and limitations of the international human rights movement over the previous half century, including how its center of gravity had moved away from grassroots and religious organizations and toward smaller circles within the professional class:

> As the human rights movement grew and its activism, reports, and criticisms got increased attention, governments, at least the less threatened ones, responded by dramatically increasing the number of international treaties, mechanisms, and judicial processes. These promised, and in a few cases delivered, some modest advances but, intentional or not, these government-approved pathways were slow and time consuming and often seemed designed to keep human rights workers diverted from more threatening domestic forms of generating political pressure.
>
> Donors also responded to the march of human rights by giving some of the key organizations financial resources beyond their wildest dreams. This made it possible to begin hiring more and more professionals who got their training not from time spent in grassroots movements and struggles but increasingly from university programs usually set up in law schools. Human rights began to shift from a cause to a career. The discourse on human rights began to shift from a moral one—accessible to all—to a legal one, accessible to a few. . . .
>
> There is no doubt this professionalization of human rights produced some immediate and important results. But over the longer term, human rights changed from a universal idea that concerned all human beings and was relevant to nearly every serious issue facing them—a moral idea related to and supported by virtually every religious tradition, calling on people of all backgrounds to join a universal fight—into one more specialized legal discipline with its own peculiar language and methodology, not needing activists as much as it needed financial donations to support experts.[4]

The professionalization of human rights occurred within the larger rise of the nonprofit industrial complex, with its wealthy benefactors, evasive tax structure, and close ties to the corporate world. Joan Roe-lofs, a political scientist who studies the history of philanthropy, writes that by the 1970s, "radical activism often was transformed by grants and technical assistance from liberal foundations into fragmented and local organizations subject to elite control. Energies were channeled into safe, legalistic, bureaucratic and, occasionally, profit-making ac-tivities."[5] Of course, grassroots organizers, especially poor ones, had to take money where they could get it, and many continued to do good work. Similarly, there were plenty of grant makers and foundation officers who funded visionary projects. The problem wasn't any one individual operating within this paradigm but the paradigm itself.

The codependent relationship between powerful granters and needful grantees was a boon to the wealthy, who preferred that the poor and their allies fight for resources and advocate for specific and isolated policy issues, rather than focus on fundamental questions of economic and political power. Over time, many poor people's orga-nizations morphed into, or were usurped by, nonprofit organizations that mimicked the structure of Fortune 500 companies and were less accountable to actual bases of people. The effect was one of division and containment: potentially transformational human rights organiz-ing was often fractured and channeled into more acceptable forms of advocacy, offering very small answers to very big problems.

EVERYBODY IN, NOBODY OUT

Today, with societal instability and authoritarianism on the rise at home and abroad, some in the political sphere have abandoned the framework of human rights altogether. We are now being forced into an ever-more-defensive posture to protect the rights we still enjoy instead of imagining and championing all of the rights that we in-trinsically possess. But poor people's movements across the world are still holding the line. Members of these movements know that beyond the rarified world of lawyers and experts, and the limits of the nonprofit industrial complex, human rights, including economic rights, still offers a vision for the future where everybody has the right to live and thrive.

I've worked alongside many of these movements in this country. These groups—including the Michigan Welfare Rights Organization in Detroit and Highland Park, the Coalition of Immokalee Workers in southwest Florida, and the Vermont Workers' Center—continue to be on the cutting edge of human rights organizing. Over the last two decades, they have pioneered innovative models of movement building among the poor and helped revitalize the fight for human rights in the United States.

Water Is a Human Right: The Michigan Welfare Rights Organization

"They had to take away our democracy before they could take away our water." Claire McClinton, one of the founders of the Flint Democracy Defense League and a member of the Michigan Welfare Rights Organization (MWRO), once shared these words with me. Called "Squeaky" by friends, McClinton is a labor organizer who was politicized in the 1960s and has worked for decades alongside other poor and working-class organizers in Michigan, including General Gordon Baker, Marian Kramer, and Maureen Taylor (all mentors of mine).

Baker was the first person to publicly burn his draft card during the Vietnam War and was a labor leader with the Dodge Revolutionary Union Movement, the League of Revolutionary Black Workers, and the United Auto Workers Local 600. His widow, Kramer, got her start in the civil rights and welfare rights movements in the 1960s and 1970s. She is also a close comrade of Taylor, one of the most clear-eyed and militant people I've ever met. In the 1960s, Baker famously convinced Taylor, then a young radical, to put down a Molotov cocktail during a street protest and instead join the workers' movement.

Over the last couple decades, McClinton, Baker, Kramer, and Taylor have taught me about a two-fold human rights crisis that has swept across Michigan: the crisis of democracy and the crisis of clean and affordable water. Starting in 2000, the state government in Lansing began placing cities into "receivership," suspending local democratic processes and empowering nonelected emergency managers to govern in their place (all of these cities are majority Black and became impoverished after auto jobs began drying up decades ago). These emergency managers had unlimited power to unilaterally cancel union contracts, sell public assets like libraries, and suspend and privatize sanitation services—anything to pay back the bonds and debts owed by these cities to Wall Street.[6] Through unilateral decision-making, they had full discretion to further enclose the "commons" of urban Michigan: public space and infrastructure that could be captured by the private sector. The cities that were put into receivership became tiny fiefdoms for the interests of companies like Nestlé, Whirlpool, Ford, Stellantis, and General Motors, rather than democratically run communities.

The 2014 Flint water crisis—in which over one hundred thousand disproportionately poor Black people were exposed to poisoned water, including ten thousand children[7]—occurred under the watch of an emergency manager. Bemoaning that the cost of piped water from Detroit was too high, he switched the water lines from the Detroit Water System to the Flint River. Local supply pipes were corroded after the switch was made, allowing lead to seep into the water now flowing into people's homes. Because democracy had been suspended in Flint, the emergency manager never had to consult with the community.

Meanwhile, in Detroit and Highland Park—a small, separate municipality within the bounds of Detroit where my mom was born and raised*—the privatization of their water systems was a looming threat throughout the 2000s and 2010s. Both cities have old and battered water infrastructure that have long needed to be updated. But rather than receive financial support from the state or federal government to

---

* In a stroke of serendipity, General Baker and my mom were high school classmates.

improve their water systems, the neoliberal solution in the 2000s was austerity. Detroit and Highland Park both began jacking up utility prices and cutting off the taps of people who couldn't pay. In Highland Park, an emergency manager in power from 2001 to 2018 also imposed extreme municipal cuts: closing the library and recreation center, limiting the work hours of public employees, and stripping city officials of their power to legislate the city budget. For months, she even refused to authorize the expenses involved with turning the lights on at city hall.[8] When she closed the city's district court, public safety officers accused her of creating a pay crisis to destroy their union. In an interview with my partner, Chris, and me in the midst of this crisis, Kramer noted they "don't have people checking fire hydrants anymore. When there is a fire, everyone is afraid. Whole blocks burn because the fire hydrants are not working. Neighboring cities' fire departments refuse to help. Who will pay them? They just let the city burn."[9]

A few miles away in Detroit, an emergency manager was appointed in 2013, when the city shut off an unprecedented forty-four thousand household taps, often sealing valves with cement for good measure.[10] In order to survive, residents became experts in water sharing and other forms of community solidarity. When I was regularly visiting with the Michigan Welfare Rights Organization at the height of the crisis, it was not uncommon to see garden hoses hanging between the open windows of two neighboring houses. Residents called this and similar survival strategies "cutting their water back on."

The implications of these intolerable conditions extended far beyond just the immediate effects of shutoff taps. In Detroit, the city administrator added delinquent water bills to the property tax owed for a home, empowering the city to foreclose on people who couldn't pay their water bills.[11] Meanwhile, children were seized from parents who couldn't afford to keep their taps on and placed in foster care.[12] Teachers, in fact, often began the school year by instructing students that they could use the sinks and bathrooms before and after school but to not tell them if the water was shut off at home; as "required reporters," they would have to report their students' parents to Child Protective Services.

In 2014, both the United Nations special rapporteur on the human right to water and sanitation and the special rapporteur on the right to adequate housing visited Michigan. In a joint statement after the visit, they denounced Michigan's water shutoffs and forced evictions as contrary to human rights:

> We were deeply disturbed to observe the indignity people have faced and continue to live with in one of the wealthiest countries in the world and in a city that was a symbol of America's prosperity. We were also distressed to learn from the low-income African American residents of the impossible choices they are being compelled to make—to either pay their rent or their medical bill, or to pay their water bill.[13]

Leaders with MWRO, mostly poor Black and Brown women, have been at the forefront of this human rights struggle. When the crisis first broke out in Flint, they worked with mothers to ring the alarm that they were being poisoned, using hashtags like #flintwatercrisis and #flintlivesmatter to go viral online and garner national media coverage before anyone was paying attention. They organized marches from Flint to Detroit calling for the city and state to switch the Flint water source from the Flint River back to the Detroit Water System, in the process making connections between poisoned water in Flint and water shutoffs in Detroit and Highland Park.

Long before national figures like Barack Obama, who famously drank filtered Flint water during a 2016 press conference, visited the city, the women of MWRO invited leaders from other poor communities to visit. People from as far as Texas and Louisiana heeded the call, bringing pallets of bottled water with them. I was particularly moved when a community facing coal ash contamination in West Virginia heard about the situation in Flint. They fundraised for bottled water and then drove up with the donated water in their cars and minivans. This kind of solidarity was evidence of just how radical human rights can be in the hands of poor and dispossessed people. These mostly poor white West Virginian families didn't travel hundreds of miles out of pity or sympathy. Rather, they saw their own lives and livelihoods reflected in the fight for water and life in this majority Black city.

In Highland Park, MWRO helped build a broad and racially diverse coalition called the Highland Park Human Rights Coalition. They held "Water Town Hall Meetings" to which residents were encouraged to bring their water bills and expose the affordability and shutoff crisis in front of local TV and radio broadcasters. In the state capitol in Lansing, they organized a "State of the People Address" that mobilized large numbers of affected residents to lobby the governor and state legislature. MWRO also led numerous acts of nonviolent civil disobedience in front of local water departments and pursued legal action in the form of a "Complaint for Administrative Relief" against the city agencies responsible for water and sanitation services.

Over the years, MWRO and their allies have focused on the interlocking nature of the death of democracy and the gross violation of human rights. By speaking out about the confluence of civil, political, and economic rights, they have articulated a powerful rebuttal against the undemocratic attempt to strip away the remaining public assets in their rustbelt cities. The organization has also called into question why water costs anything at all when it falls freely from the sky and they are surrounded by the largest freshwater lakes in the world.

Back in 2007, Maureen Taylor, the state chairperson of MWRO, explained: "Access to water, access to the means of survival is supposed to be one of the tenets that democracy is built [on]. When you have a class of people that are denied the ability to live, that is a straight-up democratic fight. Your children are under attack. Your survival is under attack."[14] Two years earlier, MWRO helped craft the country's first comprehensive water affordability plan, which was passed by the Detroit city council but never implemented.[15] About this plan, Taylor said:

> When Michigan Welfare Rights first started negotiating with the water department around a new way to structure water rate charges, we contacted some groups of attorneys we knew. We had a number of meetings to pull together language that would be a systemic change in how water rates are charged. After many months, we found a legal expert out of Boston, Mass., specializing [in] developing language for affordability programs. We sent him packages of notes, this is what it should be, this is what it should say, and this is the outcomes, and he put something together and it is brilliant. We are very proud of it. We made copies and took it to members of city council, took it to the water department. People looked at it and scrutinized it, and couldn't find anything wrong with it.[16]

Nearly two decades later, MWRO's vision is finally being taken more seriously. In 2023, after a temporary pandemic-era moratorium on water shutoffs expired, Michigan legislators authored the first statewide water affordability bill, drawing on the research and advocacy of MWRO and their allies.[17]

MWRO has at times been pressured to frame their organizing around water as only a struggle for civil rights and racial justice rather than human rights. On this point, they have demonstrated farsighted leadership. They are clear that in Michigan, it is poor Black people who have overwhelmingly suffered from the water crisis, and they speak passionately about the racism that is killing their communities. But just like their experience during deindustrialization, they understand that they are harbingers of a national crisis that is intensifying for tens of millions of people of every racial and ethnic background. Food and Water Watch estimates that about fifteen million people have their water shut off every year, and a 2023 study from the US Geological Survey found that half of America's drinking water was contaminated with synthetic "forever chemicals" (to say nothing about the crisis of our nation's shrinking aquifers).[18] This national emergency will only be solved when we reorient our society's relationship with water systems and the natural world, including guaranteeing safe and accessible drinking water for everyone. And this kind of lasting solution will only be achieved when we finally treat water as a human right instead of as a waste bin for industrial poison and a commodity to be traded by C-suite executives on the backs of the poor.

Farmworkers' Rights Are Human Rights: The Coalition of Immokalee Workers

The Immokalee region of southwest Florida is famous for its tomatoes and infamous for the labor abuses of its farmworkers. Over the years, these workers, who are mostly Guatemalan, Mexican, and Haitian, have lived in conditions that might shock even the most experienced human rights lawyers. Back in the 1990s, young men, far from everyone and everything they knew, sometimes lived twelve to a trailer and were paid as little as $7,000 a year, most of which they sent back home to their families. Every day, each of these workers filled hundreds of buckets of produce by hand, trapped in the fields not just by their low wages but through indentured contracts and even in slavery rings. Some workers were forced to pick tomatoes from sunup to sundown and then chained in the back of shipping containers over night. The situation was so bad that a US attorney once called Immokalee "ground zero for modern slavery."[19]

In 1993, a small group of workers and organizers began meeting in a local church to make a plan to fight back. These included Lucas Benitez, a farmworker who came from Mexico when he was fourteen and has since become an international human rights leader; Greg Asbed, an organizer who was first politicized while working with peasant movements in Haiti and later won a MacArthur "Genius" Fellowship for his work in Immokalee; and Laura Germino, Asbed's partner and a brilliant public service lawyer. Out of these meetings,

Benitez, Asbed, and Germino, and dozens of others founded the Coalition of Immokalee Workers (CIW).

They began with hunger strikes and work stoppages, not just in the fields but across the community, recruiting families and concerned neighbors into their struggle. They have since grown into a sophisticated human rights organization, skillfully building a mass base among some of the poorest and most dispossessed people in the country: people with various legal statuses, who speak multiple languages and come from different ethnic and religious backgrounds. Over the last two decades, CIW has busted multiple slavery rings and won successful wage campaigns against some of the largest buyers of the produce they pick, including fast-food and grocery giants like Taco Bell, McDonald's, Burger King, Chipotle, Whole Foods, and Walmart.

I first met CIW leaders at the Highlander Center for the "North-South Dialogue," the meeting of poor people's organizations that KWRU pulled together before the 1998 New Freedom Bus Tour. A year later, seventeen of their members walked the entire route of the March of the Americas. After the march, Benitez, Asbed, and Germino invited Chris and me down to Immokalee to help them figure out how to harness the still new frontier of digital media to advance their efforts. At the time, very few people from outside Immokalee had visited the region, and CIW was especially concerned with how to break through their isolation, including the media blackout that made their work largely invisible to the world. We traveled back and forth to Immokalee multiple times, training CIW on early internet tactics like website design and video editing, which they then ran with beyond our wildest dreams. For example, they outfitted the flatbed of a pickup truck with a projector and an improvised screen and drove from one labor camp to another at dusk, playing educational and recruitment videos for their fellow workers. They also streamed these videos online and delivered them to a wide audience years before YouTube and TikTok. This was a groundbreaking use of very new information and communications technologies to organize grassroots campaigns.

In 2001, CIW conducted an analysis of the relationship between the country's largest tomato producers and commercial buyers. They had little leverage with producers who commanded near total power in the fields and had no public profile, but they realized they could influence the business practices of buyers, including Taco Bell, which was in the middle of negotiating a new contract with the company that supplied its tomatoes. If Taco Bell would agree to pay one penny more per pound for its tomatoes and pass that money on to the farmworkers, it would double their wages. CIW learned that Taco Bell was spending $250 million a year in ads to its most popular demographic, eighteen- to twenty-four-year-olds, so we developed a hybrid online/ offline campaign to reach young people on college campuses across the country.[20] This included a 2002 national bus tour, the Taco Bell Truth Tour, that drew from our experiences on the New Freedom Bus Tour a few years earlier. Organizers also led protests at local Taco Bell restaurants and community hearings, where immigrant workers and college students deployed a little creative political jiujitsu. At the time, Taco Bell's mascot was a chihuahua and one of their corporate slogans was "yo quiero Taco Bell." CIW went viral after they changed the slogan to "yo NO quiero Taco Bell," forcing the company to retire the yappy dog.

Over the next four years, CIW led a highly publicized national boycott of Taco Bell. During our early visits to Immokalee, Chris and I had met with local students and religious leaders who wanted to get involved. Now, CIW leveraged these relationships, as well as our connections with national faith organizations and denominations, to garner wider support. They convinced the United Church of Christ to pass the first denominational overture endorsing the boycott, and the Presbyterians, Episcopalians, the United Methodist Women, the National Council of Churches, and others soon followed. We also encouraged Sunday school classes to send letters of support to CIW, pressured Taco Bell shareholders in congregations to use their power at shareholder meetings to raise the demands of the farmworkers, recruited local faith leaders to join marches and bus tours, and enlisted Catholic bishops from the US and Mexico to write proclamations of support for the cause. These efforts demonstrated to the farmworkers that religious communities in Florida and elsewhere could show up on the side of love and justice, rather than on the side of extremism and corporate greed.

In 2005, after significant pressure, Taco Bell and its parent company, Yum Brands, agreed to all of CIW's demands, including ongoing payments directly from Taco Bell to tomato pickers and guarantees that the company would work with its suppliers to ensure its workers' human rights were protected. CIW also won recognition from Yum Brands as a participant in future contract negotiations. This was a significant development for farmworkers who have long been excluded from the protections of the National Labor Relations Board and weren't formally employed by Taco Bell. Building on the success of this campaign, CIW helped start other national human rights organizations, like the Alliance for Fair Food and the Student Farmworker Alliance. They also launched the Fair Food Program, now the international gold standard for fair labor practices across the entire length of agricultural supply chains. Fourteen multinational corporations have since signed onto the program.[21]

Because of the highly contingent and exploitative nature of the agricultural industry, CIW cannot afford to organize only at the point of production. Instead, they've innovated an organizing model that involves their entire community and uses direct action and mass media to win others to their cause. Their fair-food campaigns, a masterful combination of on-the-ground organizing and communications tactics designed to win hearts and minds, have helped galvanize a revival in farmworker organizing in the United States. These campaigns have also inspired other workers who have been historically excluded from

the traditional labor movement, like day laborers and domestic workers, to experiment with a similar organizing model. Through these
efforts, CIW has emerged as an important leader in an insurgent wave
of labor organizing that now includes the Amazon Labor Union,
Starbucks Workers United, the Union of Southern Service Workers,
and the United Auto Workers. Nestled deep in the rural South, they
have demonstrated that an organization led by the poorest and most
dispossessed workers in the country can force some of the world's
biggest companies to the bargaining table. And win.

Healthcare Is a Human Right: The Vermont Workers Center

When Green Mountain Care was signed into law in 2011 in Vermont,
it became the first and only state-level, single-payer healthcare system
in the country. The victory hadn't come easily. The Vermont Workers'
Center (VWC), which led the fight for years, faced relentless opposition from corporate interests, austerity politics, and an entrenched
belief among some Vermonters that people don't have rights they
can't afford to pay for.

VWC was formed in 1998 by a group of young, low-wage workers
in central Vermont. At first they focused mainly on workplace issues
like wage increases, but over time they broadened into other efforts:
keeping community schools open, challenging lead paint in Burling-
ton rental units, and even attempting to organize a downtown workers'
union in the small city of Montpelier. In 2008, VWC leaders, including James Haslam, Kate Kanselstein, and Sarah Weintraub, launched
their Healthcare as a Human Right campaign. The lack of affordable healthcare was a crisis that unified thousands of people across
the state. Sixty-six thousand Vermonters, including eleven thousand
children, did not have healthcare in 2008. Another 180,000—or nearly
one-third of the state's population—were underinsured.[22] These tens
of thousands of people were foregoing preventive care, dental care,
surgeries, and other life-saving treatments because they couldn't afford
to pay. When one VWC member lost her job, for example, she also

lost her healthcare. However, she was ineligible for Medicaid because of her previous income. Despite having serious health problems after years of working in a factory, she had no way to access affordable care.

VWC's previous work had mainly kept them in Vermont's cities, but they realized that to build statewide power, they needed to reach into the many poor, rural communities that are usually made invisible in liberal imaginings of Vermont. Workplace organizing had made sense in the cities, since they were home to the largest employers, but it wasn't going to allow VWC to develop a footprint in areas where industry had long since disappeared. Their new healthcare campaign used an explicit human rights framework to assert the rights of everyone in the state and indict a political and economic system that was abrogating these rights. VWC emphasized five fundamental human rights principles—universality, equity, transparency, accountability, and participation—to claim that all Vermonters were entitled to comprehensive, quality healthcare, distributed according to need, not ability to pay.

During the first year of the campaign, VWC organizers fanned out across the state, going door-to-door in every county. They held community meetings and hearings, bringing together local religious leaders, healthcare professionals, and community-based partners to hear directly from impoverished Vermonters, and they gathered over 1,200 responses to a survey on the state of healthcare in Vermont. Through this activity and more, they built organizing committees at the county level in a way that went far beyond traditional workplace organizing. Suddenly, the entire state was organized as a "workplace" that was failing its workers.

In 2010, after two years of rigorous base building, VWC organized candidate meetings, asking politicians if they believed healthcare was a human right. Many candidates were initially dismissive or skeptical. But thousands of poor people turned this supposedly impossible idea into a viable political demand. After intense public pressure, Vermont governor Jim Douglas, a Republican, allowed Act 128, which created a study to determine how universal healthcare could be designed and funded, to pass into law without his signature. This process identified single-payer healthcare as the most efficient way to provide universal healthcare to all Vermonters. Finally, in 2011, a bill began making its way through the statehouse that would legislate the single-payer approach. After the bill passed the House, a last-minute amendment was adopted in the Senate to exclude undocumented people, even though they made up a very small percentage of the state's population. By offering healthcare to most, but not all, residents of Vermont, this amendment was a clear attempt by some state legislators to divide the communities that were organizing for universal healthcare.

But VWC was prepared. In fact, they'd started preparing two years earlier, when they held trainings and political education sessions on how the wealthy and powerful often use racism and xenophobia as a tool to derail and splinter popular poor people's movements. After the amendment was introduced, VWC quickly mobilized, bringing members and partners together to demand that lawmakers remove the exclusionary language. They organized a massive 2011 May Day rally at the capitol, which I attended with my daughter, and called for the legislation to pass in the spirit in which it had been intended: everybody means everybody, universal means universal. The human rights framework both allowed and required them to make this demand. Two days later, Act 48, establishing Green Mountain Care, was passed, with the exclusionary amendment removed.

VWC gained a lot of notoriety in those days. As happens with so many scrappy organizations after a big win, money started flowing in from foundations and they began staffing up and further institutionalizing their operation. These were very optimistic days. But shortly after Green Mountain Care was enacted, the legislation faced a swift counteroffensive, not just from state-based businesses but multinational corporations. To finance the plan, the Vermont legislature originally included a tax hike on the wealthy, which business interests vigorously opposed. Six years earlier, IBM, the largest employer in the state, sat its workers down and warned them that single-payer healthcare would drive up taxes and force businesses to decamp to more "pro-business" states.[23] Other companies echoed this sentiment during the legislative battles of 2011. But the source of their opposition went deeper than just the issue of taxation; the universal healthcare plan was a direct challenge to the profit motive of the market and therefore a fundamental threat to the way corporations were accustomed to being treated. If they allowed the new law to stand in Vermont, who knew what its ripple effects would be across the country? Peter Shumlin, a Democrat who had replaced Douglas as governor, was won over to corporate concerns. He claimed universal healthcare would be too great of a financial shock to the state's economy and tabled the effort in 2014, even though the financing study found that over 90 percent of Vermonters would benefit economically from the plan.[24] Adding insult to injury, he pursued austerity measures to cut costs on other social welfare spending.

Shumlin's actions were a gutting setback for VWC and the group fell into a state of disorganization. Resources that were once flush waned as foundations turned elsewhere, and the group entered a funding crisis, losing both money and staff capacity. The leadership of VWC made three critical decisions during this crisis: (1) they studied their own history, the healthcare industry, and larger economic processes in order to better understand the forces they were up against; (2) they redoubled their efforts to organize among the poorest residents of Vermont, who they believed would serve as their most disciplined and committed leaders; and (3) they began looking outside Vermont to forge relationships with other poor people's human rights organizations. In the aftermath of a nationally coordinated corporate attack, they realized that the fight for healthcare as a human right in Vermont was indelibly connected to a national fight for the same.

VWC reorganized around a long-term vision for national universal healthcare. These were the years when my colleagues and I at the Poverty Initiative, the organization I cofounded at Union Theological

Seminary, got even closer with VWC. We helped connect them with other poor people's organizations, including Put People First! PA, a Pennsylvania-based group that was founded in 2012 and also took up a healthcare is a human right campaign. In 2020, VWC joined the Nonviolent Medicaid Army, a multistate organizing drive launched by Put People First! PA to unite poor people as a leading force in the fight for universal healthcare. By then, VWC was also playing a leadership role in the Poor People's Campaign: A National Call for Moral Revival.

In all of these efforts, VWC carried the lessons of the Green Mountain Care fight with them: (1) poor and dispossessed people are often the least likely to be swayed by corporate propaganda and the most likely to take transformative action to drive forward a human rights struggle; (2) a human rights framework remains a strategic, unifying, and powerful vehicle for poor people to secure the rights of all; and, finally, (3) a discrete victory in a single state on a fundamental issue like healthcare will never stand on its own; it will face massive and lavishly funded pushback. The size and severity of this opposition mean that poor people need to organize and unite not just at the local and state levels but at a national and even international scale. It has to be everybody in and nobody out.

CHAPTER FIVE

THE STRUGGLE IS THE SCHOOL

On a clear winter day in West Virginia in 2007, a group of us climbed up the spine of Kayford Mountain, which was slated to be cut open, blown up, and demolished so an energy company could access the seams of coal within it. Our guide, a small, compact white man, then in his early sixties, was Larry Gibson, the Keeper of the Mountain. Gibson was eager to show us both the beauty of the land and the horror that threatened to destroy it. As we walked, there was never any danger we'd lose sight of him: Gibson's hat and T-shirt were both the same brilliant shade of fluorescent yellow and on his shirt he had printed a message in massive black and bolded script: "WE ARE THE KEEPERS OF THE MOUNTAINS. LOVE THEM OR LEAVE THEM. JUST DON'T DESTROY THEM." After these words, he added an invitation, "IF YOU DARE TO BE ONE TOO," followed by two phone numbers where aspiring mountain keepers could reach him. With an entire mountain to protect, he did not have the luxury of being subtle or discreet.

Gibson's extended family had lived on Kayford, the ancestral lands of the Cherokee people, since the late 1700s, and over three hundred of his relatives were buried in a small cemetery on the mountain.

When he was a boy, his parents struggled to make ends meet and they moved often, hopping from coal town to coal town across the Appalachian region until his father was hurt in a mining accident. Gibson never worked in the mines. As a young man, he made his living at a General Motors factory in Ohio until a workplace injury sent him back to Kayford in the 1980s. At the time, the coal industry was just beginning to poke its head above ground, shifting from the dangerous and labor-intensive process of longwall mining to the new method of blowing up and leveling mountains. For the coal barons of West Virginia, mountaintop-removal mining, which replaced large numbers of miners with explosives and high-tech machinery to allow them to reach deeper into the mountains, minimized both labor costs and the threat of worker organizing.

The coal companies weren't wrong to fear the power of their workers. During the West Virginia Mine Wars in the early 1900s, entire communities of miners and their families faced off against their employers, who ruled the mountains with an iron fist and were backed by the state government as well as a private army of armed thugs and detectives. For over twenty years, these Black and white, immigrant and non-immigrant miners led a tireless campaign of land occupations, wildcat strikes, and union organizing drives, coming together across racial lines in a time of widespread racial segregation. When they marched, they wore red bandanas as a symbol of their solidarity, a little-known source for the often derogatory term "redneck." During the Battle of Blair Mountain in 1921—one of the largest uprisings of the poor in US history—the military flew planes as a scare tactic over thousands of striking miners, the only time American military airpower has been brought to bear on a domestic rebellion.[1] This legacy of miner resistance continues to shape an acute sense of class consciousness and militancy among poor and dispossessed people across the state.

By this measure, Gibson was clearly a son of West Virginia. In the 1980s, Massey Energy, at its height the largest coal company in the region, started knocking on his and his neighbors' doors, offering them small payouts to buy their land and the valuable mineral rights beneath it. He was the sole holdout, and over the years, as Massey rolled in its equipment, Kayford became one of the last untouched mountains in a vast graveyard of dead land. From his mountain-island, Gibson—a lifelong member of the Sierra Club, a board member of the Ohio Valley Environmental Coalition, and the founder of the Keeper of the Mountains Foundation—staged a multi-decade standoff with Massey, which continued coming back with increasingly higher dollar offers, eventually totaling in the millions. Each time, he refused the offers, not just to keep hold of his family's land but to protect the earth from being destroyed. Massey and some of his neighbors weren't pleased, and Gibson endured dozens of death threats and attacks on him, his dogs, and his property over the years. He started wearing a bulletproof vest and armored the door to his trailer to defend himself against intruders.

Over the years, Gibson became one of the nation's leading grass-roots activists against mountaintop removal. He traveled everywhere, speaking to anyone who would listen, while back home he welcomed thousands of people to Kayford. In 2007, the group of us gathered on the mountain included seminarians, faculty, and grassroots organizers connected to the Poverty Initiative (relaunched as the Kairos Center in 2013). Larry seemed right at home with us. "I'm poor too," he told us, without a trace of shame in his voice.

We started our tour in a pavilion not far from the trailer where Gibson lived. He taught us about the history of the region and the power of the coal companies, drawing connections for us between poverty, economic exploitation, workers' rights, and environmental degradation. He linked our personal complicity in the process of fossil fuel extraction (including our reliance on laptops and other electronics dependent on lithium batteries and other materials derived from fossil fuels) with a broader call for corporate responsibility and policy change. And while the public debate about poverty and communal disrepair in

Appalachia has focused on the supposed backwardness of its impoverished residents (think J. D. Vance and his *Hillbilly Elegy*), Gibson reminded us that it was coal bosses, not miners, who were to blame for immiserating the mountainous communities and exploiting the earth (not to mention the pharmaceutical companies that have flooded the region with opioids over the last few decades). In his condemnation, he skillfully undercut powerful propaganda by the coal industry that has long attempted to pit miners against environmentalists. Instead, he focused on the predatory actions of Massey's CEO, Don Blankenship, while at the same time contexualizing Blankenship within larger economic processes that were hurting the vast majority of the state's population.* Gibson made it clear that he expected us to do more than just listen and learn. "If you're not going to do something with all this information," he warned, "don't waste my time."

He then readied us to cross through Hell's Gate, the point on his property where the surrounding mountain ranges came into view. This was the dramatic climax of his tour. The minute I stepped through the clearing, I saw it. Across the vista, there was a mountain that had been cleaved in two. On one side, the land was still alive—all shades of green shrubbery and birds flying overhead. The other side was shaped like a mountain, but there was no greenery or birds, only the jagged accumulation of rock and debris that the company had piled back up after the land was detonated.

Our group was shocked into silence. Standing at Hell's Gate, I was reminded of the folk song so common in West Virginia, written and sung by coal miners during the Mine Wars: "Which side are you

---

* Blankenship was the CEO of Massey Energy Company from 2000 to 2010. His tenure ended when he was imprisoned for worker-safety violations after an explosion at one of his mines killed twenty-nine workers. At the time, Blankenship was the highest-paid coal executive in the country. He was released a year later, in 2011, and he has since run two unsuccessful campaigns for the US Senate in West Virginia. (Trip Gabriel, "Ex-Executive Donald Blankenship Is Indicted in Disaster at Coal Mine," *New York Times*, November 13, 2014).

on? Which side are you on?" It was clear to me that taking Gibson's side, and the side of others like him, meant taking the side of life. To take the other side, the side of Massey and other coal companies, where nothing would grow for hundreds of years under the artificial sod placed over the rocks, was to take the side of death.

Although it was gutting, there was also something clarifying, even galvanizing, about the experience. No matter who we were, where we came from, or what issue we were most immediately concerned about or organizing around back home—immigration, wages, housing, healthcare—the destruction of the earth by a company hungry for greater profit felt like an existential foreshadowing of the world to come if we did not band together to fight back.

Walking back down the mountain, I marveled at the courage and tenacity of our guide. I was also struck by how open his heart was after all these years. Gibson had seen this view tens of thousands of times, and just earlier that day he had taken another group up the mountain. Still, as he stood next to us, surveying the land, he was visibly devastated. He seemed to feel the loss of life as if he was experiencing it for the first time. He had not grown numb. This, I have learned over the years, is a key ingredient of leadership within a movement—the ability of a person to see far, feel deeply, and help others to do the same.

After that first visit, the Poverty Initiative continued bringing groups back to Kayford Mountain. A year later, we returned with students and faculty members from a dozen other universities and seminaries, all interested in the intersection of theology and public life. We visited Gibson for the Fourth of July hootenanny he organized every year, and in New York City we hosted him and delegations of grassroots leaders from West Virginia, Kentucky, Virginia, Tennessee, and Ohio when they brought human rights cases against the coal companies to the United Nations and held actions outside the Fifth Avenue apartment of another coal boss. And when he died in 2012, after decades of holding the line at Kayford, we held a memorial service for him at Union Theological Seminary.

How do we build powerful movements that can grow and sustain themselves over time? Larry Gibson was one answer to this question. Through his leadership, he modeled not only an ethic of unyielding resilience in defense of the mountain but an understanding that he couldn't do it alone. He was committed to helping other people become the leaders that all of our struggles—interconnected as they are—need.

PEDAGOGY OF THE POOR

Building power among poor and dispossessed people requires many leaders who are clear, committed, competent, and connected to one another and to communities in struggle. Developing these four *c*'s of political leadership involves more than workshops on knowing your rights, building tactical skills, and creating campaign plans, although these are all important tools in an organizer's tool kit. Leadership development is a constant and collective educational process that helps everyday people see the world and themselves more clearly: who they are, why they are hurting, how power is formed and wielded, and what it will ultimately take to end their suffering. Our friend Phil Wider, a brilliant organizer and political educator from Philadelphia, likes to say that in the analogy of a staircase, leadership development isn't just a step on the path to greater power—it is the entire staircase.

Without a continual process of learning, reflecting, and growing intellectually, our organizing is reduced to mobilizing, an exercise in moving bodies without supporting existing leaders and developing new ones. Don't get us wrong: mobilizing people is important, but when it becomes our sole focus, we sacrifice long-term power for short-term action. Indeed, much of what is called organizing is actually mobilizing as many bodies as possible or—given the significant turn toward digital campaigning at the expense of on-the-ground work—mobilizing as many names as possible. In the process, we end up treating people as empty vessels for political objectives. This is especially true during election cycles, when political parties, foundations, and wealthy donors pour hundreds of millions of dollars into canvassing, door knocking, and operating phone banks, and hundreds of millions more into advertising and digital outreach, only to shut down these activities after the elections.

Confusion, doubt, apathy, fatigue, and resignation can set in when people are not given the conceptual tools to make sense of their lives and the political work they are involved in. Conflict and burnout are common when people are not offered pathways toward making larger commitments and assuming greater leadership in determining the strategic direction of that work. This reality is, unfortunately, commonplace in the world of grassroots organizing, and if we are going to organize an effective and durable fight against the systems that produce poverty, we need to do everything we can to counter this phenomenon. We need to move both bodies and minds.

The deepest kind of learning doesn't happen in the classroom but in the crucible of the struggle itself. In 2010, the Michigan Welfare Rights Organization helped organize the US Social Forum in Detroit, a gathering of twenty thousand social justice activists from across the country and the world. During a session led by the Poverty Initiative, General Gordon Baker, the longtime labor organizer from Detroit, spoke about a series of organizing drives and wildcat strikes he helped lead at the city's Chrysler plant in the 1970s. He reflected on a challenging internal dynamic that the workers consistently encountered as they organized: "The sixties left us with two types of people. Those who fought and refused to think. And those who thought and refused to fight. It took us [another] twenty years to turn fighters into thinkers and thinkers into fighters." He explained further: "We have to have the theoretical struggle, but the struggle is the school itself. You have to study, but you [also] have to struggle, because out of the struggle comes the real lessons that you apply to things that you study. That way it becomes real and alive to you."[2] Like Phil Wider, Baker always emphasized leadership development and political education not as an isolated or theoretical practice but as an integral part of every action taken within a movement.

In *Where Do We Go from Here*, Dr. King frames the tension between "fighting" and "thinking" this way:

> Education without social action is a one-sided value because it has no true power potential. Social action without education is a weak expression of pure energy. Deeds uninformed by educated thought can take false directions. When we go into action and confront our adversaries, we must be as armed with knowledge as they. Our policies should have the strength of deep analysis beneath them to be able to challenge the clever sophistries of our opponents.[3]

Willie Baptist has a blunter way of putting it: "It doesn't matter if you're right if you're *dead* right." A smart analysis, he means, is necessary, but it is meaningless in the face of power, unless it is backed up by a power of its own.

"The struggle is the school" is a useful shorthand for our approach to leadership development and movement building. Over the years, I've worked with thousands of leaders waging different struggles and campaigns, each with specific and concrete goals. I've done whatever I can to support these efforts, but I've also never seen them as ends in and of themselves. Instead, I've always understood them as vehicles for further amassing the experience and political consciousness that can translate current efforts into greater strength over time.

A campaign victory might be a genuine stepping stone toward sustained power, but if we don't have the necessary leadership to secure, protect, and expand that victory, it can also paradoxically spell doom. A victory given or conceded by those in power can often just as easily be taken away. If we are focused only on whatever concessions we can win right now, we risk losing our bearings and the leaders we need for the fights to come. Folks in our work sometimes call this

"losing by winning." For example, in the mid-1990s, the Kensington
Welfare Rights Union won housing for over seven hundred people
in Philadelphia, a hard-fought victory we were incredibly proud of.
But we were entirely unprepared for the consequences of our success. Many of our members stopped organizing after they were given
public housing, which generally turned out to be inadequate and
fleeting. Eventually, many of them ended up on the streets again,
this time without an organization to back them up. The city also used
our "victory" as an opportunity to split up our members and move
them into far-flung neighborhoods across the city—we called this
tactic "spatial de-concentration"—atomizing our base and leaving us
weaker in the long run.

In *Pedagogy of the Poor*, Baptist reflects on a similar dynamic that
played out during the demise of the National Union of the Homeless
in the 1990s. At the time, drugs were flowing into unhoused communities and city officials in Philadelphia and elsewhere offered cushy
housing jobs to a few key unhoused leaders in an effort to defang the
organization:

> Underneath all of that, the main lesson for building an organization
> or a movement is that at its initial stage the question of finding
> committed leaders and developing their clarity and competence is
> key. We just didn't know that. We were inexperienced and couldn't
> deal with it. Not having a core of experienced and clear leaders left
> us unprepared to deal with the maneuvers of the powers-that-be
> and the all-around assault of the drug epidemic and then one
> chapter [of the Homeless Union] folded after another. The key
> lesson we learned from this was to focus on developing leaders so
> the movement doesn't have to be compromised by any individual
> who gets compromised.[4]

Conversely, there is a lot to learn and even be gained from losing
campaigns. In August of 1996, KWRU marched to the state capitol

in Harrisburg after the passage of state legislation that would cut 250,000 Pennsylvanians from medical assistance benefits.[5] Once we got there, we set up a month-long encampment inside the state house, demanding public action to address the poverty and homelessness that was only going to worsen after these cuts. We called our encampment "Ridgeville" after then Republican governor Tom Ridge, harkening back to the history of the Great Depression when unemployed workers organized mass "Hooverville" encampments disdainfully named after President Herbert Hoover.[*]

KWRU suffered defeat after defeat in that campaign. In late September, a month after we arrived in Harrisburg, a federal judge evicted us from the state house. We moved our encampment onto the ornate steps of the building and attempted to resume our protest during business hours when the public was allowed inside. Refusing to back down or dialogue with us, the Ridge administration officially rewrote the legislature's rules to prohibit events on the capitol premises after 8 p.m., including the steps, which until then were open to the public twenty-four hours a day. A few days later, our members took a public tour of the governor's mansion—maintained at a cost to taxpayers of $1 million a year—and observed that his dogs were living better than unhoused people across the state. Meanwhile, the state capitol police used the opportunity to confiscate the tents, sleeping bags, and supplies we had left on the steps. We were eventually forced

---

[*] The largest Hooverville was organized by ten thousand politicized World War I veterans who occupied the Anacostia Flats outside Washington, DC, in the summer of 1932 to demand that Hoover pay a bonus promised to them fifteen years earlier. This nonviolent movement of Black and white veterans called itself the Bonus Army, and their encampment, which lasted over a month, was perhaps the most racially integrated place in the country at the time. Eventually, Hoover ordered their violent eviction, a decision that was then successfully used by Franklin D. Roosevelt to undercut him in the 1932 elections. The Bonus Army's demands were ultimately met by FDR, and its militant protest presaged nearly a decade of explosive organizing among the poor. "The 1932 Bonus Army," National Park Service, https://www.nps.gov/articles/the-1932-bonus-army.htm.

back to Philadelphia without a legislative breakthrough and with new restrictions on our right to preacefully protest.[6]

The experience was a tough pill to swallow. But our persistent protest that summer, as well as our callous treatment by the government, was ultimately a boon to KWRU. During our initial march to Harrisburg, we met with religious leaders, students, labor organizers, and community activists who all felt connected to the issues of our march. Once we arrived at the state house, these people and others joined us for various actions and rallies during our encampment. This preliminary work meant that by the time the police kicked us off the steps, we had already won the hearts and minds of thousands of Pennsylvanians who were now further outraged by our eviction and even more willing to fight alongside us. We called this "winning by losing."

Years later, in New York City, I worked closely with the leadership of Domestic Workers United (DWU), a citywide group of nannies and housekeepers from the Caribbean, Latin America, and Africa. Over seven years, from 2003 to 2010, DWU built a coalition of workers, community members, and clergy to fight for the nation's first Domestic Workers Bill of Rights. In the beginning, as with most grassroots organizing efforts, DWU had a mountain to climb. At the time, the city's domestic workers spent long and demanding hours in far-flung neighborhoods, often with low pay, scant workplace protections, and with their own families to care for back home. Sometimes only five or ten people showed up to DWU's meetings, and the organization regularly struggled to hold employers responsible for abusive actions. The fruits of their organizing often felt bitterly insufficient.

However, amid the wins and losses, DWU refused to get sidetracked from their central task, which was building up the power and leadership of their fellow workers. Over time, with each new step in their campaign, they gained more experience and exposure, proving to the public that the seemingly far-fetched idea of a workers' bill of rights was moral and necessary. They also proved to their fellow workers that they weren't going anywhere, and as they slowly earned the trust of the community they succeeded in bringing a groundswell of new leaders into their organization. Finally, in 2010, they won. The Domestic Workers Bill of Rights in New York was a historic victory, but DWU also knew it was just the first step. After the legislation passed, they continued organizing to ensure that what was written into law was enforced in practice. Protections for domestic workers in one state also needed to be fortified by protections elsewhere, so they supported and trained similar groups in other states as they waged their own bill of rights campaigns. Years later, this work helped set the stage for the birth of the National Domestic Workers Alliance, a national network that now organizes domestic workers across the country.

So far, in this and previous chapters, we have used the word *leader* without actually defining it. Leadership can mean many things, and whether it is in our homes, schools, workplaces, houses of worship, community groups, or local governments, we all have experience working with leaders of many styles, stripes, and temperaments. In the context of movement building, though, our experience is that the most important attribute of a leader is their ability to teach other people how to lead. Rather than telling people what to do or doing things for them, a leader in a movement helps the people around them discover their own voice and sense of self. This kind of leader supports people not just by meeting their immediate needs but by offering them the tools to deepen their political awareness and help them understand that they are powerful—that they are people who can make and shape history.

Poor people's movements will never have the financial resources, media might, or political relationships of the wealthy and well-connected. Their greatest resource is the untapped power of their numbers. To unleash this power, these movements need a lot of poor people to believe that it is possible to end poverty and systemic injustice and that they are the ones who can effect this change. We need leaders—as many of them as we can get.

This kind of leadership—the kind that is committed to developing others as leaders— requires patience and a willingness to do the unsung, often unseen work of consciousness raising and community building. It also requires discipline and principled discernment. Anyone who does grassroots organizing encounters all kinds of people— people who are scared, proud, generous, desperate, eager, angry, stable, in crisis, and so forth. Our organizing must be visionary enough to include the needs and aspirations of every person we meet, but that does not mean that everyone is ready or able to lead.

One of our favorite examples of this approach to leadership development was taught to us by S'bu Zikode, a cofounder of Abahlali baseMjondolo (AbM), the South African shack dwellers movement. Zikode, now in his early fifties, was propelled into politics as a young man through the anti-apartheid struggle and he has since continued organizing in the shadow of repressive post-apartheid governments. In 2005, he began working among the three thousand informal settlements and encampments scattered on city outskirts throughout the country, in the process helping build one of the largest poor people's movements in Africa. Today, AbM counts among its members tens of thousands of shack dwellers who face constant surveillance and abuse from the police and government, even as they fight for the basic human right to housing (a right enshrined in the post-apartheid constitution). A number of their leaders have been assassinated over the years and others, including Zikode, have been forced underground on multiple occasions.

I visited with Zikode in South Africa in 2007, and over the years I've hosted him and other AbM leaders in the United States for various events, teach-ins, leadership schools, and human rights gatherings. He once told me about a key policy of AbM. When an individual asks to join the shack dwellers' movement, they're told to go back to their community and recruit fifty others to come along with them. Only once they are successful are they and their community recognized as an official chapter of the movement. The idea is not to dissuade people from joining, but to break through any individualistic illusions among AbM's base and emphasize the reality that they are only strong through their collectivity. In the encampments outside Durban, Johannesburg, and Cape Town, leaders are not top-down messiahs or saviors—they are shack dwellers who have the trust of their community and know how to find and develop other leaders like themselves.

THE LONG HAUL

Here in the United States, one popular educator whose thinking has shaped generations of grassroots leaders is Myles Horton, the founder of the Highlander Folk School (now the Highlander Research and Education Center). The school was opened by Horton and a handful of seminarians and organizers in the summer of 1932, deep in the mountains of eastern Tennessee. Within a few years, it emerged as a cradle for transformational organizing. During the late 1930s and early 1940s, Highlander served as the official education arm of the industrial labor movement in the South, led by the Congress of Industrial Organizations. Over the next two decades, it played an even bigger role in supporting the Civil Rights Movement.

Hidden in the leafy folds of the Great Smoky Mountains, Highlander was one of the few interracial meeting places in the South, and it was there where organizers and community leaders came to learn and strategize together across racial lines. It was at Highlander where the organizer and educator Septima Clark first experimented with the literacy programs that became the movement's citizenship schools, a network of close to nine hundred community-based schools that taught tens of thousands of Black Southerners how to read and pass the Jim Crow literacy tests that were compulsory for voter registration. Highlander was also where Rosa Parks studied as a young organizer before the Montgomery bus boycott.

Horton, the child of poor white Tennesseans, was raised in the Presbyterian church. As a young man, he left the South and made his way to Union Theological Seminary in New York City, where he was quickly immersed in a melting pot of religious thought and political activity. Still, he couldn't shake a nagging itch of dissatisfaction. He understood that this kind of educational space would never be fully welcoming to poor people like him, nor could it provide them with the tools to collectively pursue their own emancipation. Horton dreamed of starting an education center where poor people would be given the power to shape the educational process alongside their teachers and where they would experience living in a democratic setting that valued their opinions and encouraged their leadership, for perhaps the first time in their lives.

This vision struck a chord with others at Union, including his friend Don West, with whom Horton had traveled to Denmark to learn from that country's folk school tradition, a cornerstone of Scandinavian worker movements in the 1800s. Just a year after arriving at Union, Horton, West, and a few other seminarians packed up their things and headed south. Meanwhile, in New York City, one of their former professors, the renowned ethicist and moral philosopher Reinhold Niebuhr, organized Highlander's first fundraising appeal. In a letter to prospective funders, Niebuhr candidly explained their purpose: "We are proposing to use education as one of the instruments for bringing about a new social order."[7]

I read Horton's autobiography, *The Long Haul*, for the first time when I myself was a twenty-something-year-old student at Union Theological Seminary. By then, I had already visited Highlander multiple times. KWRU stopped there for a night during the 1998 New Freedom Bus Tour. Sitting around a campfire, we wrote the lyrics to "Rich Man's House," one of my favorite movement songs, which is included as an epigraph at the beginning of this book: "I went down to the rich man's house and I / Took back what he stole from me. / I took back my dignity. / I took back my humanity. . . . / Ain't no system gonna walk all over me." This song is now widely sung across social movements in the US; in 2024, we heard it in college encampments calling for a ceasefire in Gaza.*

The Long Haul is a slim volume, but its pages are full of ideas that have stuck with me, including Horton's pedagogical approach to political education. Horton used to talk about teaching with "two eyes."[8] With one eye, he endeavored to look at the world the way his students saw it: to understand what they cared and worried about, what they thought about themselves, and why they believed what they believed. Seeing through this eye, Horton explained, is the starting place for any political education process, just as it is for leadership within a movement. For political educators and organizers, it doesn't matter what we believe is true if the people we are trying to organize are not moved to come along with us. We have to begin where our people are, not where we want them to be.

As Horton's first eye scanned the present, his second eye was firmly fixed on the horizon. This eye, he proposed, was concerned with seeing who poor and dispossessed people could become and what marvelous things they could do when their consciousness was encouraged to grow and the muscles of their political acumen were strengthened. The way I understand it, this second eye wasn't interested in forcing a prescribed ideology onto people. Rather, it was the watchful eye of the lookout on a ship, first spotting from the crow's nest new territories that the crew would chart together.

Horton always tried to position Highlander in that crow's nest as well. He writes: "We avoided implementing programs that other

---

* For more on this song and others like it, check out *Songs in the Key of Resistance*, a songbook curated by our colleague Charon Hribar. Hribar is a leading cultural organizer within the movement to end poverty. https://kairoscenter.org/wp-content/uploads/2023/10/Movement_Songbook_2023.pdf.

less cutting-edge organizations or institutions were doing. We tried to find ways of working that did not duplicate what was already being done."[9] Horton and his colleagues paid close attention to the moment, assessed what other people were already doing, and tried to stay just ahead of the curve, constantly adjusting their educational process and pushing the community leaders they worked with to think and act more expansively. To this day, I have tried my best to emulate Horton and stay on the cutting edge of movement work. For three decades, I have advocated for new political positions, created new organizations and campaigns, and developed new educational processes. I have then moved on to other issues and plans when those ideas reached a broader consciousness and other groups stepped in to take on the mantle of leadership—or when my approach wasn't working and there was a need to change course.

I have reread *The Long Haul* many times over the years, and I am always struck by how Horton describes the inextricable relationship between leadership development and movement building. At one point, he recounts a long-standing debate between himself and Saul Alinksy, the legendary organizer and his contemporary:

> Saul and I differed because my position was that if I had to make a choice between achieving an objective and utilizing the struggle to develop and radicalize people, my choice would be to let the goal go and develop the people. He believed that organizing success was the way to radicalize people. We were both trying to do the same thing, but we differed in method. When I look at a situation in order to decide whether to work with an organization, it's essential to consider whether that organization is moving toward structural reform or limited reform. If it's moving toward structural reform, I'll work with that organization. If it's just limited reform, I would hesitate, because I don't think valuable learning comes out of winning little victories, unless they are calculated steps toward the large goal and will lead to structural reforms.[10]

Even though they had significant disagreements, Horton respected Alinsky. But he worried that many of Alinsky's followers had lost his radical vision for society and were mechanically implementing his organizing methods. He also worried that they had taken Alinsky's teachings and domesticated them by placing them into a tidy little box they called the "Alinsky Method." They focused mainly on small and winnable campaigns, bargaining for minor reforms and carving out careers that were rarely oriented around building mass movements centered on the leadership of poor and dispossessed people. Horton, on the other hand, believed it was the contagious energy and hope of a movement that transformed little victories into big ones, and people into leaders:

> It's only in a movement that an idea is often made simple enough and direct enough that it can spread rapidly. Then your leadership multiplies very rapidly, because there's something explosive going on. People see that other people not so different from themselves do things they thought could never be done. They're emboldened and challenged by that to step into the water, and once they get in the water, it's as if they've never not been there. People who work to create a decent world long for situations like this, but most of the time we are working with organizations. We cannot create movements, so if we want to be part of a movement when it comes, we have to get ourselves into a position—by working with organizations that deal with structural change—to be on the inside of that movement when it comes, instead of on the outside trying to get accepted. [. . .]
>
> In a social movement, we are clearly part of a collective struggle that encourages us to increase our demands. One of the dynamic aspects of a social movement as opposed to an organization is that quite often in the latter, you'll bargain down to make concessions in order to survive. You have a limited goal, and you might say, "Well, we want to get ten street lights," and you'll get together and figure that you won't get ten, but you probably can get five. So you

decide to tell them you want ten in order to get five. In a social movement, the demands escalate, because your success encourages and emboldens you to demand more.[11]

I recognize myself in Horton's words. After a childhood of wading in that encouraging and emboldening water with my socially active family, I fully submerged myself in the movement in Philadelphia in the 1990s, and I never returned to the dry land of a so-called normal life.

CONDITIONS + CONSCIOUSNESS

Willie Baptist has a teaching analogy: Imagine you have to travel unexpectedly to Chicago to visit a sick family member in the hospital. You buy a train ticket, stuff some clothes in a bag, and rush out of the house. Once you get to the station, though, you mess up and get on the train to Atlanta. At first you don't realize your mistake, and, as the train gathers speed, you watch the passing world through the window, anxious but glad you will soon be with your loved one. By the time you hear the conductor announce the destination, it's too late. Now, the speed of the train causes only dread. No matter how much you wish it were different, every precious mile means you are headed further in the wrong direction.

When he is working with new organizers, Baptist likes to use this parable to impart a simple lesson: the formula for momentum (speed + direction x mass) is a helpful one for movement building. Sometimes we as activists and organizers act with a strong sense of moral indignation, but without a clear analysis of the root causes of the problem we're facing or of the best ways to build power in response. Too often, we conflate morality with strategy. We barrel ahead with a lot of energy and motion, and at first all of that activity can feel really constructive and exciting. At the very least it can feel good to actually be doing *something*. And in the short term, our efforts might work. We might recruit some people over to our cause and move some people into action. We may even win some of our demands. But, although we are working very hard, little seems to change in the long run. Or things actually get worse. We have speed, perhaps some mass, but no sense of strategic direction. To gain momentum, a movement needs all three.

Another way of putting it is that the emergence of a movement that can actually realize transformative change depends on the combination of conditions and consciousness. Conditions have to be right, which often means they have to be so wrong that society is objectively being unsettled and shaken up. The speed of the escalating crisis generally has to be swift and dramatic enough to compel a critical mass of people into action and allow them to take advantage of fractures within the status quo. But conditions alone are not enough. To fully meet the moment, we also need conscious and connected leadership. This is especially true for poor people's movements, which attempt to organize the most disorganized section of society and contend with very wealthy, entrenched, and sophisticated oppositions.

We live in an incredibly pragmatic society, one in which immediate and tangible concerns are usually prioritized over big-picture and historically grounded thinking. For the majority of us, this pragmatism encourages acting from a place of instinct and reaction rather than analysis and discernment. The result is a rather stunning current of anti-intellectualism that runs throughout our society. This anti-intellectualism is certainly, if paradoxically, true of our education system, which has always been standardized and oriented around teaching practical and employable skills rather than supporting young people to learn how to think and act for themselves.

In organizing spaces, deep political education is often ignored or considered an afterthought for the "real work." I can't tell you how many organizing campaigns I have been part of that appear committed to growing the knowledge and understanding of their members only to brush this commitment aside when deadlines arrive and taking action, by whatever means necessary, feels irrepressibly urgent.

This dismissiveness is rarely made with bad intent; money needs to be raised and measurable progress needs to be made. But without rigorous and honest intellectual labor, we as organizers and community leaders are left with a shallow understanding of the forces that have created our present reality and that are already shaping the future. Without the compass of growing consciousness, it is impossible for us to chart a course of strategic action.

Throughout my years of anti-poverty organizing, I have found that this narrow pragmatism also plagues the church. The actions even very well-meaning congregations take to address poverty often lack a real analysis of economic systems and fail to develop a deeper consciousness among parishioners and those served by the church's social ministries. Meanwhile, in pulpits and study groups, the Bible is often decontextualized and presented piecemeal. We are given small and hyper-spiritualized parables and inspirational messages, but we lose the deeper meaning of what Jesus and his disciples have to say about love and justice and what is required of a Christian in a world where hate and idolatry are alive and thriving. It is also the case that across many denominations and Christian traditions, congregants and people of faith are not expected or empowered to contribute to an understanding of what Christianity can and must look like in the modern world. More often than not, we get theology from the top rather than an organic liberation theology that emanates from the collective wisdom of the community.

RAISING UP GENERATIONS OF LEADERS: THE POVERTY INITIATIVE

During the twentieth century, Union Theological Seminary established itself as the nation's leading progressive seminary and the birthplace of American liberation theology. Liberation theology is often associated with the Peruvian priest Gustavo Gutiérrez, who in the late 1960s was developing his notes on the "preferential option of the poor"—the idea that the teachings of the Bible instruct society to prioritize the needs of poor people. In the same decade, Union

professor James Cone was breaking new ground with his Black liberation theology. Gutiérrez and Cone were both living in contexts riven
by social unrest and political suppression, and they were searching for
a theology that matched their communities' deep need for change.
The animating question of their spiritual and political inquiry was
brilliantly simple: Where is God in history? For the two theologians,
independently working three thousand miles away from one another
and worlds apart, the answer was the same: God is present among
poor and dispossessed people, and the infinite spark of divinity can
be discovered in their struggles for freedom.

Union's fertile tradition of liberation theology felt like home.
When I arrived at the seminary in 2001 after spending the first half of
my twenties in Philadelphia, I teamed up with two movement friends,
Paul Chapman and Cathlin Baker, to continue organizing in New
York City. Baker, who had worked with the National Union of the
Homeless and the Kensington Welfare Rights Union before studying
and working at Union, was one of the loudest voices advocating for
me to go to seminary. Chapman, a seafarers' rights organizer, welfare
rights activist, and Baptist minister who had been deeply involved
in the Civil Rights Movement, helped organize the New York City
programming for both the 1998 New Freedom Bus Tour and the 1999
March of the Americas. As I settled into my new life at Union, I spoke
about my organizing experience with classmates and discovered how
many other seminarians yearned to get involved in economic and
racial justice work through their churches and denominations, but
didn't have the training or a clear entry point.

A couple years earlier, Chapman conducted a national survey investigating the anti-poverty pedagogy of American seminaries. The
results were predictably lamentable. Most seminaries had very few
courses that explored poverty and none with a central focus of equip-
ping faith leaders to partner with those most affected by economic
injustice and work toward abolishing poverty. Seminaries also rarely
seemed to consider that many students were themselves poor and,

because they were deeply connected to impoverished communities, were often strategically positioned to play leadership roles within those communities. We were left with a clear sense that our fledgling movement needed more and better ways to identify, train, and connect new generations of faith leaders and grassroots organizers. So we put our heads together and started an organization that could serve as the education and leadership development arm of the movement to end poverty. Many at Union were eager to join us, and after some concerted organizing and fundraising on my part, Willie Baptist moved up to New York City, where he was invited to become Union's first poverty scholar in residence, a position we created for him.

The name we chose for our new organization was intentionally straightforward: The Poverty Initiative. Those first years were unglamorous, full of half starts and trials and errors. We held immersion trips like the one to Kayford Mountain and leadership schools that brought people together into what we called the "poverty scholars" network. We offered technical assistance and behind-the-scenes support for new and emerging poor people's organizations. We led national poverty tours and held truth commissions on poverty, modeled after the Peruvian and South African truth and reconciliation commissions. We taught classes on the theory and methods of anti-poverty organizing to a new generation of pastors and clergy, who later deployed to pulpits, schools, food banks, and community organizations across the country. And we traveled abroad to compare notes with other poor people's movements like the Landless Workers' Movement in Brazil (Movimento dos Trabalhadores Rurais Sem Terra, or MST) and Abahlali baseMjondolo in South Africa.

Ella Baker, the longtime leader within the Black Freedom Struggle, often spoke about the "spadework" of organizing: the daily, unheralded preparatory tasks that a movement is built on. For us, the spadework involved working with hundreds of community leaders across the country and encouraging the full expression of their innate talents, carefully agitating and pushing them beyond their comfort zones and, through them, further popularizing the vision of poverty abolition. We didn't always know what we were doing or where it was going, but those initial years with the Poverty Initiative were indispensable. From the outside looking in, it may have been difficult to see, but we were slowly breaching the brittle topsoil of our communities, growing deep roots in the form of organized poor people who were increasingly connected to one another and prepared to fight and lead for the long haul.

LEARN AS WE LEAD, WALK AS WE TALK, TEACH AS WE FIGHT

We were inspired not just by Highlander but also by the MST in Brazil, the largest social movement of the poor in the Western Hemisphere, made up of over one million landless workers and their supporters. In Brazil, there is a remarkable tradition of radical popular education led by and for the poor. At the same time that Horton was building Highlander in the 1930s and 1940s, Paulo Freire was laying the groundwork for his "pedagogy of the oppressed" in the Brazilian state of Pernambuco. Freire drew from many sources, including his Catholic upbringing, and he made invaluable contributions to the practice of popular education both in Brazil and around the world.

In the early 1980s, the MST formed around semi-permanent worker occupations of vast land estates controlled by big landowners and agribusiness and covering millions of hectares across the Brazilian countryside. The MST has drawn deeply from Freire, and over the years they have broken new pedagogical ground by organizing regional and national schools for their own leaders as well as international schools for other social movements (we've sent dozens of leaders to learn with the MST over the years). For these landless workers, political education is critical to cultivating and sustaining their leaders, and it offers them a continual opportunity to practice the complex art of popular democracy at a time when the forces of authoritarianism and Christian nationalism are clamoring with fury all around them.

I visited the MST in the summer of 2003 and was impressed not just by their formal educational process but by what one could call their "spirit of struggle." At the heart of their movement is a soulful culture, known as *mistica*, which draws on Christian and Indigenous practices, music, visual art, and performance to create a sense of collective meaning and identity. At their meetings, the MST often begin with mistica rituals layered with their people's histories, their many cultural identities, the various forms of their oppression, and their visions of freedom. For some members, these rituals are connected to God, and for others they are connected to a secular but reverent belief in the dignity and value of all life. This is spiritual and pedagogical practice in service of social transformation.

There has always been an analogous, organic culture at the center of the organized struggles of the poor in the United States. We weave song, art, and prayer together, not just into our actions and protests but into the daily ways we relate to one another. We bring this spirit of struggle, this fighting culture of the poor and dispossessed, into our homes, our families, our celebrations, and our most difficult and intimate moments. When we pray, chant, and sing, our voices become an access point, a sixth sense, for the *feeling* of power and liberation, which we then channel back into our organizing.

In the Poverty Initiative, our educational spaces were always infused with this spirit. In 2009, we held a leadership school at a youth camp in the mountains of West Virginia. One hundred and sixty grassroots organizers and faith leaders, many who had never traveled before, came from over a dozen states. We were Black, Latino, white, Asian, and Indigenous; religious, agnostic, and atheist; young and old. The school was organized along five educational tracks: Human Rights, Multi-Media Production, Arts and Culture, New Labor Organizing, and Bible Study. Outside of the classroom, we built a lively sense of community, swapping stories, singing songs, and offering blessings and prayers from various faith traditions. Anyone who was there will agree that the school was alive with an electric pulse of possibility. There was an intangible energy permeating the air, borne out of a shared spirit of struggle that felt bigger than the simple sum of its parts. And we carried that spirit with us when we brought the whole school to nearby Kayford Mountain and sang freedom songs with Larry Gibson, the Keeper of the Mountain.

―――――――――

We took the study part seriously. In classes and schools, including that leadership school in West Virginia and others in Pennsylvania, Ohio, Michigan, and elsewhere, our poverty scholars studied the untold history of poor people's movements in this country, harvesting encouraging and cautionary lessons from the past. We learned about the centrality of systemic racism in our national life and about the divide-and-conquer strategies that reinforce white supremacy and keep the poor disunited. We wrestled with the nuts and bolts of economics, something that has been intentionally left out of most of our education. We invited people to participate in a process we called "poverty mapping," in which participants explored their own experience with poverty and systemic racism and how that mapped onto the larger systems that ordered their lives. And we dove deep into the religious traditions and sacred texts that are precious to so many in our communities, innovating a new approach to liberation theology that we called "Reading the Bible with the Poor."

When we first started experimenting with this approach to biblical interpretation, more professionalized, secular organizers raised concerns about us mixing organizing and religion. Others, even clergy, didn't see how deeper political education, including studying the Bible, could strengthen grassroots campaigns and lead to policy victories. And many questioned what good could come from reading the Bible at all, a skepticism that was understandable given that the majority of people were more familiar with regressive theologies and false moral narratives that blame people of color, immigrants, LG-BTQ+ people, and the poor for society's problems. These responses revealed the degree to which organized religion, especially Christianity, has hurt people, even as so many still hunger for spiritual meaning and connection.

But what I'll say is that among our people, including the multiracial and multifaith leaders of significant grassroots organizations, our Bible studies were groundbreaking. We pulled together pastors and lay leaders from all kinds of churches and other houses of worship; people who were deeply spiritual but not engaged in organized religion; folks who had harrowing experiences with religion, especially Christianity, and every reason to steer clear; community leaders and human rights activists who understood the moral and strategic importance of religion, even if they didn't adhere to one; and a healthy number of poor folks who loved the Bible and organized their lives around it.

Our method was aimed at reading the Bible as an entire text that is focused on the liberation of poor and dispossessed people, as well as reimagining popular biblical passages. Rather than deriving biblical interpretation only from clergy and scholars, we emphasized the leadership of our participants and encouraged them to see themselves as moral prophets and theologians. Given the ways Christianity has been perversely used to justify and sustain social and economic oppression, we began our studies with the simple assertion that Jesus was a poor man living under Roman imperial rule. We articulated together how what happens to Jesus and the prophets, as told throughout the Bible, shares striking similarities with the lives of the poor today. This includes the experience of being surrounded by and finding shelter among other poor people, being concerned about debt and the sharing of resources, valuing dignity over money, critiquing charity as the chief response to injustice, and taking new and unsettling action to disrupt and transform an inhumane status quo.

In "Reading the Bible with the Poor," we drew a direct line connecting the actions of prophetic leaders in the Bible to other freedom struggles throughout the ages, including our own. Our experience with these Bible studies proved that poor people could reinterpret our religious texts and revive our moral traditions across vast differences of experience, identity, formal education, and theological persuasion. The Bible itself is probably one of the most important mass-media texts ever produced that has something good to say about the poor. Through our bottom-up theology, we were proving it.

CHAPTER SIX

THE BATTLE FOR THE BIBLE

C edar Monroe is covered in tattoos. Their ink may seem irreverent to some clergy, but for Monroe, a white nonbinary chaplain from rural Washington, it has always served a higher purpose. When they founded Chaplains on the Harbor, a small outpost of the Episcopal diocese of Olympia, they got a new tattoo every time a member of their community died: of a healthcare or housing crisis, a drug overdose, an injury sustained from police brutality. In seaside Grays Harbor County, this kind of unnecessary and violent death is commonplace. In a county of sixteen thousand, there are about a thousand unhoused people, mostly white, but also Indigenous and Latino.[1] A sprawling tent encampment once straddled the local river until county authorities demolished it. Jobs are scarce and the police are heavily armed. For many young people the future feels like a dead end, school an irrelevancy; in 2015, the county had the highest truancy incarceration rate in the state.* White power gangs, both in and out

---

* At the time, juvenile courts in Washington led the nation in jailing young people for non-criminal offenses like truancy. In Cedar Monroe's autobiography, they write, "In 2015, Grays Harbor led the state on this count, with 77.2 percent of their arrested children incarcerated for truancy charges. That year, they incarcerated 541 children for truancy. Meanwhile King County, an urban county with a population over two million, incarcerated only 180." *Trash: A Poor White Journey* (Minneapolis: Broadleaf, 2024).

of prison, prey on young people, offering them safety and belonging in exchange for loyalty.

In the decade that Monroe worked as a street chaplain in Grays Harbor County, they lost track of the number of funerals they had to officiate, including ones they had to perform because the first funeral was led by clergy who, standing over their graves, chastised the deceased for their supposedly bad decisions and blamed them for their own deaths. So with each new funeral, a new tattoo. Monroe's body became a living memorial to the stolen lives our society would prefer us to ignore or forget.

One hundred years ago, the county's port in the city of Aberdeen was the timber export capital of the world. A lot of money flowed through the port in those days, although the greatest profits were always made and held by a few prominent families. The rest of the community, including workers flocking in from all over the world, fought one another for whatever scraps were left. By the time Monroe was a kid, the timber industry was already packing up and moving to the Global South. Not much remained and no new industry came in to fill the gap. Over the next couple decades, an underground economy sprang up as the only way many people could survive. There was a big boom in the production and selling of drugs, but that was soon shut down by federal authorities. In the 1990s, the flow of drugs reversed and opioids flooded the community, both illegally and through overprescription by doctors who responded with blunt force to the chronic pain and lifelong injuries that the timber industry left in its wake. The response of the local and state government to this crisis only added fuel to the fire: rather than build new businesses and hospitals, they built a new prison, along with an expanded network of local and municipal jails.*

---

* This phenomenon is common in rural counties that often rent their jail beds to overcrowded federal and state prisons, as well as immigrant detention facilities, as a source of income generation to supplant a waning tax base. For more on this, read *The Souls of Poor Folk*, a 2018 report from the Poor People's Campaign: https://www.poorpeoplescampaign.org/resource/the-souls-of-poor-folk-audit/.

I met Monroe through a student of mine named Aaron Scott. Scott, a white trans man who is now in his late thirties, was born in a working-class town in upstate New York and grew up attending a poor rural church in the foothills of the Adirondack Mountains. His mother and grandmother were both labor organizers and his father was a small-town preacher. By the time Scott arrived at Union Theological Seminary in 2007, he was eager to more deeply understand the religion he'd been brought up in. On the first day of his orientation, he joined a Bible study led by Willie Baptist and me and soon after he became a work study student with the Poverty Initiative.

After seminary, Scott moved to Washington State and began the process of becoming a deacon in the Episcopal Church. He met Monroe at a social justice conference hosted by the local diocese in 2013. They bonded quickly, in part because they were the only poor and queer people in the ordination process, and Monroe told Scott about the street outreach and hospitality work they had begun to do among unhoused folks in Aberdeen, where they themselves lived on and off the streets. The two spoke at length about the traditional work of chaplaincy among the poor—such as feeding people and offering spiritual guidance—and how they both understood that the work of a chaplain is also to be an organizer. They agreed that a chaplain has a moral responsibility to support their community not just through individual acts of care but by fighting alongside them for better conditions.

In 2014, Scott invited two colleagues of mine at the Poverty Initiative, Colleen and John Wessel-McCoy,* to visit Grays Harbor while they were in Washington presenting to a conference of Episcopal deacons. Cedar and Aaron drove them around and told them about their dream of doing deeper organizing in the area. Cedar pointed out

---

* Colleen is an ethicist and the author of *Freedom Church of Poor: Martin Luther King Jr.'s Poor People's Campaign* (Lanham, MD: Lexington Books, 2021). John is a longtime political educator and popular historian in the movement to end poverty.

an Episcopal church that had recently been shuttered and sat directly next to a food pantry.* The four agreed that it was a good location for street-based organizing. When Cedar and Aaron reached out to the local diocese to inquire about the vacant church, they were nervous about the response they would receive. It was a pleasant surprise when the diocese handed them the keys to the front door.

Monroe and Scott were never interested in proselytizing to people or bringing them to church on Sunday. Their goal, as Aaron explained to Noam and me, was to become "a ministry of presence for folks who were struggling."[2] In Grays Harbor, there are very few physical spaces where poor folks can legally gather in large groups without being surveilled. After decades of the neoliberal enclosure of public institutions and social supports, the community services on offer are mostly owned and operated by a network of far-right churches and clergy. Before Chaplains on the Harbor existed, hungry and unhoused people were forced to sit through patronizing services and Bible studies if they wanted a meal or a bed to sleep in. Some people chose to sleep on the streets rather than submit to this paternalistic control.

When Monroe and Cedar founded Chaplains on the Harbor, they understood that the Bible has been a contested text, a terrain of struggle, as long as Christians have been on these shores. Its varied interpretations have always been at the center of conflicts over the nation's moral and political values, for Christians as well as the many

---

* In rural Washington, as in other parts of rural America, churches are often some of the last communal institutions still standing, offering not just formal worship but all manner of direct services. Today, nearly half of all churches in the country feed the poor, and over 60 percent of all food pantries are housed in faith-based institutions. (Brad R. Fulton, "Nearly Half of all Churches and Other Faith Institutions Help People Get Enough to Eat," *The Conversation*, October 28, 2021. https://theconversation.com/nearly-half-of-all-churches-and -other-faith-institutions-help-people-get-enough-to-eat-170074).

millions more whose lives are impacted by Christianity. Power in this country has often been won or lost through this battle for the Bible, pitting theologies of the poor and dispossessed against theologies of the Christian elite. Today, the religious and political aspirations of the nation's most powerful Christians are expressed through the resurgent power of Christian nationalism, not just in the Pacific Northwest but across the country, even in so-called liberal enclaves. Liberatory theologies, and the communities they emerge from, are suffering mightily under this ideological assault.

On the rural coast of Washington, Monroe and Scott did the opposite of the local Christian nationalist elite. They opened the doors of their small church and welcomed everyone in need. They started by experimenting with different "projects of survival": partnerships with the food bank, harm reduction and first aid for people without healthcare, mental health chaplaincy, popular education classes, prison visits, and community led de-escalation of violence instead of involving law enforcement. According to Chaplains on the Harbor's website, projects of survival

> are more than a handout to people in need—they are a way of regularly gathering struggling people together to meet immediate needs, as well as to build relationships and strategize and organize around issues of injustice. . . . We know that the people with the greatest insights and leadership to offer on poverty, homelessness, and incarceration are the people who have lived through those things themselves. Projects of survival are a way of gathering those directly impacted leaders together.[3]

For the first two years, this is all Monroe and Scott did. Rather than enter the community with grand political pronouncements, they listened to the people walking through their doors. They listened as people told them about their hurts and traumas, their joys and desires, their petty squabbles and savvy observations. They listened and commiserated and gossiped and cracked jokes and, when the moment seemed right, they asked searching questions. Scott's favorite was borrowed from the legendary civil rights activist Ruby Sales: "Where does it hurt?"

The answers these two young chaplains received shaped the projects of survival they offered, which in turn deepened trust between them and their base: the poorest and most stigmatized people in the community. Sitting in the church's sanctuary, people discussed the latest indignities they and their families were facing: police sweeps in the local encampment, the passage of anti-homeless municipal ordinances, vigilante violence by local militias acting with near impunity from (if not through outright collaboration with) county officials. After trading notes, Monroe, Scott, and the community members would plan an appropriate collective response.

Over time, Chaplains on the Harbor developed a strong core of politically conscious leaders by building up their sense of power and ownership over the church space. They invited people to cook and clean and do repairs in the old church building, and eventually many of these same people stuck around long enough to become staff and volunteer leaders with the organization. As Chaplains grew, so did their footprint in the community, and Monroe and Scott made a significant impact in an area that previously had almost no progressive and socially active clergy.

In 2018, the city of Aberdeen attempted to ban family members, service providers, advocacy groups, and clergy from visiting an encampment of unhoused people that was slated for demolition. Monroe and two other community members sued the city in federal court, and the judge, a Republican, agreed with them that the city's ban was unconstitutional on the grounds of freedom of religious expression and association. The city, the judge concluded, was being run "like a jail."[4] The lawsuit was soon followed by a second, which focused on the demolition of the encampment itself. In this second case, Monroe stood as a plaintiff alongside ten unhoused people who were residents of the encampment. They argued that the city was in violation of the Eighth Amendment and that through repressive ordinances, camping bans, and encampment sweeps, the city was inflicting "cruel and unusual punishment" on its unhoused residents.* They also cited violations of sovereign treaties that protect the right of Indigenous peoples to "erect temporary structures" along their ancestral fishing grounds, since a few of the plaintiffs were enrolled tribal members of the Quinault Indian Nation. Unhoused people had never sued anyone in Grays Harbor before.

I visited Grays Harbor for the first time in the spring of 2017. I had helped organize a learning exchange between Chaplains on the Harbor and a delegation of faith leaders, veterans, unhoused organizers, and Movement for Black Lives activists from Ferguson and Miami. On our first day, Monroe led a memorial service for a young man who had died on the streets. Afterward, we gathered in the church to participate in a mock human rights trial indicting the government for the region's shameful poverty and housing crisis. On the front stoop of the church, Monroe and Scott had placed a doormat with a message for police officers that made it crystal clear who they stood with in the community: "Come Back with a Warrant."

After decades of public ministry among the poor, I was not new to memorial services and other end-of-life rituals that recognize the

---

* This legal battle is not unique to Grays Harbor. On June 28, 2024, the US Supreme Court decided *Grants Pass v. Johnson*, the most important case about homelessness in decades. The case concerned the town of Grants Pass, Oregon, a six-hour drive south of Grays Harbor. Grants Pass had previously outlawed sleeping or resting anywhere on public property, even when no shelter beds were available. The city claimed that the Eighth Amendment did not impose any substantial limitations on its ability to criminalize its unhoused residents. The court ruled in the city's favor, laying the groundwork for other local and state governments to follow in Grants Pass's footsteps and threatening a dramatic rise in the criminalization of homelessness and poverty across the country.

dignity and worth of lives that were never treated as such. This service, in particular, got me thinking about the revolutionary nature of spiritual acts of collective care among the poor. I was reminded of the underground community associations organized by poor people in the shadow of the Roman Empire. One of the key functions of these organizations was to ensure the burial and memorializing of their members, taking on the role of mutual aid societies and offering financial support for those too poor to provide for their own funeral. These burial societies were often considered dangerous by the Roman Empire since they brought poor people together in a time of rampant inequality and social polarization. The imperial government understood a timeless truth: when oppressed people spend enough time together, beyond the repressive bounds of an empire's influence, the winds of dissent and uprising often follow.

As part of their burial rituals, these associations offered a libationary toast to the deceased, often with the words "We do this in memory of . . ." When Jesus teaches his followers to practice what we now call communion (instructing them to break bread and to "do this in remembrance of me"), he is likely drawing inspiration from rituals that the poor of his day were already using to honor their dead. While I listened to Monroe eulogize their friend, I was struck by the thought that the ancient practice of communion had more in common with the work of this community of poor and unhoused people than with the rarified celebrations of communion served in shiny goblets and on silver platters in many churches. Others agreed. Bob Zellner, a native Mississippian who was the first white field secretary of the Student Nonviolent Coordinating Committee in the 1960s, had traveled with us to Grays Harbor. He was floored by the beauty of the memorial service amid so much unnecessary death. "I imagine this is what heaven feels like," he marveled.

Over the years, Monroe and Scott have described Chaplains on the Harbor in a number of ways: as a grassroots organization, a chaplaincy program, a mission station of the Episcopal Church. My personal favorite is when they call themselves a "freedom church of the poor."* When it comes to religion, the community members who first gathered around Chaplains on the Harbor were an eclectic bunch. Among them were Christians, former Christians who were mistreated by the church, occultists, spiritual seekers, agnostics, and athiests. Although many of these people weren't Christian or religious, the organization was able to earn their trust because, as Scott told us, they were "building sacraments and rituals that honor the struggle and dignity of our base."[5] These rituals, like funerals, may seem insignificant in the work of building a movement, but they are enormously significant for people who have been constantly subjected to words and deeds of dehumanization. Rituals sanctify the present by building bridges to the past and the future; they invite a dignified presence into our lives that ennobles the spirit, no matter who we are. In a society that so often treats the lives of the poor as expendable, life-affirming rituals are acts of tender resistance. From the very beginning, Monroe and Scott understood that the rituals of their religious tradition were just one way to help people feel loved and respected, and, through that nurturing feeling, cultivate a vibrant sense of communal power.

Since the 1970s, many churches in places like rural Washington have made a sharp turn toward the theology of Christian nationalism. Alongside this religious extremism, political extremism has flourished. In 2021, Monroe and Scott discovered that the brother of a local

---

* Years ago, the Poverty Initiative was inspired by this concept, which we encountered in a December 1967 speech given by Dr. King titled "Nonviolence and Social Change." Laying out his vision of a massive organizing drive among the poor, he described the emerging Poor People's Campaign as a "nonviolent army" and a "freedom church of the poor." Here, he was likely drawing on the legacy of the African Methodist Episcopal Zion Church, the denomination that his wife, Coretta Scott King, belonged to. Since the days of abolition, the AME church has been an enduring home to radical Black social activism and is colloquially known as the "freedom church."

county commissioner flew thousands of miles to DC to participate in the January 6 insurrection. Back home, that same commissioner constantly belittled and harassed poor and unhoused people. A second commissioner, who repeatedly blocked funding for lifesaving shelter programs, frequently leveraged her faith and her church's charitable works as a way to deflect from the policy-driven violence she committed against poor residents of the community. The actions of these two county commissioners were just the latest eruption of a volcano that has been smoldering for decades. The oppressive atmosphere in Grays Harbor County has emerged in no small part due to its history of resistance among the poor. During the heyday of the timber industry, the city of Aberdeen was a hotbed of multiracial labor organizing, which was met with crushing violence by the timber companies. More often than not, though, the actual dirty work of beatings, bombings, and murders were carried out by other poor and middle-income white people, with the direction and backing of the region's white elite. The same is true today.

Religion is a key factor in this reactionary all-white, cross-class alliance. Although many of the people who have attacked Chaplains on the Harbor are not religious, they have no problem allying themselves with Christian leaders and institutions. One prominent local church hosted meetings for a "concerned citizens" group that harassed, stalked, filmed, and live-streamed poor and unhoused people in Aberdeen. Monroe and Scott denounced the violence of these Christians, emphasizing for their community the themes of justice and freedom that are present on almost every page of the Bible. "Know that when you hear clergy say these things about the Bible, they are lying," the two chaplains reminded their community members. "They are just here to hold on to a sense of propriety and a sense of position. It's not biblical."[6]

The unwavering insistence of these chaplains on reclaiming and championing the most radical roots of the Bible has had the important effect of weakening the credibility of these clergy and politicians in the eyes of the poor and unhoused folks who are under attack. In a community whose power brokers have long relied on the fact that their political and religious positions usually go unchecked, one little church, with a group of streetwise chaplains, has made a world of difference.

THE BATTLE FOR THE BIBLE

The theological fight waged by Chaplains on the Harbor in rural Washington is not unique to that place nor to this moment in American history. From abolition to the Social Gospel to the Black Freedom Struggle to countless labor campaigns and other movements of the poor, the Bible has served as a wellspring of liberatory imagination and democratic awakening.[*] The theologies at the heart of these bottom-up struggles have always been reconstructive in a dual sense: they have demanded that society be rebuilt in the image of God's abundance and insisted that the revolutionary teachings of the Bible be recovered from the detritus of biblical distortion.[†] Indeed, Jesus spends the lion's share of his ministry preaching the Good News of redemption to those made poor by systemic oppression, calling out the hypocrisy of a society that neglects the poor, and admonishing the powerful for their idolatrous worship of wealth. Condemnation of idolatry in the Bible is almost always a critique of governing authorities: those who cloak themselves and their administrations in the garb of divinity in order to justify their hoarding of resources and legitimize their acts of violence and control.

---

[*] Non-Christian theologies have also always animated movements of poor and dispossessed people in this country. This chapter focuses on Christianity and the Bible because of its particular uses and abuses throughout American history.

[†] It is worth noting that the Jesus movement was itself a project of social and theological reconstruction. Despite the disastrous Christian distortions that followed, this was a Jewish renewal movement that attempted to reclaim the liberative theologies of the Torah and make them relevant for impoverished subjects of the Roman Empire, both Jewish and non-Jewish alike.

Woven throughout our nation's history there is a central thread of this idolotry—a long and evolving story of Christian nationalism that has enabled an elite strata of mostly white Christian men to rule society and amass enormous power and wealth. These Christians have always anointed themselves, and legitimized the social order they have benefited from, with the lie of divine righteousness and of their being chosen as God's representatives on earth. To maintain this charade, they have brandished the Bible like a cudgel, bludgeoning poor people, people of color, Indigenous people, women, LGBTQ+ people, and others with tales of their supposed sinfulness that are meant to distract, demean, divide, and dispossess.

The roots of this idolatry reach back centuries, before the founding of the nation, to the conquest of Indigenous lands by European invaders. In 1493, after Spain landed its ships on the islands of the Caribbean, Pope Alexander VI issued the Doctrine of Discovery, a series of papal bulls granting all newly "discovered" lands to its Christian conquerors. These church documents asserted the supposed "godlessness" of Indigenous peoples, smoothing over the ruthless colonial campaign of extermination with a veneer of moral virtue.* Centuries later, Manifest Destiny drew on the same religious underpinnings as the Doctrine of Discovery, popularizing the belief that white Christians were destined by God to control, and therefore redeem, the lands of the West. Manifest Destiny not only valorized the violence of westward expansion but sanctified and made exceptional the emerging project of American imperialism. God, the argument went, had chosen this nation to be a beacon of hope, a city upon a hill, for the whole world.

Alongside the dispossession and attempted extermination of Indigenous peoples, invocations of God and the Bible were used to

---

* In 1823, the US Supreme Court upheld this doctrine in *Johnson v. McIntosh*, affirming that Indigenous peoples did not have a right to sovereignty over their ancestral lands.

justify the enslavement of African peoples and their descendants. Slaveholders cherry-picked passages from the book of Ephesians— "slaves obey your earthly masters"—and other lines from the Apostle Paul's epistles to claim that slavery was ordained by God. They ripped out from the Bibles they gave to their enslaved workers the pages of the Exodus from Egypt, huge sections of the prophets, and even Jesus's inaugural sermon praising and elevating the poor and dispossessed. These "Slave Bibles" serve as evidence of just how dangerous the unadulterated gospel was to the legitimacy of the slave-holding planter class.

White Christians also grafted the Bible onto the racial pseudo-science of the day. Consider their use of Genesis and the Curse of Ham. In this biblical story, Ham, the son of Noah, discovers his father in a drunken state of nakedness. Noah is humiliated and condemns Ham's son, Canaan, and his son's descendants, into slavery. Although this curse is never directly affirmed by God in the text, slaveholders used the story to claim that Africans were the descendants of Canaan and consecrate American slavery through the fabrication of race and racialized difference (they pointed to Canaan's brother Cush, who is often identified with the lands just south of Egypt, as evidence that people with darker skin were cursed by God).

The planters' twisted theology served their political needs in another way: by obscuring the common interests of enslaved Black workers and poor Southern whites. Readings of the Bible that claimed God had singled out Black people for slave labor helped the Southern ruling class turn the region's majority of poor whites into zealous defenders of a system that relegated them to marginal lands and poverty wages. After the fall of the Confederacy, the Bible remained core to the new system of racialized divide and conquer in the South. Embedded in the legal structure of Jim Crow were moral and religious arguments that vilified and pathologized people of color, most of them poor, as fundamentally inferior, and threw poor white people the meager bone of spiritual superiority. Drawing directly on slaveholder religion, segregationist theology emphasized the Curse of Ham as evidence of God's preference for separation and "purity" of races.

Pro-segregation preachers, no longer able to use the Bible to defend slavery, also turned to stories like the Tower of Babel, which they claimed was proof that God desired not just linguistic difference but racial segregation and abhorred intermarriage across racial lines. In 1954, the Baptist preacher Carey Daniel wrote a pamphlet titled *God the Original Segregationist,* in which he explained: "When first He separated the black race from the white and lighter skinned races He did not simply put them in different parts of town. He did not even put them in different towns or states. Nay, He did not even put them in adjoining countries."[7] The pamphlet was distributed widely by the White Citizens' Councils and eventually sold over a million copies.

A decade later, at the end of the 1965 march from Selma to Montgomery, Dr. King offered a vivid description of this religiously infused strategy of division:

> If it may be said of the slavery era that the white man took the world and gave the Negro Jesus, then it may be said of the Reconstruction era that the southern aristocracy took the world and gave the poor white man Jim Crow. . . . And when his wrinkled stomach cried out for the food that his empty pockets could not provide, he ate Jim Crow, a psychological bird that told him that no matter how bad off he was, at least he was a white man, better than the black man. . . . And his children, too, learned to feed upon Jim Crow, their last outpost of psychological oblivion.[8]

The metaphorical bird described by King was seasoned and cooked in a volatile mix of "race science," economic control, and religious extremism. In fact, its progenitors retained their enormous power in part by using the Bible and an oppressive form of Christianity to validate their worldview. The effect on the majority of Southerners has always been terrible: the Bible Belt—sweeping across the South and parts of the Midwest and Appalachia—has long been the most contiguous area of poverty in the country. Today, one-third of the nation's poor live in the South.[9]

Parallel to theological justifications of Jim Crow, a national theology of industrial capitalism emerged in the late 1800s and early-to-mid-1900s. During the Gilded Age, the prosperity gospel and its theology of muscular Christianity flourished among the white upper class. Amid the excesses of the Second Industrial Revolution, they celebrated their own hard work and moral rectitude and bemoaned the personal failings of the poor. When the economic bubble finally burst in 1929, and the New Deal ushered in an unprecedented era of financial regulations and labor protections, the nation's corporate elite once again turned to the church to fight back on their behalf and cosign their free market aspirations. In *One Nation Under God: How Corporate America Invented Christian America*, historian Kevin M. Kruse writes that in the 1930s and 1940s:

> Corporate titans enlisted conservative clergymen in an effort to promote new political arguments embodied in the phrase "freedom under God." As the private correspondence and public claims of the men leading this charge make clear, this new ideology was designed to defeat the state power its architects feared most—not the Soviet regime in Moscow, but Franklin D. Roosevelt's New Deal administration in Washington. With ample funding from major corporations, prominent industrialists, and business lobbies such as the National Association of Manufacturers and the US Chamber of Commerce in the 1930s and 1940s, these new evangelists for free enterprise promoted a vision best characterized as "Christian libertarianism."[10]

The phrase "freedom under God" captures the tension at the heart of the long battle for the Bible in this country. Within this battle, there have always been two diametric visions of freedom: on one side, the freedom of the vast majority of people to enjoy the fruits of their labor and live with dignity and self-determination; on the other side, the freedom of the wealthy to control society, sow division, and hoard the world's abundance for themselves. Poor people, disproportionately poor people of color, have always been on the front lines of this battle, as both canaries in the coal mine and prophetic leaders. So go their lives, so goes the nation.

A PEOPLE'S HISTORY OF MODERN-DAY CHRISTIAN NATIONALISM

The question of what "freedom under God" means is once again being debated with potentially dire consequences for American democracy. Christian nationalism is gaining in power.[11] The leaders of this movement and their wealthy benefactors weaponize the Bible and mythologize a past that never was in order to effectuate a future unfettered by secularism, democratic expression, and economic regulation. The Christian nationalism of our day is the inheritor of the old theologies of the rich and powerful—the theologies of colonization, enslavement, and industrial capitalism. But it is also a modern creation of its own.

The roots of modern-day Christian nationalism reach back to the mid-twentieth century. At that time, a new movement of radical conservatism was ascendant. This movement, which included activists like Richard Viguerie, Phyllis Schlafly, and Paul Weyrich (who cofounded the Heritage Foundation, the American Legislative Exchange Council,* and the Moral Majority), was dead set on rolling back the gains of the New Deal and Great Society programs, together with the gains of the civil rights and women's rights movements. But to advance their emerging neoliberal agenda, the leaders of this

---

* Since 1973, ALEC has served as the legislative workshop of wealthy conservatives. Its corporate members draft template legislation that they then export to state legislatures across the country. This "corporate capture" of government is intimately connected with the rise of Christian nationalism, as evidenced by Weyrich's leadership in both ALEC and the Moral Majority.

right-wing movement needed a social base—an army of true believers. With the backing of powerful corporate patrons, they set their sights on organizing white evangelical and Catholic communities.

In 1971, they struck gold. That year, the Supreme Court ruled that private, white Christian schools, which exploded in numbers after *Brown v. Board of Education*, could lose their tax exempt status if they remained segregated. White evangelical and Catholic leaders in the South were outraged by the ruling, which meant the integration of Black students into their schools, and it finally opened them up to overtures from the Right.[12] But in the age of civil rights it was clear that uniting a broad movement of white evangelicals and Catholics around the issue of overt segregation was not a winning strategy. Two years later, *Roe v. Wade* arrived as if an act of divine intervention. In the years leading up to the ruling, white evangelicals were famously split on the issue of abortion. The Southern Baptist Convention, evangelicalism's most storied denomination, took moderate positions on abortion in the 1950s and 1960s, while leading Baptist pastors and theologians rarely preached or wrote on the issue.* But things changed after *Roe v. Wade* thrust abortion directly into the public eye and abortion rates climbed as access expanded. By the end of the 1970s, a growing number of white evangelicals expressed reservations about legalized abortion, joining a loud chorus of outraged Catholics.

This was the reactionary context from which the Christian Right emerged. Over the next few decades, the movement invested hundreds of millions of dollars into anti-abortion organizations and campaigns to advance its social values, while asserting the racist and sexist myth of dependency and individual failure to advance its free market

---

* A 1970 poll by the Baptist Sunday School Board found that "70% of Southern Baptist pastors supported abortion to protect the mental or physical health of the mother, 64% supported abortion in cases of fetal deformity, and 71% in cases of rapes." ERLC Staff, "5 Facts About the History of the SBC and the Pro-Life Cause," January 17, 2020, https://erlc.com/resource/5-facts-about-the-history-of -the-sbc-and-the-pro-life-cause/.

dreams. In the 1980s, Reaganomics, which championed austerity and deregulation, was packaged and sold in part through a trickle-down theology, demonizing workers and unions and levying salacious and moralizing attacks on the poor, especially poor people of color.

This "moral" crusade deployed culture wars—a phrase popularized by Christian Right operative Pat Buchanan—to forge new political unity among white evangelicals and Catholics. The effects on policy were seismic and hit the most marginalized communities of the poor first. The Christian Right's war on welfare, for example, was waged with debilitating efficiency throughout the 1980s and 1990s, conditioning the ideological visions of both political parties. Bill Clinton's 1996 Personal Responsibility and Work Opportunity Reconciliation Act (PRWORA)—riddled with language that disparaged single parents, sex and pregnancy out of wedlock, and more—was a generational triumph for the Christian Right and a pivotal inflection point for neoliberalism.

On its path to national power, the Christian Right worked diligently to capture the country's churches and co-opt the Bible to advance its policy goals. In the 1990s and first decades of the 2000s, it prosecuted a religious fight within mainline Protestant denominations, like the Southern Baptist Convention, United Methodist Church, and the Presbyterian Church (USA), accusing them, as well as many seminaries and congregations, of being too liberal. Successful campaigns by the Christian Right replaced moderate and more progressive clergy, presidents, professors, and department heads of seminaries, churches, mission groups, and other affiliated institutions with leaders from within their own ranks.

In 1996, the same year as welfare reform, the Presbyterian Church—the denomination in which I was raised and ordained—amended a section of our polity to bar people having sex outside of marriage from being ordained. The new stipulation, specifically written to target

LGTBQ+ people, revealed and emboldened a kernel of bigotry that has always been present in some circles of my denomination. It was also a deft strategic move by the Christian Right to split the Presbyterian Church and weaken our ability to take the offensive in advancing a moral agenda that could expand the rights of LGBTQ+ people, women, people of color, immigrants, and the poor. Young people left the church after the decision and LGBTQ+ clergy suffered years of prosecutions and punishments from church leadership. As a result, liberal and progressive Presbyterians were forced into a deeply defensive posture and many of my friends in the church valiantly spent the lion's share of their time during the 2000s fighting to recover the most basic rights of LGBTQ+ Presbyterians.*

These and other maneuvers by the Christian Right have left this movement with an impressive national infrastructure: a loosely held but disciplined network of churches and para-church organizations, including media companies, seminaries, discipleship ministries, evangelistic crusade associations, Bible study groups, prison ministries, disaster-relief organizations, and direct-service operations like feeding programs. Through this network, the Christian Right reaches tens of millions of people, including millions of middle- to upper-income white Christians who have always served as an important base for conservatism in this country and who have teetered in the last decade ever more closely to outright Christian nationalism and authoritarianism. This movement has also made worrying inroads in socially conservative Black and Latino communities, as well as poor white communities in small cities and rural areas like Grays Harbor, Washington, where the neoliberal assault on government has pulverized public institutions and the base of the old industrial economy

---

* After a hard-fought thirteen-year battle, the Presbyterian Church amended its polity in 2009 to once again allow LGBTQ+ people to be ordained. Unfortunately, Presbyterians and other mainline Protestants are waging similar battles around LGBTQ+ rights, reproductive rights, and gender justice today.

has collapsed. Far-right churches and para-church organizations have skillfully stepped in to fill the gap, responding to emergencies and attending to the very real needs of people for material support and communal belonging, even as they support policies and practices that hurt the poor and other historically oppressed communities.

––––––––––

The Christian Right has inaugurated a new, gilded era of Christian nationalism, drawing on the neoliberal playbook while increasingly eschewing democratic values all together. The election of Donald Trump in 2016 was a major coup for this movement, whose leaders leveraged their newly developed relationship with Trump, the mercurial businessman turned messianic strongman, to take full control of the Republican Party. Six years later, in 2022, the *Dobbs v. Jackson* decision, which gutted the right to abortion by overturning *Roe v. Wade*, affirmed their multi-decade plan to commandeer the Supreme Court. In 2023, the selection of Louisiana representative Mike Johnson, a tried-and-true son of the Christian Right with strong theocratic bona fides, as the Speaker of the House served as their latest coronation within the halls of Congress. A year later, in 2024, the re-election of Trump catapulted this emboldened movement, and the nation as a whole, into uncharted waters.

A few key beliefs animate modern-day Christian nationalism in the US, including these: (1) a highly exclusionary form of Christianity is the only true religion; (2) the country should be ruled by this form of Christianity and the separation of church and state is anti-Christian and must be undermined; (3) white supremacy, along with patriarchy and heteronormativity, is "the natural order" of the world and must be upheld in our personal lives as well as in public; (4) militarism and violence, rather than democratic expression and diplomacy, are the right ways for the government to exert power domestically and internationally; (5) scarcity is the economic reality of life and we (Americans vs. the world, Christians vs. non-Christians, natural-born citizens vs.

immigrants, etc.) must compete for resources; (6) people who are oppressed by systemic violence are, in fact, to blame for the deep social
and economic problems of the world; that is, the poor are at fault for
their poverty, LGBTQ+ people are responsible for disease and social
rupture, documented and undocumented immigrants are "rapists and
murderers" who are stealing so-called American jobs, and so forth; and
(7) the Bible is the source of moral authority on these and other issues.[13]

The recent ascendance of modern-day Christian nationalism is
mirrored by the international rise of religious nationalism and authoritarianism in countries as disparate as Brazil, Hungary, India, and
Israel. Here in the US, the worst may be yet to come. After decades of
neoliberal plunder—possible only through the participation of both
Republicans and Democrats—the Christian Right and its wealthy
patrons now have their eyes set on an even more ambitious power
grab. In 2023, the Heritage Foundation published its infamous 2025
Presidential Transition Project, otherwise known as Project 2025.[14] In
over nine hundred pages of painstaking detail, the influential right-
wing think tank outlined an astonishingly expansive blueprint for
the next Republican administration, with the political and financial
firepower to back it up.* More than half of the project's listed authors,
editors, and contributors were part of the first Trump administration,
and among its original sponsors were a number of key Christian nationalist organizations and billionaire funders.[15]

Project 2025 lays out a vision of wholesale state capture, couched in
a religiously regressive worldview that has only become more vitriolic
since the 1990s. Although its authors claim to be pro–working class
and unabashedly deploy the language of conservative populism—they
decry wokeness, cultural Marxists, and a dozen flavors of the elite

---

* Since the 1970s, the Heritage Foundation has published various neoliberal
policy agendas, including its influential 1980 "Mandate for Leadership," one of
the intellectual anchors of Ronald Reagan's first term as president. Project 2025
dwarfs Heritage's previous agendas in both scope and scale.

("Washington elites," "establishment elites," the anti-Semitic trope of "globalist elites," and so on)—the plan is chiefly concerned with how to wrestle even greater control of people and resources into the hands of a small minority of mostly white and wealthy Christians. Before the 2024 elections, this faux populism was unmasked by polling that found opposition to Project 2025 grew across party lines the more people learned about it.[16]

The longest section of Project 2025 focuses on "general welfare," including proposals to significantly cut back the Departments of Agriculture, Health and Human Services, and Housing and Urban Development. Popular and successful programs like Head Start and Housing First would be eliminated, while a "life agenda" and a "family agenda" would further curtail access to abortion and other reproductive rights, as well as LGBTQ+ rights (all of which would hurt the poor first and worst but ultimately touch every corner of society). To secure these and other proposals, Project 2025 envisions an increasingly anti-democratic and militarized form of governance. In other sections of the plan, the authors call for political power to be centralized in executive authority and for every branch of the military to be expanded, including for domestic deployment.

Although Trump half-heartedly distanced himself from the plan late in the 2024 campaign, the network that produced the document is the ideological and organizational center of the MAGA movement that Trump himself represents. His running mate, former venture capitalist J. D. Vance, was chosen directly from the Project 2025 ecosystem. On the campaign trail, Trump also proudly championed the Christian nationalism at the heart of Project 2025. At a Turning Point USA Rally in July 2024, he unabashedly told the audience: "I love you Christians. I'm a Christian. I love you, get out, you gotta get out and vote. In four years, you don't have to vote again, we'll have it fixed so good you're not going to have to vote."[17]

Project 2025 now represents the political horizon of the Republican Party, a hardened extremism that assures only deeper national turmoil in the years to come. And, despite popular distaste for the plan's proposals, significant parts of Project 2025 have already been implemented at the federal and state levels. In the summer of 2024, for example, the US Supreme Court released a string of bombshell decisions reflecting its increasing despotism: *Loper Bright Enterpises v. Raimondo*, which upended decades of precedent on the government's ability to regulate corporations, including the fossil-fuel industry; *Grants Pass v. Johnson*, the historic anti-homeless ruling that has only intensified the hostile terrain facing unhoused and precariously housed people; and *Trump v. United States*, which granted Trump near-total immunity from criminal prosecution.

In 2024, Republican-held state legislatures in dozens of states drafted and passed laws attacking reproductive rights, LGBTQ+ rights, public education, and social welfare programs, anticipating key proposals of Project 2025. A multistate Republican strategy also emerged to preempt the creation of new anti-poverty programs. At least ten states challenged universal basic income plans through legislative bans, funding restrictions, constitutional challenges, and court injunctions, while four states (Arkansas, Idaho, Iowa, and South Dakota) completely prohibited such plans. These legal and legislative maneuvers are evidence of the significant political power that Christian nationalism already wields at the state and local levels.[18]

With Trump's re-election in 2024, we can expect this movement to only grow and consolidate in national power, backed by a vengeance-obsessed administration that is better organized than in 2016 and has now fully disciplined the Republican Party. Among those who stand to benefit are the super-rich, who are already reaping the rewards of a second Trump presidency. On November 6, 2024, the day after Trump won the election, the ten richest people in the world increased their wealth by a single-day record of $64 billion, as Wall Street investors anticipated the likelihood of more tax cuts and deregulation.[19]

FAILURES OF LIBERALS AND THE LIBERAL CHURCH

The rise of modern-day Christian nationalism is the result of both the successes of the Christian Right and the failures of the liberal establishment and its most powerful institutions. The experience of Grays Harbor, Washington, is illustrative. Before 2016, the county was one of the longest-running blue-voting districts in the country, having not voted for a Republican candidate since Calvin Coolidge in 1924. In 2016, Grays Harbor flipped from Obama to Trump, surprising many pundits in the historically liberal state. Cedar Monroe, Aaron Scott, and the crew at Chaplains on the Harbor were less surprised. Trump's victory finally made plain a communal crisis they had been decrying for years, a crisis that until then had mostly been ignored by liberals and has only worsened since 2016.

The long-standing economic catastrophe battering Grays Harbor has both conservative and liberal authors. Decades of policy decisions by Blue Dog Democrats—like NAFTA and welfare reform—have wrought havoc on poor people in the region, including those who were once more comfortably nestled in the middle class of the timber industry. For decades leading up to 2016, Democrats largely dismissed or thumbed their noses at these very people. As conditions worsened, the active derision of liberals and the absence of progressive organizations and churches left a political vacuum that Christian nationalism and the MAGA movement were all too happy to fill.

We saw the same story unfold in 2024, although this time Trump succeeded in speaking to the economic pain of not only poor white people but some poor people of color as well. Indeed, Trump won in 2024 by building a diverse coalition that included poor and dispossessed people of every race, while the Democrats emerged as the party of the better-educated and better-off. While Trump's policies are unlikely to help the poor and dispossessed, he at least acknowledged their material struggles on the campaign trail, particularly in relation to high inflation and the cost-of-living crisis. Meanwhile, Joe Biden and Kamala Harris regularly appeared to deny people's lived experience and offer only happy talk about the strength of macroeconomic indicators like GDP and official unemployment rates.[20]

The Christian Right may have very little to offer communities like Grays Harbor in terms of actual plans to resolve the deep social crises they are facing. But its leaders and institutions are often the only ones on the ground providing people material aid, spiritual care, and political direction. I am reminded of my uncle, a born-again Christian, who as a young man struggled with drugs and finding good-paying work. While living in Illinois in the 1990s, he joined the Promise Keepers with his wife and three kids. These Christians, who preach a patriarchal and anti-LGBTQ+ theology, embraced him like a brother, offering him not only a sense of belonging but access to youth programming, family support, and medical aid. When he got sick with cancer and after he died, his family didn't have to worry about meals for months. Their community ensured the refrigerator was always stocked with food and their living room was filled with comforting friends.

It is often said that folks like my uncle are motivated by white grievance amid demographic change and that people like him vote against their best interests. While this first point might be true, it is also true that some of my uncle's most immediate interests *were* addressed by the Promise Keepers. The care and devotion that he and his family received would have been hard to find from many liberal institutions or churches. And while I don't know if or how he voted, the argument that working-class white people vote against their best interests glosses over the fact that millions of poor and low-income people across race vote sporadically or not at all. This lower-than-average voter engagement is at least in part because they don't hear politicians from either party speaking about the issues and concerns that actually shape their lives. After the 2020 elections, a report from the Poor People's Campaign found that relatively small increases in voter turnout among poor and low-income people could have equaled or surpassed the margin of victory in multiple swing states.[21] Although Trump improved his margins with poorer voters in 2024, there were still millions of poor and low-income people who didn't vote at all. If this sleeping giant of potential voters is ever awakened in a sustained way and brought into a mass movement that recognizes them as political actors and addresses their economic and social concerns, the political landscape election outcomes could be transformed for a generation.

————————————

Among liberal institutions, the liberal church has often failed the poor and paved the way for extremism. Within mainline liberal denominations there has always been a troubling current of paternalism and anti-poor moralizing, especially among the whitest and wealthiest. This religiously motivated condescension has been meted out unequally, most intensely toward poor people of color but also toward poor white people. Before Monroe founded Chaplains on the Harbor, they received a scholarship to attend an Episcopal seminary. In their autobiography *Trash: A Poor White Journey*, they write about their harrowing experience upon arriving in the seminary halls of one of the wealthiest and most liberal denominations:

> I was expected to leave my past and my people behind. I was expected to be grateful that the coffers of the Episcopal Church had ensured my path toward respectability. I would never again have to live with poor people, and I could enter the American Dream and never look back. It was another proffer of salvation. . . . I could learn to enunciate words correctly—"no accents!" my liturgy professor urged us—and I could bargain for a good salary and live a good life. Poor white people were failures: beyond hope of redemption, racist beyond saving, best left to die out in their hollers and trailer parks. But maybe a few, like me, could be saved.[22]

This lofty disdain has become perhaps even more insidiously pervasive in the neoliberal age, with its hyper-individualism and racialized explanations of poverty. As the Christian Right swept onto the scene, the liberal church got pulled into the quicksand of their vicious finger-pointing and talk of personal responsibility. After welfare reform in 1996, for example, many liberal churches unknowingly became the frontline troops of austerity and privatization through a provision of the PRWORA called Charitable Choice. The provision stipulated that if a state used private or nonprofit contractors to deliver social services, that state must also include religious congregations in the competitive contracting process. On paper, this provision appeared to many clergy, liberals included, as a recognition of the historic role churches and other houses of worship have played in providing direct services to people in need. Lots of folks in the church agreed that they were best positioned to care for their communities since they knew them better than the government. But in practice, this provision and others that followed, like the Bush-era "faith-based" initiatives, provided moral cover for politicians to tear apart the welfare system and off-load the remaining pieces to civil society and the private sector. From the start, government funds delivered through Charitable Choice were narrow and insufficient. Rather than address the full breadth of need within poor communities, the provision became an ideological tool of neoliberalism.

If over the last few decades the Christian Right has fought for the heart and soul of the church and the nation, many liberals and progressives have simply left the battlefield, allowing these extremists to claim a monopoly on God and morality. The media has played into this dynamic, reporting on only a few issues as "moral" or "religious," such as marriage, abortion, gun rights, and the protection of private property. Many journalists also make the mistake of identifying only right-wing leaders as "Christians" in their reporting, while the liberal and progressive Christians who are actively fighting in the public square are often painted as "activists." With the moral high ground conceded, liberals often appear satisfied with levying condemnation. During the 2024 elections, many decried the threat that Project 2025 and Christian nationalism posed to democracy without offering a proactive vision of their own that spoke to the actual needs and dreams of most people (let alone investing in the on-the-ground infrastructure necessary to go toe to toe with this authoritarian movement). The same has been true in previous election cycles, when other extremist agendas were on the ballot. Within this dynamic, the liberal church has largely failed to offer vibrant and biblically sound theologies, although there are many heroic clergy who are struggling under immense pressure to hold the theological line.

This failure is significant, considering that the biblical positions espoused by Christian nationalism are not just reactionary but heretical to the teachings of Jesus. Opposition to abortion, for example, is never mentioned in the Bible. In fact, there is strong historical evidence that abortion was regularly practiced across the Roman Empire, by both its impoverished subjects and its prosperous rulers.[23] One would have to imagine that if this were a concern of Jesus's, it would have appeared somewhere in his teachings. What does appear in his teachings, however, is condemnation of politicians and religious leaders who neglect the weightier matters of justice and act as priests of the empire rather than chaplains for the movement.

THE LEAST OF THESE IS ALL OF US

To achieve a new moral vision for society, we need to build it. We need to fight for people by offering them not just political direction but physical protection, material and emotional support, and spiritual belonging. This is the focus of a 2022 report commissioned by the Kairos Center and MoveOn titled *All of U.S.: Organizing to Counter White Christian Nationalism and Build a Pro-Democracy Society.** MoveOn, a secular, progressive advocacy organization, may appear an odd bedfellow for a report on Christian nationalism, but the report

---

* The *All of U.S.* report was authored by Stosh Cotler, a visionary Jewish organizer who served as the CEO of Bend the Arc, the largest progressive Jewish organization in the country, from 2014 to 2022.

actually originated out of conversations they initiated with Noam and me after the January 6 insurrection. Although they anticipated the threat of political violence following the 2020 elections, the organization was caught off guard by the Christian nationalist fervor at the heart of the insurrection.*

Our team conducted interviews with grassroots organizers—many in rural areas and the South—who described conditions of rising political violence and repression within their communities, as well as the erosion of public services and communal infrastructure. Repeatedly, we were reminded that the places where Christian nationalism has emerged are not as monolithic or as ideologically hardened as many liberals assume. As we write in the report, for example, "Rural organizing requires far less persuasion to galvanize support for issues we would associate with a pro-democracy/anti-authoritarian agenda than non-rural people often think. Instead, what is needed are resources to energize and organize people who are already aligned, but who remain unorganized."[24] In fact, policies that are often considered more progressive—like racial justice, expanded healthcare, higher wages, and taxing the wealthy——are fairly popular in many of the geographic areas that are often written off by liberals. One organizer told us: "We did polling that actually showed the Democratic Party brand had lower favorability than Black Lives Matter protestors among rural battleground voters in 2020. The Democrat brand is worse for progressive policies than progressive policies are for the Democratic Party."

To tap into the latent power of these communities, we identify three key strategic interventions for countering Christian nationalism: (1) Organize more holistically. That is, broaden and sustain grassroots movement building by attending to people's material, emotional, and

---

* After the 2020 elections, Speaker of the House Mike Johnson and other Christian Right leaders within both Congress and civil society emerged as the architects of the "Stop the Steal" effort. The evidence of their Christian nationalism was undeniable during the insurrection itself. Protestors held up Bibles, crosses, and Christian flags, while proudly confessing their theocratic beliefs on camera.

spiritual needs. (2) Contest and invest. In other words, stop ceding geographic, political, and moral space to Christian nationalism. (3) Plan and coordinate for deeper crisis. Take the steps to prepare our communities for greater uncertainty, chaos, and possible large-scale crisis.

The model offered by Chaplains on the Harbor is a promising place to start on all three strategies. Consider the impact this one little freedom church has made in a region that has long been neglected by liberal politicians, activists, and clergy. Through their organizing, Chaplains on the Harbor has asserted that everybody has a right to live, reminded society that "baby Jesus was homeless," and refused to back down despite significant pushback and repression. Now consider what it might look like if there was a church like Chaplains on the Harbor in every county in coastal Washington, Washington State, the Pacific Northwest, even the entire country. What might be possible if so many churches were operating not in isolation, but in coordination with one another. Imagine the power of this vast network to shake things up and assert the moral, intellectual, and political agency of poor and dispossessed people. Food pantries could become places not just to fill bellies but launch protests, campaigns, and organizing drives; superstorms and forest fires could become moments not just for acute disaster response but for sustained community care and relationship building, repairing the societal fissures that worsen extreme weather events.

The many nodes of this network would not all need to be churches. Poor people's organizations often serve a similar function as a church, offering their members connection, sanctuary, and a sense of higher purpose. In fact, these organizations regularly blend spiritual and political labor and deliberately do so outside of institutional religion, which has often been a source of terror and trauma in their communities. We are reminded of something that S'bu Zikode, the founder of Abahlali baseMjondolo, the shack dwellers' movement of South Africa, once told us. During a visit to New York City in 2018, he explained: "We claim the God of the poor. We claim God as ours, as being on our side."[25] In their encampments, the members of this movement, many of whom are Christian, have chosen to take God out of the formal church, which has little relevance to their lives, and instead to bring God into their daily struggles for housing and land. In the process, Abahlali baseMjondolo has become a sacred space of its own. This is what Zikode calls "living politics"—a politics that speaks to both the material realities and spiritual concerns of his people.[26]

As Monroe and Scott learned in Grays Harbor, we can't rely on social media outreach or expect to win people by parachuting in and out of their communities, knocking on their doors and asking them to join our campaigns as so many political operations do every election cycle. In the places where Christian nationalism is rearing its ugly head, we need to prove to people that we are committed to being with them through thick and thin. We need to attend to the material, spiritual, and emotional needs of vulnerable and struggling communities, even as we plant the seeds of political consciousness and emboldened leadership. In this era of social isolation and communal fracture, we need what church can offer, even if it's not church in name or form.

There are, of course, essential roles for people of all faiths, and people who don't subscribe to any faith, to play in building the living politics that these times demand. There is a heightened need in this moment for us to forge new relationships across religious and cultural divides. Moral movements, broadly defined and inclusive to all, have always inspired the greatest national transformation. But today's ongoing political crisis reminds those of us who are Christian that we can no longer afford to sit out the battle for the Bible. The experience of Chaplains on the Harbor underscores that there is an indispensable role for a multiracial freedom church of the poor to play in beating back the rising tides of Christian nationalism—and cultivating the deep community connections, organizing infrastructure, and spiritual sustenance that are necessary to mount an effective fight to end poverty. We need bottom-up moral movements, led by people who are not waiting to be "saved" but who are taking lifesaving action where violence and death proliferate.

CHAPTER SEVEN

OUR KAIROS MOMENT

Sharon Lavigne almost leaped from her porch chair in surprise when she heard the voice of God in her right ear. She had been praying a lot lately, often in bed after a bath, but it had been a while since God had spoken back.[1]

It was the fall of 2018. Over the previous few years, the sixty-eight-year-old special education teacher had watched as an unnatural sickness slowly consumed her community. At school, her classroom was filling up with new students beset by asthma and other illnesses that disrupted their ability to learn. When she wasn't working, she was going to funerals, sometimes several a week, of friends and neighbors who died riddled with cancer. The sickness was also invading her home. In 2016, Lavigne was diagnosed with autoimmune hepatitis, a liver disease, and doctors discovered irregular levels of aluminum in her body. Like her students, her grandchildren were developing breathing problems, and when they played outside their skin broke out in rashes. In her yard, Lavigne's beloved persimmon trees had begun to turn barren.

Lavigne, a Black woman now in her mid-seventies, is a lifelong resident of the fifth district of St. James Parish, which sits on a gentle curve of the Mississippi River fifty miles upstream of New Orleans. When she talks about her childhood, it glimmers with idyllic luster. She recalls: "That was the good old days. That was the clean years."[2] In the 1950s and 1960s, the persimmon trees of St. James bore fruit that was tangy and plentiful. Other trees, too, flowered generously: oranges, figs, pecans. Lavigne's father kept a big vegetable garden, and her family lived off the abundance of the land, eating and selling their crops and raising pigs, chickens, and cattle. The river offered a similar bounty, teeming with fish and shrimp. There wasn't a lot of money to go around, and the mostly poor Black community was still haunted by the unresolved legacy of Louisiana's slaveholding past, but the natural world provided sustenance and income, a small mercy in an often unmerciful world.

Everything changed when the first petrochemical plant was built in the river parishes by Gulf Oil in the late 1960s. Many in the community, including Lavigne's father, a civil rights activist who integrated the local school system, welcomed the arrival of an industry whose representatives promised new jobs and economic development. Over the next few decades, dozens of other companies followed, chewing up the land and transforming St. James and the neighboring river parishes into a sprawling industrial web of two hundred plants and myriad pipelines, oil depots, and landfills—composing one of the largest sites of petroleum production in the country.[3] The sky was pierced by bright pillars of orange fire and the air around the plants became thick with the sulfuric stench of rotten eggs.

Despite the transformation of her surroundings, Lavigne did not know the true extent of the damage being done to her region until decades later. The puzzle pieces finally came together when she joined a local community organization in 2015. She sat through meeting after meeting where residents discussed the plants, twelve of which were a short drive from her home. Lavigne learned that the river parishes, which sit on an eighty-five-mile stretch of land between New Orleans and Baton Rouge, have some of the highest rates of industrial-borne cancer in the country. The Environmental Protection Agency estimates that the risk of cancer in the area can run as high as seven hundred times the national average.[4] Some residents, who had been organizing against the petrochemical industry for decades, called their home "Cancer Alley."

And there were plans to build new plants. In 2014, the local parish council amended the land-use plan for the fifth district to accommodate more industry. On the official maps, Lavigne's community went from being a strictly "residential" zone to a mixed "residential/industrial" zone. Among the companies poised to build were a $1.25 billion plastics plant owned by the Chinese company Wanhua and a $9.4 billion plant owned by the Taiwanese company Formosa, the second of which was slated for construction in the unincorporated community of Welcome, just two miles from her home and one mile from a public school.[5] The Formosa plant, which would span sixteen facilities and consume 2,400 acres of land, proceeded to be marketed as the "Sunshine Project," an Orwellian attempt to paper over its toxic implications with a sheen of cheery PR spin.[6] The reality of the proposed plant, however, is grim. WWNO, the NPR affiliate in New Orleans, reported that "when the Louisiana Department of Environmental Quality granted its air permits in 2019, it authorized the plant to release 13.6 million metric tons of greenhouse gasses every year, the equivalent of 3.5 coal-fired power plants."[7]

Lavigne didn't consider herself an organizer, but in September 2018 she and a few friends convinced the local community group to organize a march to protest the proposed plants. After the march, however, leaders with the group claimed there was nothing more they could do. A few weeks later, she sat on her porch, worriedly turning over her options, when she heard a voice unlike any other. She explains:

That's when God spoke to me, sitting on my front porch. When I asked him if I should sell my home, he said no. And then I asked him if I should sell my land, the land that he gave me, and he said no. And it startled me. Because he was sitting or standing on my right side. I didn't see him, but I knew he was there. And I knew it was his voice. It wasn't no other voice. People sometimes say, "This voice is not from God." Oh baby, when you come from God, you will know it's God's voice. From that moment I felt like I was transformed into another person.[8]

Within a few weeks, Lavigne was a woman on a divine mission. In October, she invited friends and family over to her house to discuss the Formosa plant. About ten people showed up, and her oldest daughter served as notetaker. Together, they brainstormed what actions they could take to fight back. After that first meeting they held others, their numbers growing as people caught wind of this latest wave of local resistance. Their new organization, named Rise St. James, did a little bit of everything: they held marches and rallies, attended parish council meetings, connected with lawyers and larger environmental organizations, and even put up billboards for anyone driving through the parish to see. One billboard simply read: "St. James is our home. No Formosa."

As their work progressed, they began hearing from other people in the surrounding parishes, some of whom were also organizing against the plants. In St. John the Baptist Parish, Robert Taylor, a Black retired contractor, had founded Concerned Citizens of St. John's Parish in 2016 to protest a plant owned by DuPont, the multinational chemical company. Lavigne, Taylor, and other residents of the river parishes decided they would be stronger if they joined forces, so in 2019 they formed the Coalition Against Death Alley, a variation on the theme of Cancer Alley. At one point, Sharon advocated for an even more scathing nickname: the Coalition Against Death Row.

———————

The tentacles of the fossil fuel industry in southeast Louisiana extend in all directions, not just across the lands of the river parishes but deep into the Gulf of Mexico. In 2010, the British Petroleum Company (BP) famously lost control of its Deepwater Horizon oil platform, pouring more than 200 million gallons of oil and 225,000 tons of methane into the sea's warm waters.[9] The spill was one of the worst human-made environmental disasters in history: eleven workers, hundreds of thousands of animals, and millions of plant life were killed, the livelihoods of fisherman and other sea-faring workers were thrown into disarray, close to 2 million additional gallons of oil dispersant were showered onto the crime scene, and over 150 million gallons of oil were never recovered.[10] BP was forced to pay $20 billion in fines, a historic sum—but, for a company as wealthy as BP, that amount was ultimately a speedbump. Since the BP spill, the US has become the world's largest producer of petroleum, with new and expanded drill sites by BP pockmarking the Gulf of Mexico.[11]

After the spill, folks across the gulf region sprang into action to defend their communities and demand accountability. One such organizer was Cherri Foytlin, a Diné-Cherokee woman who lived in the oil town of Rayne, Louisiana, a two-hour drive west of St. James. Foytlin's husband worked on a different deepwater oil rig and she was concerned for him and his colleagues. She was also worried about the health of the water and land and recognized within herself a spiritually rooted responsibility to be a good steward for future generations, just as her ancestors had been for her. On the spill's one-year anniversary in 2011, Foytlin—already a well-known organizer and independent journalist in the region—set out on a 1,200 mile walk from Louisiana to Washington, DC, to demand that the Obama administration mobilize a more rigorous and fulsome response to the disaster.

My colleagues and I at the Poverty Initiative also mobilized after the spill. We connected with local organizers and did what we could to bring them into relationships with other poor people organizing across the country, including those who were similarly impacted by polluting industries. We met Foytlin when she attended a human rights film festival we organized in 2012 at Union Theological

Seminary. Like us, she understood that what was happening to her home was ultimately caused not by one company but by larger economic processes requiring a nationwide response from people like her. At an international convening on the human right to water that we organized in Biloxi, Mississippi, in 2014, she put it this way: "I realized it's bigger than the Gulf. If we're ever going to win in the Gulf we have to bring people together from all over the place. It's not about starting a new group, but about supporting the communities and the groups that are already out there fighting."[12]

For Foytlin, this understanding was reinforced by other trips we took together, including visits to Flint, Michigan, and West Virginia. She was deeply affected by these trips. In Flint, I remember watching her collect poisoned water to mix with the blackened water she had carried from her home, a lethal cocktail that evoked the inseparable nature of our water systems and the many millions of lives that rely on them. During our visit to the mountains of West Virginia in 2015, Foytlin traveled with Catherine Coleman Flowers, a Black organizer from Lowndes County, Alabama, who I have known and worked with for years. Over the last decade, Flowers has helped bring attention to the crisis of failing sanitation services in poor rural communities like Lowndes County, where public infrastructure has crumbled, septic tanks are prohibitively expensive, and human waste sometimes sits untreated in people's lawns and next to freshwater sources.[13]

Foytlin and Flowers, who both became founding members of the Poor People's Campaign's Steering Committee in 2017, were moved when they learned how much they had in common with one another, as well as with poor white people in Appalachia. The two women became fast friends, and in 2016 they traveled with my colleagues to the Oceti Sakowin Camp on the edge of the Standing Rock Sioux Reservation to bear witness to the Indigenous-led resistance movement against the Dakota Access Pipeline. Two years later, in 2018, Foytlin was living in the swamplands of Southeast Louisiana, having set up an encampment to protest the construction of the Bayou

Bridge Pipeline on the ancestral lands of the Houma, Chitimacha, and Chahta peoples. The pipeline, which was completed a year later and runs straight through St. James Parish, is co-owned by Energy Transfer Partners, the same company that co-owns the Dakota Access Pipeline. Like the water protectors at Standing Rock, Foytlin and her comrades—who included Indigenous organizers, veterans, low-wage workers, and LGBTQ+ leaders—endured constant, militarized abuse from local and state authorities.

Police raided the encampment on multiple occasions, and in response to the protest the Louisiana legislature changed the law to make trespassing a criminal offense rather than a misdemeanor when it occurred on property the government considered "critical infrastructure."[14] To avoid criminal prosecution, the water protectors got creative. They climbed up the old cypress trees rooted along the proposed path of the pipeline and built platforms between the trees where they could sit and even sleep. These "sky pods" were a clever innovation—Energy Transfer Partners owned the trees but not the space in between them. The residents of the airborne encampment echoed the rallying cry of Standing Rock, where people had declared *Mni wiconi*, "water is life," in the Lakota language. In the heart of Cajun country, they used Louisiana Creole instead: *L'eau est la vie.*

It didn't take long for Foytlin and Lavigne to meet. In a region like Southeast Louisiana, people who are standing up to the fossil fuel industry are hard to miss, and both women became leaders in the fight against the Bayou Bridge Pipeline and Formosa. During a public hearing concerning the plastics plant in December 2018, an attorney with the Louisiana Office of Coastal Management turned off the sound system after Foytlin stepped up to the mic and decried their complicity in the corporate abuse of poor, Black, and Brown communities. "This is a dog and pony show," she exclaimed, "and everybody in this room knows it."[15]

That same winter, my colleagues and I visited the river parishes a number of times to learn how we could help. A few years earlier, Foytlin had introduced us to a local pastor who then introduced us to Lavigne and other community leaders. In January 2019, they invited the Poor People's Campaign, which had launched a year earlier, to organize a mass meeting and memorial service alongside Rise St. James and the Coalition Against Death Alley. We brought as many people and media as we could muster. Eight months later, Wanhua abandoned its plans for construction in St. James before the Parish Land Use Commission could vote on whether or not to green light the project and before a lawsuit by Rise St. James could go to court. It was clear the pressure was working.

Two years later, Rise St. James won an even bigger victory when a judge in Baton Rouge terminated Formosa's air permits, citing the company's failure to accurately report data on the polluting effects of their proposed plant. The judge, who also learned from the plaintiffs that the plant was slated to be built atop the old burial sites of enslaved people, defended the residents of St. James with unusual vigor: "The blood, sweat, and tears of their ancestors is tied to the land. . . . Their ancestors worked the land with the hope and dream of passing down productive agricultural untainted land along the Mississippi to their families."[16]

The fight against Formosa isn't over yet. The Taiwanese plastics giant challenged the 2022 ruling, and in January 2024 a state appeals court sided with the company.[17] Rise St. James has vowed to continue contesting the plant in court, and although the second ruling was disappointing, Lavigne is undeterred. God's voice is still ringing in her ear. She is certain they will win, a conviction reflected in the movement's anthem, sung to the tune of the old church hymn "Victory Is Mine Today." In the original lyrics, Satan is named as the ultimate adversary. In the shadow of the petrochemical industry, Lavigne made one important tweak: "Victory is mine, victory is mine, I told Formosa to get thee behind, because victory today is mine."

It is not an accident that the fossil fuel industry sets up shop in poor communities like St. James, which have the least amount of leverage and influence in government committees and corporate boardrooms. There are no multibillion-dollar plastics plants in wealthy communities. The wealthy people who did once live nearby these industries are also the first to leave when they see the writing on the wall, as happened in the river parishes in the late 1960s and 1970s, when the white and well-off residents who lived along the Mississippi River moved to safer ground. Most of the public investments made by the local and state government in the ensuing decades followed them to their better-off neighborhoods.

In a world transformed by the climate crisis, poor people—disproportionately poor children, women, and people of color—are being hit first and worst. As superstorms, wildfires, heat waves, floods, droughts, and other climate-related disasters intensify in the coming decades, the poor will continue to suffer the most, both from primary harm and secondary ripple effects. Already, the damage is not reserved to those living near polluting industries. Without a major and immediate shift in how we produce and consume energy, the unnatural heating of our world is only going to widen economic inequality through plagues of famine, water scarcity, job loss, health emergencies, and mass displacement. Adding insult to injury, the handful of fossil fuel executives responsible for these conditions are the very same people who simultaneously profit off war, champion the wholesale deregulation of the economy, and advocate the further gutting of social programs. They are also some of the biggest funders of Christian nationalist politicians. Rising fascism in the twenty-first century is fueled by Big Oil.

In the age of corporate-driven global warming, the lives of the poor are harbingers of an existential crisis that implicates all of our struggles and all of our futures. The fight for peace, living wages, affordable housing, healthcare, food, water, and other fundamental rights runs directly through the fight for a transformed economic system that no longer dominates the earth through extraction or people through immiseration. If our human rights have always been inextricably bound together, the connective threads linking our communities are only tightening. As the climate crisis threatens all of us, the long-standing demands of the poor are increasingly becoming the demands of humanity. After decades of ravage and ruin raining down from those situated at the top of society, an anthem from the Poor People's Campaign resounds with thunderous clarity: "When you lift from the bottom, everybody rises."

For years, poor and dispossessed people, so often women of color and Indigenous women like Lavigne, Foytlin, and Flowers, have been doing just that—lifting from the bottom of society and standing in the breach like the prophets of old. Not only have they been ringing the alarm of a nation in crisis but they have consistently offered concrete solutions that would yield broad societal benefits. They have also organized their communities to demand that these proposed solutions become government policies. In response, those in positions of greatest political and economic power, and moral authority, have committed a crime denounced throughout the ages: "They have treated the wounds of My people like they were not serious, saying 'peace, peace,' when there is no peace" (Jeremiah 6:14). Even as the life-or-death stakes of the present moment become clearer, members of both political parties waste precious time denying the climate crisis, or worrying more about its perception than its reality, while continuing to prioritize corporate profits and financial markets over everyone's well-being.[18]

Noam and I find the Bible useful in times like these. Consider the Exodus story. When the Israelites first begin their abolition campaign, God tells Moses that although he must go to Pharaoh with their demands, the ruler will not assent. Then, as God summons plagues of hunger, illness, ecological devastation, and death, God does a curious thing: God "hardens Pharaoh's heart" (Exodus 7:3-4). People have wrestled with this moment for centuries. Why must a society suffer for the sins of a few, and why must its ruler become crueler as conditions deteriorate? Why would God make things harder for the very people God claims to love and protect?

We have always thought of this moment in Exodus less as an ethical quandary and more as an accurate depiction of a society riven by deep inequality. Yes, we might wish for an easier narrative, but the story is useful to us because of how it unfolds. As our friend Dan Jones, a Jewish organizer and poor people's scholar of the Torah, writes, "What use could we make of a version of the Exodus where things don't get worse before they get better? What use would we have for this story if Pharaoh let the Israelites go simply because he saw the error of his ways and not because he was forced to do so? Our long experience tells us that only a society in crisis is a society ripe for transformation."[19]

This is the truth of plagues in the Bible: they tear down the flimsy whitewashed walls of false narratives to expose the foundations of injustice. Before a plague, God always sends prophets, usually sick and impoverished themselves, to tell the powerful to reject wickedness, stop oppressing the poor and the vulnerable, and turn toward peace and justice. But when the vision and action of prophets are not enough—when the powerful double-down on deceit and violence— God speaks and acts through plague to force us to see the terrible truth of our society and remove oppressors from power. Plague in the Bible is not a storm weathered before a return to normalcy. It is a call for people to come together in new ways in order to survive, hold the powerful responsible for the lies they tell to cover up their wrongdoing, and rebuild society on stronger and more sustainable foundations.[20]

Jones puts it this way:

> We don't celebrate the deaths and the suffering of pandemics or war or of any of our other plagues today. We don't celebrate the hard-heartedness of presidents, generals, CEOs, and shareholders.

But we know that plague is what happens when injustice pushes a society to its breaking point. And we know that breaking points are what force oppressed people to tear down old ways of doing things and replace them with a society organized around their needs. The question for us is not whether the hard-heartedness of the rich and powerful will intensify as they cling to power, but what we will do in response. Will we be organized to move with unity, like the Israelites did, when moments of historic possibility present themselves?[21]

KAIROS TIME

In the days of antiquity, the ancient Greeks taught that there are two ways to understand time: chronos and kairos. Chronos is quantitative time—the measured, chronological time of a clock. Kairos, on the other hand, is qualitative time—the special, even transformative time of a moment. Kairos is all about seizing opportunity through unwavering action; in biblical terms, kairos can be considered a moment when, as German American theologian Paul Tillich wrote, "the eternal breaks into the temporal, shaking and transforming it."[22] During this heightened form of time, the old and often oppressive ways of the world—dominant systems and institutions—are dying as new understandings struggle to be born.

Greek archers were trained to recognize the kairos moment, the opening, when their arrow had the best chance of reaching its target. The image of the vigilant archer remains a powerful one, especially because kairos time is full of both tremendous possibility and danger. If the archer seizes the moment, they may hit their target. But if they fail to do so, they may just as quickly become the target themselves. With the right kind of decisive action, kairos time can yield the triumph of justice. In the wrong hands, it can foreshadow the arrival of new forms of wickedness. Positive change is not chronological and it is never promised. It is a choice that must be made; an action that must be taken.

Tillich popularized the modern use of the word kairos in describing the period between the First World War and the rise of fascism. He recognized the existential stakes of that transitional moment and warned against the societal failure to stem the tide of fascism in Germany, Italy, and Spain. The history of the 1930s reminds us that fascism metastasizes in moments of great change and instability, when those in power can no longer safely rely on the levers of liberal democracy to maintain their power, and the floor of the economy is falling out from beneath the feet of everyday people. In moments like these, demagogues and false prophets often appear, alongside a whole host of other morbid symptoms, including religious nationalism, war and environmental destruction, the undermining of the formal mechanisms of democracy, and attacks on poor people, people of color, LGBTQ+ people, women, religious minorities, and political dissidents. These are the moments when strategic and decisive action are of utmost importance.

I first learned about the concept of kairos time from my mom. When I was a child, she was involved in international solidarity organizing with the anti-apartheid movement. She was taken with the prophetic vision of a group of Black and white South African theologians and clergy who published the KAIROS Document in 1985, after decades of mass resistance and still years before the fall of apartheid. In the document, they challenged the Afrikaner elite, who were instrumentalizing religion to legitimize the social and economic structures of apartheid, and church leaders who were either defending or acquiescing to the status quo:

> The time has come. The moment of truth has arrived. South Africa has been plunged into a crisis that is shaking the foundations and there is every indication that the crisis has only just begun and that it will deepen and become even more threatening in the months to come. It is the KAIROS or moment of truth not only for apartheid, but also for the Church.

We as a group of theologians have been trying to understand the theological significance of this moment in our history. It is serious, very serious. For very many Christians in South Africa, this is the KAIROS, the moment of grace and opportunity, the favorable time in which God issues a challenge to decisive action. It is a dangerous time because, if this opportunity is missed, and allowed to pass by, the loss for the Church, for the Gospel, and for all the people of South Africa will be immeasurable. Jesus wept over Jerusalem. He wept over the tragedy of the destruction of the city and the massacre of the people that was imminent, "and all because you did not recognize your opportunity (KAIROS) when God offered it" (Luke 19: 44).

A crisis is a judgment that brings out the best in some people and the worst in others. A crisis is a moment of truth that shows us up for what we really are. There will be no place to hide and no way of pretending to be what we are not in fact.[23]

The words of these rebel theologians are often on our minds these days. It seems clear we are living on the precipice of, or already within, a similar kairos moment, with implications not just for us here in the United States but for billions around the world. These are years that feel like centuries, in which multiple systemic crises are converging and destabilizing our world. Within this kairos moment, our movements have experienced both stirring victories and crushing defeats—and we are still in flux, waiting to see how our movements, and humanity as a whole, will emerge through this transitional period.

The decade after the 2007–2008 Great Recession produced one of the greatest sustained periods of mass protest in world history, often led by poor and dispossessed people yearning for a more just and humane world.[24] People mobilized in record numbers, from the Occupy encampments to the Arab Spring to the Pink Tide protests that swept across Latin America. Here in the US, the 2012 murder of Trayvon Martin in Florida gave birth to the Movement for Black Lives, while

in 2013, the Forward Together Moral Movement in North Carolina—
also known as the Moral Mondays Movement—emerged as the largest
sustained human rights struggle in the South since the 1960s. In the
early-to-mid 2010s, low-wage workers organized successful living wage
campaigns at fast-food chains; water protectors risked life and limb in
an insurgent climate movement with Indigenous people at the lead;
and immigrants erupted in action across the country, proclaiming they
were "undocumented and unafraid" and refusing to allow older family
members to be pitted against young "dreamers."

In 2013, when my colleagues and I relaunched the Poverty Initiative as the Kairos Center for Religions, Rights, and Social Justice,
we wrote:

> No statistics can fully capture the desire manifested in so many
> struggles—from Occupy to Moral Mondays to Ferguson—for a
> radically different, just, and moral society and world. To build a
> movement large enough, broad enough, and deep enough to change
> the policies and structures that create injustice and suffering re-
> quires boldly applying what we have learned over the past decade
> to the dynamic challenges we face today.[25]

We were struck by the deeply moral, even spiritual, dimensions of
the many struggles for justice breaking out. Everywhere we looked, poor
and dispossessed people, along with people of conscience from every
walk of life, were articulating their discontent through moral language
and action—in terms of right and wrong, love and hate, life and death.
These movements were elevating the normally bitter world of politics
to the transcendent world of the beloved community. In the process,
many millions of ordinary but extraordinary humans were drawing
on, and transforming, age-old cultural, ethical, and religious traditions.

This groundswell of popular protest and movement building continued through the late 2010s and into the 2020s, even amid the
shutdowns and economic shocks of the COVID-19 pandemic. In

the summer of 2018, the Poor People's Campaign launched "40 Days of Moral Action" in over thirty states, one of the largest coordinated waves of nonviolent direct action in US history (I was arrested multiple times during those six weeks and Noam and I were arrested together on the steps of the Supreme Court). Two years later, in the summer of 2020, the Black Lives Matter uprising exploded after the murder of George Floyd in Minneapolis, with tens of millions of people hitting the streets in nonviolent protest in over five hundred towns and cities.[26] A 2024 report in the *Personality and Social Psychology Bulletin* found that these racial justice protests had a considerable and positive impact on opinions about race among white Americans.[27]

Around the same time, low-wage workers ignited a bottom-up resurgence in labor organizing despite the continued decline in nationwide union membership. Impoverished warehouse workers at Amazon and low-income baristas at Starbucks built new unions from the bottom up, while teachers organized walkouts and fundraisers for their beleaguered schools. The radical spirit of the labor movement was also rekindled through the United Auto Workers' groundbreaking 2023 "Stand-Up Strike," which involved strikes, intentionally organized to be hard to predict, at multiple plants owned by the Big Three auto manufacturers: General Motors, Ford, and Stellantis. The creativity and potency of these strikes shocked the companies, forcing them to make significant and unexpected concessions to their workers.

In 2024, when Israel began dropping thousands of American-made bombs on Gazan civilians, these movements for racial and economic justice found new expression through the ceasefire movement and its demand for peace and a free Palestine. High school and college students who were first politicized during the Black Lives Matter uprising in 2020 and the failures of the government's response to the pandemic joined Palestinian and Jewish communities in widespread nonviolent protest. Meanwhile, low-wage worker organizations and labor unions called for solidarity with the poor and dispossessed people of Gaza. In the electoral arena, hundreds of thousands of voters in Michigan, Minnesota, Wisconsin, North Carolina, Colorado, and other states cast "uncommitted" ballots during the Democratic primaries, demanding that the Biden-Harris administration respond to international calls for the US to divest from the war effort and use its considerable political power to broker a ceasefire.

These advances in movement-building have offered hope in hard times, but the urgency of this kairos moment demands that we also recognize the swift and well-funded counterreaction that is already well underway and will likely only worsen under a second Trump administration. Midway through the 2020s, we are witness to a sharp rise in militarized and highly punitive forms of political repression. During the ceasefire movement, for example, universities and city governments in both Democratic and Republican strongholds mobilized large and heavily armed police responses to peaceful student encampments, terrorizing young people with military-grade weapons and leaving many with bruises and broken bones.

In October 2024, after a year of these and other protests for a ceasefire in Gaza, the Heritage Foundation released Project Esther, a complement to Project 2025 trumpeted by the organization as a "blueprint to counter antisemitism in the United States." But rather than targeting the most dangerous and alarming manifestations of antisemitism, most notably from within Heritage's own Christian nationalist circles, Project Esther is a blueprint for the government-led dismantling of not just the Palestinian liberation movement but progressive movements more broadly. In the document, Heritage recommends the further weaponization of anti-racketeering charges, counter-terrorism statutes, hate speech provisions, and immigration laws, among others, to target pro-Palestinian activists and non-profit organizations. These same tactics, which directly echo the Red Scare of McCarthyism, could then be used to increase public pressure and legal attacks on other progressive groups that work on

all manner of issues, from workers' rights to racial justice and reproductive freedom.[28]

Project Esther is only the latest attempt to diminish democracy
and the power of popular social movements. Over the last decade
or so, the country has been consumed by Republican-led efforts to
criminalize the constitutional rights to suffrage and the freedom of as-
sembly and protest, often with only tepid resistance from Democrats.
Since the Voting Rights Act of 1965 was gutted in 2013 by the Supreme
Court, dozens of states have introduced hundreds of voter suppression laws. In 2021, one expert explained that this was potentially the
"biggest assault on voting rights since the end of Reconstruction
[after the Civil War]."[29] Meanwhile, by 2024 nineteen states codified
"critical infrastructure" laws like the one passed by Louisiana in 2019
to undermine the *L'eau est la vie* encampment and other pipeline
protests (efforts that have enjoyed generous lobbying support by the
petrochemical industry). Back in 2017, the Georgia legislature used the
2015 white supremacist Charleston church shooting in neighboring
South Carolina as justification to expand its definition of domestic
terrorism to include the destruction of property. Since then, according to journalist Adam Freedman, "21 states have passed legislation
to enhance penalties and fines for common protest-related crimes,
such as trespassing or blocking highways," while a total of "300 anti-
protest bills [were] introduced in state legislatures since 2017, 41 of
which passed."[30] Beginning in 2020, Georgia deployed such laws to
attack and criminalize young people protesting the construction of
the $90 million Atlanta Safety Training Center, a sprawling police
training center otherwise known as Cop City.[31] Other states have
mirrored these militarized police actions in their own confrontations
with protestors.

Such legislative attacks on democratic expression cannot be seper-
ated from wider efforts to criminalize the survival strategies and
physical movements of poor and dispossessed people. Growing legal attacks on the unhoused by both Republican and Democratic

politicians, like state-sanctioned encampment sweeps and land evictions, and bipartisan crackdowns on immigration are emblematic of an anti-democratic approach to American governance that is increasingly reliant on force and violence to establish social control. In practice, this punitive approach to American lawmaking is undermining the human rights of millions of people.

These are precipitous times. Amid tremendous ecological, social, and economic dislocation, traditional American institutions and political alignments are losing their meaning for tens of millions of people who rightly feel that those in positions of power in both major parties have left them high and dry. The majority of people know things are not well in this country. They can feel it not just in our violent and vitriolic political environment but in their bank statements and debt sheets, in their rising rent and utility bills. MAGA leaders in the Republican Party often seem more willing to give voice to this societal unwellness, although they evade blame by pointing the finger at people of color, immigrants, LGBTQ+ people, and the poor. Meanwhile, during the 2024 elections, top leaders in the Democratic Party regularly sidestepped their own complicity and offered us rosy assessments of their own achievements, comforting us that our nation, including our economy, was actually doing well, even if most of us couldn't tell.

We hear a constant litany of stories about rising political polarization and societal fracture, which are certainly based in truth. But these stories gloss over the fact that public opinion polls consistently show that the majority of Americans support commonsense policy changes on issues like healthcare, housing, wages, and reproductive rights when they are divorced from partisan identifiers.[32] When these and other policy questions are put forward via one-person, one-vote referendums, rather than divisive party platforms, they enjoy notable success. Millions of people in this country are hungry for a more humane and robust social contract. Given the opportunity, many are even ready to take new and unsettling action together to realize it. The ground is shifting beneath our feet and we don't know what new shape the tectonic plates of our society will take once they settle back into place. We have never lived through a moment like this before. The rarefied texture of kairos time is thick in the air.

The truth, though, is that we can never be fully ready to take the kind of decisive action that is possible and necessary during a kairos moment. The best we can do is position ourselves so that when new opportunities arise, we are able to step boldly and strategically into the unknown—and then do it again, when the next opportunities come. As history teaches us, kairos time is never just one moment but a continuum of moments, each with their own pitfalls and possibilities.

PERMANENTLY ORGANIZED COMMUNITIES

The ability of poor and dispossessed people to harness the transformative potential of kairos time—as well as survive the moments when change is less possible—depends on their ability to build permanently organized communities. I first learned this concept from Fernando Garcia, founder of the Border Network for Human Rights. Garcia was born in Mexico and politicized during student movements protesting high tuition rates in the 1980s. After working as a photojournalist for a number of years, he landed in Juarez, the Mexican border city, where he witnessed countless poor people from across Latin America quietly slipping across the border into the United States in search of work and safe haven. Many of the conditions people were fleeing were caused, in part, by US interventionism in Latin America. The response from US Border Patrol was vicious: aggressive arrests, beatings, sexual violence, and murders. And once these hyper-militarized tactics—which deployed weapons of war and highly sophisticated surveillance technologies on unarmed men, women, and children—were mastered on the American border, they were imported into other poor communities in the nation's interior.

In the late 1990s, Garcia secured a visa and was living across the border in El Paso, Texas, Juarez's sister city. He built relationships with immigrant families, many who had already been organizing for years around border repression and other community issues. These families were the first leaders of BNHR, which was officially founded in 2001 and now has a presence across nine regions of West Texas and southern New Mexico, comprising more than one thousand families and forty five community-led committees. I met Garcia twenty-five years ago, when I was a young organizer working with the Kensington Welfare Rights Union. During our 1998 New Freedom Bus Tour, we drove through El Paso, where we were hosted by some of the comminity leaders who went on to form BNHR with Garcia. This visit was formative in my political development. Just a few years after NAFTA was implemented and local economies in Mexico were thrown into disarray, I witnessed large groups of young Mexican men sleeping on the streets of this American city. The evidence of widespread abandonment amid so much abundance was undeniable. Walking through El Paso, it was clear how many people were willing to risk everything for a better life and how powerful these people could become if they organized their communities to demand systemic change.

Since then, Garcia and I have regularly traded notes on organizing strategies and cosponsored human rights trainings and organizer exchanges, in the process further refining our own models of movement building among the poor and dispossessed. Garcia was involved in various actions of the Poor People's Economic Human Rights Campaign in the early 2000s, collaborated with the Poverty Initiative in the 2010s, and was another founding member of the Poor People's Campaign's Steering Committee in 2017. Garcia's leadership within these poor people's organizations and movements has been important, given that the families of BNHR—both citizens and non-citizens—live in one of the poorest and most highly militarized regions of the country. Many have made their homes in *colonias*, unincorporated border towns built on financially worthless land with little to no infrastructure. These communities often have no running water, want for health care and consistent and affordable food, and regularly lose family members to gun violence and white supremacist vigilantism. In 2018, according to Garcia, the average income for some colonia residents was between $8,000 and $13,000.[33]

Before BNHR began organizing in the colonias, the Border Patrol and local police kept the residents suspended in a state of constant fear. Garcia explains: "Border residents were experiencing violations of first, fourth, fifth, and sixth amendment rights. In practice, border patrol and other law enforcement were entering houses and confiscating property with no legal authority or permission. They were stopping people by the way they looked, by the way they walked, and relying on racial profiling."[34] In response to these hyper-militarized human rights violations, BNHR identified and trained hundreds of people in the colonias and nearby cities to become "human rights promoters." Together, they began documenting abuses by Border Patrol, initiating a multiyear grassroots campaign to hold the government accountable. A community leader with the organization described these early years this way:

> The Border Patrol used to come here every day. They used to come into the yard, into our homes. No warning, no warrant. The people would run, terrorized. The children were very afraid. Then we heard from a social worker about The Border Network for Human Rights and decided to set up our committee. The day we hung up our sign, "The Border Network for Human Rights: Reporta Abusos de la Migra, Policia, Aduanas y Otras," the Border Patrol stopped coming. They still drive by, but they don't come in.[35]

During the early 2000s, BNHR won some important victories. By coordinating hundreds of families to report clear human rights violations on the border, they succeeded in forcing local authorities to sit down with their human rights committees, including with undocumented people, and curb their most egregious abuses. But as the twenty-first century has matured, and the border has become even more politicized and militarized, BNHR discovered just how difficult it was to hold on to these victories. When the organization was first founded, in the days before the Department of Homeland Security (DHS), the government spent less than $1 billion on border enforcement. Today, the DHS budget for border patrol totals over $7 billion.[36] In Texas, New Mexico, Arizona, and California, which together comprise one of the most militarized borders in the world, this money is used for myriad purposes: hundreds of miles of fencing and walls, thousands of underground sensors, dozens of checkpoints and immigration detention centers, and a fleet of aircrafts and drones.[37] There has also been a steep rise in the hiring of government border agents and officers, from about ten thousand in 1998 to over twenty-four thousand in 2024.[38]

In the shadow of this heightened border suppression, BNHR has continued patiently growing its committees, staying proactive even as they have weathered worsening attacks. For over a decade, for example, they have led the "Hugs Not Walls" campaign, in which they have negotiated with Border Patrol a three-minute reprieve for families on both sides of the border to reunite with one another. In 2017, I joined BNHR for one of these actions. Wading in the muddy waters of the Rio Grande, I watched as families from the US and Mexico carefully waded into the middle of the river. As Border Patrol agents briefly averted their eyes, husbands and wives, parents and children, siblings and cousins held one another, sharing gentle touches and sweet words. Two years later, in late August 2019, Noam and I returned to the border after Garcia invited us and our colleagues with the Poor People's Campaign to El Paso for a weekend of political education and relationship building. While we were there, we joined hundreds of BNHR members as they led a massive community march through the city's streets in response to the Walmart massacre by a white supremacist earlier that month that left twenty-three people dead and twenty-two more people injured.[39] The "El Paso Firme Memorial

Event" continues annually, uniting immigrant communities with other El Paso residents who recgonize the interlocking relationship between rising gun violence, racism, and xenophobia.

BNHR understands their local organizing as one way to build the power neccesary to demand national systemic change. The organization has leveraged its considerable grassroots power to champion a visionary set of policy proposals on both border enforcement and wider immigration reform, which they have popularized along the border communities through caravans and grassroots events. But BNHR has never just been an immigrant rights struggle. The families that make up its base are fighting not only against state violence on the border but for all of their human rights: healthcare, affordable housing, living wages, education, and more. In a 2018 interview, Garcia described the theory that undergirds BNHR's organizing:

> In terms of the work we do within our communities, we have been in a constant consultation process. The definition of our agenda and our struggle is not done by a director but by the communities themselves. Every year these communities come together and they meet and they define [the organization's] priorities by defining their priorities. When we started the organizing process, the first thing we did [was] convene the first *congreso*, the first national, annual *asamblea*, and one of the major outcomes of that consultation was to define our struggle. Out of that consultation process, it was clear that we were eager to actually be recognized by this society, but also that immigrant families were going through multiple systems of oppression. Families were not only struggling with the immigration system, but also with healthcare, with labor conditions, with housing and education, and so we realized at that point that in an immigrant family or in an immigrant household, all of the contradictions of the system were embedded.
>
> For us it was obvious that our agenda was for more than an immigration bill. That's how we started framing our issues around

human rights. And what that means for us is that, yes, we want immigrants to be legally recognized and integrated in society, but also we want immigrants to actually be integrated with rights into a better society that encompasses all of these points of struggle, and that are also shared by other communities that are not immigrants. When we recognize that as human beings we need to fight for these potential rights, and that we need to actually organize for them, it implies that then we need to connect with other people in the same conditions and fight together. For us, we are not only an immigrant rights organization, we are a human rights organization that is fighting to change society for everybody.[40]

Two years later, in 2020, Fernando expanded on BNHR's approach to building "permanently organized communities":

We have some committees that have been meeting for years already. People, families come, they stay. Most of them stay, some of them are new. Some of them go because they need to move from one community to the other. But every week now they are meeting as if they're going to church. They are meeting to discuss the problems, their issues, to learn more about the struggle and the reality, but also to provide the solutions. The Border Network right now has 40 human rights committees that integrate close to a little less than 1000 families because our membership is a community of families. So that is the force behind the organizing structure. It's a permanent organizing structure that is not up to the whims of any particular campaign. Whatever issue they feel that they need to tackle is the priority.[41]

BNHR's organizing does not rise or fall on the basis of one victory or defeat. The families who lead the organization are always present and active in their communities, and the long-term nature of their work allows them to remain responsive to evolving conditions on the ground. The permanent nature of their organizing also enables them to remain politically independent. The families of BNHR don't rely on nonprofit structures and siloed strategies that might divert their attention or narrow their vision. The organization also doesn't rely on transactional relationships with politicians to secure one-off victories, although they navigate the political system with sophistication. Theirs is a longer view of what their communities actually need to thrive and what it will take to forge the kind of collective power that can enforce their greatest demands.

This movement on the borderlands is a living testament to what is possible when poor and dispossesed people build permanently organized communities. Even a short visit reveals the depth of their work: everywhere one turns, there are mothers, fathers, grandparents, aunts, uncles, and teenagers who are experts on human rights and who are engaged in a constant and evolving process of grassroots organizing. With their backs sometimes literally up against the wall, they have no choice but to push back together.

The Border Network for Human Rights offers a prescient example of how to organize the poor and dispossessed today. The conditions these immigrant families face may be extreme in their brutality, but Garcia has always been quick to remind people that the border is a laboratory for national methods of social and economic control. Operating in a region that has been hit hard by neoliberalism and the climate crisis, BNHR could itself be seen as a laboratory for all our movements. Indeed, from California to Appalachia, low-wage worker groups, healthcare campaigns, youth empowerment leagues, veteran associations, and other grassroots organizations have learned from their approach to combining community-wide organizing with political education, leadership development, and public advocacy.

New times require new strategies. And yet, as our society continues to transform in the shift from the industrial age to the information age, the strategies of our movements have not always kept up. During the latter decades of the nineteenth century and the first half of the twentieth century, the factory was one of the primary sites of organizing among poor and working-class people, and all kinds of communal spaces and institutions existed around it—social clubs, houses of worship, businesses, housing developments, hospitals, and more. The industrial workplace offered powerful leverage points for action, often surrounded by a densely populated community with clear, if challenging, pathways for organizing.

As today's insurgent labor movement is proving, the workplace is still a vital site for struggle. But after decades of deindustrialization, globalization, and automation, the setting has increasingly shifted away from the factory, and the communities around it, and toward the service sector: hospitals, care facilities, schools, transportation, warehouses, restaurants, and hotels, among others. These jobs are themselves becoming more difficult to organize, both because of anti-labor repression and the highly contingent and precarious nature of service work under neoliberalism. Our communities have also become more atomized since the industrial age, and many of the communal institutions that once existed have either deteriorated, been privatized, or shut down. In the Philadelphia neighborhood of Kensington, where I first began organizing as a young woman, aerial shots in the mid-1990s revealed a cityscape pockmarked by what appeared to be detonated bombs. These "bomb sites" were in fact concentric circles of industrial decay. At the center were shuttered textile factories. In ever-broadening circles around these now-defunct factories was an array of secondary devastation: dilapidated houses, churches, businesses, hospitals, and more.

Three decades later, this post-industrial devastation is still widespread. Poverty and homelessness continue to plague Kensington and politicians regularly disparage the neighborhood in what has become a ritual act of public shaming. In July 2023, then Republican candidate and biotech billionaire Vivek Ramaswamy visited Kensington while on the campaign trail. Afterward, in a *New York Post* op-ed, he maliciously painted an apocalyptic picture of drug-addled residents and decried local harm-reduction measures ("twisted cruelty masquerading as compassion") and the "extreme permissiveness" of public programs that were supposedly paying people "not to work."[42] Meanwhile, over the last decade, corporate real-estate speculators have begun buying thousands of single-family row houses and vacant properties in the neighborhood and investing in new luxury housing developments.[43] Rising property values and rental prices now threaten to further increase land speculation and accelerate the displacement of long-term residents.

The experience of Kensington shares a likeness with many other communities, both urban and rural, across the country. Today, as the cost of living continues to rise and millions of people struggle to find good-paying and reliable work—or are thrown out of the labor market as a whole—and as public services and spaces continue to shrink and disappear, our movements need new and creative vehicles for our organizing. This is doubly true in a decade that threatens far deeper levels of political repression. We will not be able to build a modern movement to end poverty if we don't adapt the old methods of trade unionism and community organizing and develop new methods of permanent, multiracial, and community-wide movement building among the poor. In the 1980s and 1990s, the National Union of the Homeless and the Kensington Welfare Rights Union, which both organized newly unemployed workers living in shelters and on the streets, articulated the need for this strategic shift earlier than most. Organizing among the poorest members of society allowed us to see what many others couldn't—the deprivation and dispossession of our members wasn't just a sad story or a moral conundrum but a signpost of the times that are now coming for the rest of our communities.

The exact form a permanently organized community takes is always contextual and can change over time. It can look like the human rights committees of the Border Network for Human Rights in Texas and New Mexico, the neighborhood groups of the Coalition Against Death Alley in Southeast Louisiana, the freedom church of Chaplains on the Harbor in rural Washington, or new low-wage worker, debtor, and tenants' unions. A permanently organized community is also not the same thing as a specific organization. Organizers and community leaders sometimes fall into the trap of giving our full allegiance to one organization or issue instead of to the pursuit of community-wide power. But the nature of organizations is that they tend to come and go. During my thirty years of grassroots anti-poverty organizing, many of the groups I've started, worked with, and included in this book have risen, fallen, shifted, and morphed over time. In the best situations, though, there were always clear, committed, competent, and connected leaders who built on previous efforts as they helped birth new ones.

POWER CONCEDES NOTHING WITHOUT A DEMAND

As Noam and I reflected on the nature of kairos moments while writing this book together, our conversations traveled back in time to a small town in upstate New York over a century and a half ago. On August 3, 1857, Frederick Douglass visited Canandaigua, New York, to give a speech to a mostly white abolitionist audience. By then, the nation was at a crisis point. A few months earlier, the Supreme Court had passed the *Dred Scott* decision, empowering the planter class to clamp down even more brutally on their enslaved workers. The direction forward for the abolition movement was unclear.

August 3 was also the twenty-third anniversary of emancipation in the British West Indies. Douglass didn't mince words. Celebrating the victory of that struggle, he beseeched the crowd to remember that abolition on the islands had come not through moral reasoning or enlightened introspection but through the organizing and rebellion of enslaved workers. Reflecting on the revolutionary actions of these

people, he offered framing words for what he believed it would take
to achieve freedom on the shores of this country:

> The whole history of the progress of human liberty shows that all
> concessions yet made to her august claims have been born of earnest
> struggle. The conflict has been exciting, agitating, all-absorbing, and
> for the time being, putting all other tumults to silence. It must do
> this or it does nothing. If there is no struggle there is no progress.
> Those who profess to favor freedom and yet deprecate agitation are
> men who want crops without plowing up the ground; they want
> rain without thunder and lightning. They want the ocean without
> the awful roar of its many waters.
>
> This struggle may be a moral one, or it may be a physical one,
> and it may be both moral and physical, but it must be a struggle.
> Power concedes nothing without a demand. It never did and it
> never will. Find out just what any people will quietly submit to and
> you have found out the exact measure of injustice and wrong which
> will be imposed upon them, and these will continue till they are
> resisted with either words or blows, or with both. The limits of ty-
> rants are prescribed by the endurance of those whom they oppress.[44]

Douglass was making a simple but fundamental point: now was
the time for even bolder agitation, whether moral or physical. But
he wasn't just calling for any kind of intensified action. He believed
that abolition in the United States would have to come, in whatever
form it took, through the leadership of enslaved people themselves.
"Who would be free," he explained in the speech, "themselves must
strike the first blow."

Douglass's perspective was certainly not the majority opinion
among Northern white abolitionists, who rarely recognized the actual
agency and political leadership of enslaved Black workers. But his
words reflected a deep and earnest engagement on his part with the
history of human struggle against social domination and economic

oppression. Through his own experience escaping from and organizing against the slave system, Douglass understood that poor and dispossessed people have always been revolutionary agents of change—through their words and their deeds. He understood that in moments of greatest peril, it is people at the very bottom of society who are first compelled to take liberatory action. These people, Douglass was saying, are the ones who make transformation and renewal possible. These are the people who make and change history.

The stories and reflections we've shared in this book are our attempt to live into the radical vision of Frederick Douglass and other freedom fighters like him. His words are especially resonant in a moment that resembles the societal crisis that engulfed the nation when he spoke them in Canandaigua. Our country has arrived at another pivotal inflection point, a kairos moment that is both existential crisis and unprecedented opportunity.

Let it not be forgotten that Reconstruction after the Civil War saw the most radical democratic experiment in US history. For roughly eight years, formerly enslaved Black workers gained a significant measure of political power and in the process attempted to rebuild the shattered South in the image of what W. E. B. Du Bois called "abolition-democracy."[45] They were joined by sections of poor white people in multiple states who, once a direct hindrance to the cause of abolition, now saw the old order crumbling and recognized the new one as a possible path forward for their own lives. Within a few years, these multiracial alliances, with formerly enslaved people at the lead, controlled state houses across the South, passing some of the most progressive education, civil rights, and labor laws in all of American history. The counterreaction to these fledgling but powerful alliances—by both the old families of the white aristocracy in the South and Northern industrialists—was swift and punishing. But for a brief moment, this historic redistribution of political and economic power offered a glimpse of what true democracy could look like on American soil.

The same is possible today, and it can be achieved through a broad and nonviolent human rights movement, but only if we heed Douglass's words and embrace the call for an intensified struggle led by the very people who seek freedom from the economic and social oppression of our own day. This, of course, is no small task. When it comes to debates about our economy and how it should be structured, we are forced to follow the leadership of those at the very top. Our society actively lionizes the wealthy, making a fetish of their hoarding of our abundant resources. Even many of the people who are skeptical of their leadership and oppose their mercenary and destructive behavior don't seem to believe that true societal transformation is possible. Even fewer seem open to the idea that poor people can unite across their differences and lead us all toward the reconstruction of a more just and whole world.

Here, we are also reminded of a 1993 speech by Diane Bernard, a Black mother and leader with the Michigan Welfare Rights Organization. At a conference celebrating the life of Malcolm X, Bernard gave her own version of Douglass's speech. She reflected on the struggle to end poverty—then at its own moment of crisis amid the early pangs of welfare reform—through the story of a poor white woman who had to jerry-rig her own heating source in the winter because she couldn't afford to pay her gas bills. One day, her house caught fire and her three children were consumed by the flames. Bernard was heartbroken for this woman, but she didn't pity her. Instead, she implored the audience to recognize that this woman, bereft of everything and everyone she held dear, could be a leader in the movement:

> Don't tell me that a white mother who witnessed her three children burned up in a house fire is unfit to lead this struggle. She has a personal vendetta against the government. She'll fight harder than anybody who's out here just reading books and talking a bunch of bull-crap because it sounds good and feels good. She will fight

because she has a personal stake, because they hurt her. Those are the kind of fighters we need, and I'll follow her anywhere, anytime. We have to embrace those mothers."[46]

Bernard believed that this mother, and others like her, could serve as the backbone of the movement to end poverty. But she wasn't simply saying that these poor mothers could be leaders as individuals. She was identifying their potential leadership at a collective level, as representatives of entire communities of poor and dispossessed people who, when organized and united, were poised to become a powerful and life-affirming force within a death-dealing society. Bernard was clear: if the abolition of poverty and economic exploitation is our North Star, then the unity and leadership of the poor is our pathway.

Our task, then, is to make that leadership irrefutable and irresistible. Those of us who believe bottom-up change is not only possible but necessary for the transformation of our society must listen to the leaders who are already engaged in impassioned struggle and will not stop because their lives depend on it. We must listen to the unhoused people seizing vacant homes in the dead of winter; the tenants on rent strike and the young people crying out for debt relief; the tomato pickers, house cleaners, cashiers, dishwashers, and home-care workers fighting for living wages; the Medicaid recipients demanding a healthcare system structured around care for people rather than profit; the students putting their bodies on the line to end war and reimagine the very meaning of collective safety; the backcountry clergy holding alight the torch of God's love amid the encroaching darkness of religious nationalism; the water protectors and grassroots leaders decrying the turning off of their water taps and the poisoning of their homes and the natural world; and the immigrants filing human rights petitions and permanently organizing their communities under conditions of extreme violence.

These leaders may be scrappy and their struggles may be messy, but they are also so much more powerful than our society allows us to believe. Like Douglass and Bernard, these leaders are tired of polite society, political prattle, and punditry. They are hungry for change and ready to seize it. The exhortations of prophets echo down through the ages. Power concedes nothing without a demand. You only get what you're organized to take.

ACKNOWLEDGMENTS

This book is a small window into a vast movement that spans generations and includes thousands of poor and dispossessed leaders. Our gratitude will always begin with these many people, who have dedicated their lives to the abolition of poverty and, in the process, influenced the lives of millions more. A full list of names is impossible, but this book reflects our deep admiration for their work and leadership. They are our best hope for a world transformed in the image of dignity, justice, and abundance for all.

Among these leaders, there are those who are no longer with us but whose contributions to the movement continue to ripple across time. We honor Akintola "Kion" Kiongozi Mapinduzi, Annie Smart, Anthony Williams, Dr. Bernice Johnson Reagon, Darryl "Waistline" Mitchell, Diane Bernard, Dick Butler, Dottie Stevens, Erro Lynd, General Gordon Baker, James Shear, Jacob George, Joe Hough, Kathleen Sullivan, Larry Gibson, Lindokuhle Mnguni, Louis Haggins, Mitchell Watson, Pamela Rush, Paul Chapman, Ron Casanova, and Veronica Dorsey, among others. May their memories be a blessing and a lesson for the rest of us.

We extend our sincere appreciation to the entire team at Beacon: Amy Caldwell, Nicole Anne-Keyton, Marcy Barnes, Susan Lumenello, Rebekah Cotton, Perpetua Cannistraro, Sanj Kharbanda, Emily Powers, Caitlin Meyer, and everyone whose time and labor made this book possible. A special thank-you to Amy for seeing its value before a single word was written and for shepherding us along so graciously.

The words in these pages were made immeasurably better through the loving attention and keen editorial eyes of a few close readers. We are indebted to Alice Markham-Cantor, Rachel Tzvia Back, Chris Caruso, Dan Jones, Shailly Gupta Barnes, Aaron Scott, Jessica Williams, Cedar Monroe, Phil Wider, Aaron Back, and Isaiah Back-Gaal. We are also grateful to everyone who opened their homes to us during the course of the writing process, including Leslie Moody and Mitch Ackerman at Rancho Gallina in New Mexico.

We wrote this book within the inspiring and supportive company of our wonderful colleagues at the Kairos Center for Religions, Rights, and Social Justice. We salute Adam Barnes, Ana Lara Lopez, Alix Webb, Charon Hribar, Chris Caruso, Ciara Taylor, Jarvis Benson, Jessica Williams, Pauline Pisano, Shailly Gupta Barnes, and Willie Baptist. We are lucky to walk alongside you every day.

There are a number of organizations that we have had the privilege of learning with and from over the years. Their efforts are the source of many of the ideas and stories in this book, and their work in the world has been invaluable. Among these groups, both past and present, we send our love and respect to Abahlali baseMjondolo, the Border Network for Human Rights, Chaplains on the Harbor, the Coalition Against Death Alley, the Coalition of Immokalee Workers, Common Defense, Domestic Workers United, Empty the Shelters, ESCR-NET, the General Baker Institute, Greater Birmingham Ministries, the Highland Park Human Rights Coalition, the Highlander Center Research and Education Center, Jesus People Against Pollution, Keepers of the Mountain, the Kensington Welfare Rights Union, the Michigan Welfare Rights Union, Movement of Immigrant Leaders in PA, MoveOn, Movimento dos Trabalhadores Rurais sem Terra, the National Domestic Workers Alliance, the National Union of the Homeless, the National Welfare Rights Organization, the National Welfare Rights Union, the Nonviolent Medicaid Army, the Poor People's Campaign: A National Call for Moral Revival, the Poor People's Economic Human Rights Campaign, Picture the Homeless, Put People First PA!, Repairers of the Breach, Rise St. James, Showing Up for Racial Justice, the Poverty Initiative, Union de Vecinos, the Union of Southern Service Workers, Union Theological Seminary, the University of the Poor, United Workers, and the Vermont Workers' Center.

Among our mentors, we want to acknowledge the singular leadership of Willie Baptist. As we write in chapter 2, Willie is an organic intellectual in the truest sense—a leader from the ranks of the poor who has committed every fiber of his being to building the unity and power of the poor. Through his brilliant marriage of theory and practice, he has mentored hundreds of leaders in the movement. Indeed, we are of the earnest belief that through his life he has forever changed the life of our nation.

Finally, to our families, who we love in innumerable ways. To Liz's family: Nancy Artinian G. Theoharis, Athan Theoharis, Jeanne Theoharis, George Theoharis, Gretchen Lopez, Gabriella Holliman Lopez, Sam Theoharis, and Ella Theoharis. To Chris Caruso, the love of Liz's life, her best friend, partner in marriage and the movement, and the smartest person she's ever met, and to their fierce, creative, and brilliant children, Sophia Theoharis Caruso and Luke Theoharis Caruso. To Noam's family: Beth Sandweiss, Aaron Back, Tamar Sandweiss-Back, and Eric Gold, who embody the meaning of home and soften the sharp edges of the world. Thank you for everything.

NOTES

INTRODUCTION

1. C. Eugene Steuerle and Gordon Mermin, *Devolution as Seen from the Budget*, New Federalism: Issues and Options for States, Series A, No. A-2, Urban Institute, January 1997, https://www.urban.org/sites/default/files /publication/66971/307034-Devolution-as-Seen-from-the-Budget.PDF.

2. Chuck Collins, "Updates: Billionaire Wealth, U.S. Job Losses, and Pandemic Profiteers," Inequality.org, March 18, 2024, https://inequality .org/great-divide/updates-billionaire-pandemic/.

3. Calculated by the Center on Poverty and Social Policy at Columbia University using data from 2023 Annual Social and Economic Supplement to the Current Population Survey. Data is retrieved from the US Census Bureau. American Indian or Alaska Native include individuals who also identify as Latino.

4. "Hunger in America," Feeding America, https://www.feeding america.org/hunger-in-america, accessed June 12, 2024; Gabby Galvin, "87M Were Uninsured or Underinsured in 2018, Survey Says," *U.S. News*, February 7, 2019; "Housing and Homelessness," Poor People's Campaign, https://www.poorpeoplescampaign.org/wp-content/uploads/2020/04 /Housing-Fact-Sheet.pdf, accessed June 12, 2024; Julia Ryan, "American Schools vs. the World: Expensive, Unequal, Bad at Math," *The Atlantic*, December 3, 2013, https://www.theatlantic.com/education/archive/2013/12 /american-schools-vs-the-world-expensive-unequal-bad-at-math/281983/.

5. Sandro Galea et al., "Estimated Deaths Attributable to Social Factors in the United States," *American Journal of Public Health* 101, no. 8 (August 2011): 1456–65, https://www.ncbi.nlm.nih.gov/pmc/articles/PMC3134519.

6. David Brady, Ulrich Kohler, and Hui Zheng, "Novel Estimates of Mortality Associated with Poverty in the US," 83, no. 6, *JAMA Internal Medicine* (April 2023): 618–19, doi:10.1001/jamainternmed.2023.0276.

7. Staff, "Mitt Romney: Tonight's Results Will Echo Far Beyond the Borders of Wisconsin," *UP Matters*, June 6, 2012.

8. "Louisiana Profile," Prison Policy Initiative, https://www.prison policy.org/profiles/LA.html#, accessed September 13, 2025.

CHAPTER I: IS IT POSSIBLE TO END POVERTY?

1. 2019 HUD Budget Fact Sheet, October 17, 2019, https://wraphome .org/wpcontent/uploads/2020/02/2019-HUD-Factsheet-10-18-2019.pdf.

2. Martha Burt et al., "Evaluation of Continuums of Care for Homeless People," US Department of Housing and Urban Development, May 2002, https://www.huduser.gov/publications/pdf/continuums_of_care.pdf.

3. State of Homelessness: 2023 Edition, National Alliance to End Homelessness, https://endhomelessness.org/homelessness-in-america /homelessness-statistics/state-of-homelessness/, accessed July 10, 2024.

4. Shailly Gupta-Barnes and Tony Eskridge, "Quick Facts on Housing," Kairos Center for Religions, Rights, and Social Justice (hereafter Kairos Center), https://kairoscenter.org/quick-facts-on-housing/, accessed August 23, 2024.

5. Mark A. Reardon, "PD&R and Public Housing," *PD&R and Edge: An Online Magazine*, Office of Policy Development and Research at the US Department of Housing and Urban Development, February 6, 2024, https://www.huduser.gov/portal/pdredge/pdredgepdrat50020624.html.

6. "Out of Reach: The High Cost of Housing," National Low Income Housing Coalition, 2024, https://nlihc.org/oor.

7. "Vacant Homes Vs. Homelessness in Cities Around the U.S.," United Way of the National Capital Area, March 28, 2023, https:// unitedwaynca.org/blog/vacant-homes-vs homelessness-by-city/.

8. Maria Heeter, "Penthouse at Manhattan's 432 Park Listed at $169 Million," *Bloomberg*, July 22, 2021, https://www.bloomberg.com/news /articles/2021-07-22/penthouse-at manhattan-s-432-park-ave-listed-at -169-million.

9. *Takeover*, dir. Pamela Yates and Peter Kinoy, Skylight Pictures, 1992.

10. Yates and Kinoy, *Takeover*.

11. Chuck Collins, "Updates: Billionaire Wealth, U.S. Job Losses, and Pandemic Profiteers," Inequality.org, March 18, 2024, https://inequality .org/great-divide/updates-billionaire-pandemic/.

12. "Wealth Tax Vital to Reduce Extreme Inequality and Tackle Climate Crisis," press release, Oxfam America, April 13, 2024, https://www .oxfamamerica.org/press/pressreleases/-tax-vital-to-reduce-extreme -inequality-and-tackle-climate-crisis/.

13. Oxfam America, Wealth Tax Vital to Reduce Extreme Inequality and Tackle Climate Crisis.

14. David Autor et al., "The $800 Billion Paycheck Protection Program: Where Did the Money Go and Why Did it Go There?" National Bureau of Economic Research, January 2022, https://www.nber.org /papers/w29669.

15. *Charitable Food Assistance Participation in 2021*, Feeding America, June 2022, https://www.feedingamerica.org/sites/default/files/2022-06 /Charitable%20Food%20Assistance%20Participation%20in%202021.pdf.

16. Susia Cagle, "A Disasterous Situation: Mountains of Food Wasted as Coronavirus Scrambles Food Chain," *The Guardian*, Thursday, April 9, 2020, https://www.theguardian.com/world/2020/apr/09/us -coronavirus-outbreak-agriculture-food supply waste.

17. Jonathan Stempel, "Tyson Foods Refusing to COMPLY with Subpoena for Meat Price Gouging Probe, Ny Attorney General Says," Reuters, August 5, 2022, https://www.reuters.com/business/tyson-foods ignoring-subpoena-meat-price-gougingprobe-ny-attorney-general -says-2022-08-03/.

18. Inequality and Taxes, Inequality.org, https://inequality.org/facts /taxes-inequality-in-united-states/, accessed June 11, 2024.

19. Annelise Orleck, "The Global Uprising for a More Equitable and Humane Labor Force," *Truthout*, February 22, 2018, excerpt from *"We Are All Fast-Food Workers Now": The Global Uprising Against Poverty Wages* (Boston: Beacon Press, 2018).

20. Orleck, *"We Are All Fast-Food Workers Now."*

21. Kasia Tarczynska, "Taxpayer Subsidies to Amazon Now Exceed $3.7 Billion," Good Jobs First, December 16, 2020, https://goodjobsfirst .org/taxpayer-subsidies-amazon-now-exceed-37-billion/.

22. Bob Lord, "Dynasty Trusts: Giant Tax Loopholes That Supercharge Wealth Accumulation," Americans for Tax Fairness, February 2022, https://americansfortaxfairness.org/dynasty-trusts-giant-tax -loopholes-supercharge-wealth-accumulation/.

23. Lindsay Koshgarian, Alliyah Lusuegro, and Ashik Siddique, "The Warfare State: How Funding for Militarism Compromises Our Welfare," Institute for Policy Studies and the National Priorities Project, 2022, https://media.nationalpriorities.org/uploads/publications/npp -warfare-state-2023-report.pdf.

24. Jim Garamone, "Biden Signs National Defense Authorization Act into Law," *DOD News*, December 23, 2022, https://www.defense.gov /News/News-Stories/Article/Article/3252968/biden-signs-national -defense-authorization-act-into-law/.

25. "Corporate Power, Profiteering, and the 'Camo Economy,'" Costs of War, Watson Institute of International and Public Affairs, Brown University, updated September 2021, https://watson.brown.edu/costs ofwar/costs/social/corporate.

26. Ashik Siddique, "U.S. Still Spends More on Military Than Next Nine Countries Combined," Institute for Policy Studies, June 22, 2022, https://www.nationalpriorities.org/blog/2022/06/22/us-still-spends -more-military-next-nine-countries-combined/.

27. Interview with David Vine, "The U.S. Has 750 Overseas Military Bases, and Continues to Build More to Encircle China," Democracy Now!, February 14, 2023, https://www.democracynow.org/2023/2/14 /david_vine_us_bases_china_philippines.

28. Neta C. Crawford, "Pentagon Fuel Use, Climate Change, and the Costs of War," Costs of War Project at Brown and Boston Universities, updated and revised November 13, 2019, https://watson.brown.edu /costsofwar/files/cow/imce/papers/Pentagon%20Fuel%20Use%2%20 Climate%20Change%20and%20the%20Costs%20of%20War%20 Revised%20November%02019%20Crawford.pdf.

29. Rasha Khatib, Martin McKee, Salim Yusuf, "Counting the Dead in Gaza: Difficult but Essential," *The Lancet*, corrected version published online July 10, 2024, https://www.thelancet.com/journals/lancet/article /PIIS0140-6736(24)01169-3/fulltext.

30. "Gaza: 15 Years of Blockade," United Nations Relief and Works Agency for Palestine Refugees in the Near East, https://www.unrwa.org /gaza15-years-blockade, accessed August 23, 2024.

31. William Hartung, "Pentagon Profiteers: Executive Compensation in the Arms," *Forbes*, December 12, 2022, https://www.forbes.com/sites /williamhartung/2022/12/12/pentagon-profiteers-executive-compensation -in-the-arms-industry/.

32. "Invest in Communities, Not Violence," National Priorities Project at the Institute for Policy Studies, November 2023, https:// media.nationalpriorities.org/uploads/publications/fact_sheet__invest _in_communities,_not_violence_(1).pdf.

33. National Priorities Project, Invest in Communities, Not Violence.

34. Arundhati Roy, "The Pandemic Is a Portal," *Financial Times*, April 3, 2020, https://www.ft.com/content/10d8f5e8-74eb-11ea-95fe -fcd274e920ca.

35. "A Poor People's Pandemic Report: Mapping the Intersections of Poverty, Race and COVID 19," Poor People's Campaign: A National Call for Moral Revival, Repairers of the Breach," Kairos Center, Howard University School of Education, and the Sustainable Development

Solutions Network: A Global Initiative of the United Nations, April 2022, https://www.poorpeoplescampaign.org/pandemic-report/.

36. Cory Turner, "The Expanded Child Tax Credit Briefly Slashed Child Poverty. Here's What Else it Did," *Morning Edition*, NPR, January 27, 2022, https://childrenshealthwatch.org/the-expanded-child-tax -credit-briefly-slashed-child-poverty-heres-what-else-it-did/.

37. Allison Bovell-Ammon et al., "I Didn't Have to Worry: How the Child Tax Credit Helped Families Catch Up on Rent and Improved Health," Kairos Center, Children's HealthWatch, and Revolutionary Healing, August 2022, https://childrenshealthwatch.org/wp-content /uploads/CTC-Report-Aug-2022-Final.pdf.

38. Jake Johnson, "Congress Just Passed $858 Billion Military Budget, But GOP Is Blocking the $12 Billion to Fight Child Poverty," Common Dreams, December 17, 2022, https://www.commondreams.org/news /2022/12/17/congress-just-passed-858-billion-military-budget-gop -blocking-12-billion-fight-child.

39. "Medicaid Enrollment and Unwinding Tracker," Medicaid, KFF, June 4, 2024, https://www.kff.org/report-section/medicaid-enrollment -and-unwinding-tracker-overview/.

40. Gabriela Parra, "Vast Majorities of Americans Intensely Support Increasing Funding for Programs," Navigator, November 30, 2024, https://navigatorresearch.org/vast-majorities-of-americans-intensely -support-increasing-funding-for-programs/.

41. Martin Luther King Jr., Report to SCLC Staff (May 1967).

42. Martin Luther King Jr., *Where Do We Go from Here: Chaos or Community?* (1967; repro. Boston: Beacon Press, 2010), 175.

43. King, *Where Do We Go From Here*, 200.

44. Martin Luther King Jr., "Nonviolence and Social Change," Massey Lectures, delivered for the Canadian Broadcasting Corporation (CBC), December 1967.

45. Sidney Lumet and Joseph L. Mankiewicz, *King: A Filmed Record Montgomery to Memphis, Documentary*, 1970.

46. Coretta Scott King, Speech, Solidarity Day Rally, June 24, 1968.

47. King, *Where Do We Go from Here*, 145.

CHAPTER TWO: THE LIES WE'RE TOLD

1. *Poverty in America: Economic Realities of Struggling Families*, House Committee on the Budget, US House of Representatives, 116th Congress, June 19, 2019.

2. Shailly Gupta-Barnes, Lindsay Koshgarian, and Ashik Siddique, *Poor People's Moral Budget: Everybody Has the Right to Live*, Poor People's

Campaign: A National Call for Moral Revival, Institute for Policy Studies, Kairos Center, Repairers of the Breach, June 15, 2020, https://www.poorpeoplescampaign.org/wp-content/uploads/2019/12/PPC-Moral-Budget-2019-report-FULL-FINAL-July.pdf.

3. "Status of State Medicaid Expansion Decisions: Interactive Map," KFF, May 8, 2024, https://www.kff.org/affordable-care-act/issue-brief/status-of-state-medicaid-expansiondecisions-interactive-map.

4. *Poverty in America: Economic Realities of Struggling Families*, House Committee on the Budget.

5. *Poverty in America: Economic Realities of Struggling Families*, House Committee on the Budget.

6. Gordon M. Fisher, "The Development and History of the Poverty Thresholds," *Social Security Bulletin* 55, no. 4 (1992), https://aspe.hhs.gov/topics/poverty-economic-mobility/poverty-guidelines/further-resources-poverty-measurement-poverty-lines-their-history/history-poverty-thresholds.

7. Shawn Fremstad, "The Defining Down of Economic Deprivation: Why We Need to Reset the Poverty Line," Century Foundation, September 30, 2020, https://tcf.org/content/report/defining-economic-deprivation-need-reset-poverty-line/.

8. "Federal Poverty Level," Healthcare.gov, https://www.healthcare.gov/glossary/federal-poverty-level-fpl/, accessed September 15, 2024.

9. Neil Schoenherr, "What We Don't Understand About America," *The Source*, Washington University of St. Louis, February 15, 2021, https://source.washu.edu/2021/02/what-we-dont-understand-about-poverty-in-america/.

10. Calculated by the Center on Poverty and Social Policy at Columbia University using data from 2023 Annual Social and Economic Supplement to the Current Population Survey. Data is retrieved from the US Census Bureau. American Indian or Alaska Native includes individuals who also identify as Latino.

11. Sewell Chan, "Mollie Orshansky, Statistician Dies at 91," *New York Times*, April 17, 2007, https://www.nytimes.com/2007/04/17/us/17orshansky.html.

12. Lawrence Mishel, Elise Gould, and Josh Bivens, "Wage Stagnation in Nine Charts," Economic Policy Institute, January 6, 2015, https://www.epi.org/publication/charting-wage-stagnation/.

13. Josh Bivens and Joi Kandra, "CEO Pay Slightly Declined in 2022," Economic Policy Institute, September 21, 2023, https://www.epi.org/publication/ceo-pay-in-2022/.

14. Dean Baker, "Correction: The $23 An Hour Minimum Wage," Center for Economic and Policy Research, August 19, 2021, https://cepr.net/the-26-an-hourminimumwage/?emci=816e6180f500-ec11-b563-501ac57b8fa7&emdi=bf508bc9-f600-ec11-b563501ac57b8fa7&ceid=4607260.

15. "Household Debt and Credit Report (Q2 2024)," Center for Microeconomic Data at the Federal Reserve Bank of New York, https://www.newyorkfed.org/microeconomics/hhdc, accessed August 23, 2024.

16. Liz Theoharis and Astra Taylor, "Why Debt Relief Matters," *Slate*, April 6, 2021, https://slate.com/news-and-politics/2021/04/debt-relief-cancelation-jubilee-biden.html.

17. Klaus Schwab, "The Fourth Industrial Revolution: What It Means, How to Respond," World Economic Forum, January 14, 2016, https://www.weforum.org/agenda/2016/01/the-fourth-industrial-revolution-what-it-means-and-how-to-respond/.

18. "The River Rouge Ford Factory: Economic Revitalization," PBS, October 10, 2016, https://www.thirteen.org/programs/dream-on/dream-river-rouge-ford-factory-dream/.

19. Nina Burleigh, "January 6 Busts a Key Myth About Trump Supporters (and Rioters)," NBC News, January 6, 2022, www.nbcnews.com/think/opinion/january-6-busts-key-myth-about-trump-supporters-rioters-ncna1287105.

20. Melanie Zanona and Ally Mutnik, "House Republican Leaders Condemn GOP Candidate Who Made Racist Videos," *Politico*, June 17, 2020, https://www.politico.com/news/2020/06/17/house-republicans-condemn-gop-candidate-racist-videos-325579.

21. Oscar Lewis, "The Culture of Poverty," *Scientific American* 215, no. 4 (October 1966): 19–25, https://users.ssc.wisc.edu/~gwallace/Papers/Lewis%20(1966).pdf.

22. Daniel Patrick Moynihan, *The Negro Family: The Case for National Action*, US Department of Labor, March 1, 1965.

23. Personal Responsibility and Work Opportunity Reconciliation Act of 1996, Pub. L. No. 104–193 (1996), https://www.govinfo.gov/app/details/PLAW-104publ193.

24. Phillip Allston, *Report of the Special Rapporteur on Extreme Poverty and Human Rights on His Mission to the United States of America*, 2018, UN Digital Library, https://digitallibrary.un.org/record/1629536?ln=en&v=pdf.

25. Ja'han Jones, "Why Joe Manchin's Complaints About 'Entitlement' Are Completely Hypocritical," *The ReidOut Blog*, October 28, 2021, https://www.msnbc.com/the-reidout/reidout-blog/joe-manchins-complaints-entitlement-are-completely-hypocritical-rcna3995.

26. Tara Golshan and Arthur Delaney, "Joe Manchin Privately Told Colleagues Parents Use Child Tax Credit Money on Drugs," *HuffPost*, December 20, 2021, https://www.huffpost.com/entry/joe-manchin -build-back-better-child-tax-credit-drugs_n_61bf8f6be4b061afe394006d.

27. Phillip Rucker, "Rick Perry, Hungry for Redemption, Says He's a 'Substantially Different' Candidate," *Washington Post*, December 9, 2014, https://www.washingtonpost.com/politics/rick-perry-hungry-for -redemption-says-hes-a-substantially-different-candidate/2014/12/09 /3c9c605a-7f20-11e4-81fd-8c4814dfa9d7_story.html.

28. Lev Facher, "Two Months Ago, This Doctor Was Delivering Babies. Now He's at the Nexus of the Obamacare Fight," *Stat*, March 3, 2017, https://www.statnews.com/2017/03/03/roger-marshall-kansas-obamacare/.

29. Tammy Ljunglbad, "Marshall Discusses the Influence of His Faith and His Police Chief Father on His Politics," *Kansas City Star*, July 19, 2020, https://www.kansascity.com/news/politicsgovernment /election/article244203212.html.

30. Paul Froese, "How Your View of God Shapes Your View of the Economy," *Religion Dispatches*, June 13, 2012, https://religionandpolitics .org/2012/06/13/how-your-view-of-god-shapes-your-view-of-the -economy/.

31. "A Christian Nation? Understanding the Threat of Christian Nationalism to American Democracy and Culture," Public Religion Research Institute, February 8, 2023, https://www.prri.org/research/a -christian-nation-understanding-the-threat-of-christian-nationalism -to-american-democracy-and-culture/.

32. Anne Bradley and Art Lindsley, *For the Least of These: A Biblical Answer to Poverty*, Institute for Faith, Work, and Economics, 2014.

CHAPTER THREE: UP AND OUT OF POVERTY NOW!

1. W. E. B. Du Bois, *Black Reconstruction in America: 1860–1880* (1935; repro. Free Press, 1999), 13.

2. Christopher Caruso, "A New and Unsettling Force: Information Technology, Popular Education and the Movement to End Poverty," *CUNY Academic Works*, 2019, https://academicworks.cuny.edu/gc _etds/3103.

3. "Hoover and the F.B.I.," *A Huey P. Newton Story*, PBS, 2002, https://www.pbs.org/hueypnewton/people/people_hoover.html.

4. Rann Miller, "Before Governor's Push on School Breakfast, Black Panthers Were Feeding Kids," *Education Next*, March 29, 2023, https:// www.educationnext.org/before governors-push-on-school-breakfast -black-panthers-were-feeding-kids/.

5. Victoria M. Massie, "The Most Radical Thing the Black Panthers Did Was Give Kids Free Breakfast," *Vox*, October 15, 2016, https://www .vox.com/2016/2/14/10981986/blackpanthers-breakfast-beyonce.

6. Sherna Berger Gluck, "Audio Interview with Johnnie Tillmon, 1991," *The Sixties: Los Angeles Area Social Movements/Activists* collection, California State University, Long Beach, https://archives.calstate.edu /concern/archives/t722hb772#.

7. Johnnie Tillmon, interview by Guida West, July 30, 1974, Sophia Smith Collection and Smith College Archives, Neilson Library, Smith College, Northampton, MA.

8. Judith Shulevitz, "Forgotten Feminisms: Johnnie Tillmon's Battle Against 'The Man,'" *New York Review of Books*, June 26, 2018, https:// www.nybooks.com/online/2018/06/26/forgotten-feminisms-johnnie -tillmons-battle-against-the-man/.

9. Guida West, *The National Welfare Rights Movement: The Social Protest of Poor Women* (New York: Praeger, 1981), 42.

10. West, *The National Welfare Rights Movement*, 44.

11. West, *The National Welfare Rights Movement*, 46.

12. For more on this story, read Annelise Orleck, *Storming Caesars Palace: How Black Mothers Fought Their Own War on Poverty* (Boston: Beacon Press, 2006).

13. Shulevitz, "Forgotten Feminisms: Johnnie Tillmon's Battle Against 'The Man.'"

14. Colleen Wessel-McCoy, "'If We Fail in Our Struggle, Christianity Will Have Failed': Beulah Sanders, Welfare Rights, and the Church," Kairos Center, April 4, 2019, https://kairoscenter.org/beulah-sanders -on-the-church/.

15. Kotz and Kotz, *A Passion for Equality: George Wiley and the Movement* (New York: W. W. Norton, 1977), 248–49.

16. Kotz and Kotz, *A Passion for Equality*.

17. Kotz and Kotz, *A Passion for Equality*.

18. Wessel-McCoy, "'If We Fail in Our Struggle, Christianity Will Have Failed.'"

19. Johnnie Tillmon, "Welfare Is a Women's Issue," *Ms.*, Spring 1972.

20. Frances Fox Piven and Richard Cloward, *Regulating the Poor: The Functions of Public Welfare* (New York: Knopf Doubleday, 1978), 328.

21. Frances Fox Piven and Richard Cloward, "Organizing the Poor: How It Can Be Done," February 1966. This paper can be found in the collection of Frances Fox Piven's writing at Smith College (https:// findingaids.smith.edu/repositories/2/resources/924).

22. Willie Baptist, *Pedagogy of the Poor: Building the Movement to End Poverty* (New York: Teachers College Press, 2011), 151.

23. Guida West, *The National Welfare Rights Movement: The Social Protest of Poor Women* (New York: Praeger, 1981), 353.

24. Marian Kramer et al., *Which Way Welfare Rights? (New Situation, New Strategy)*, Annie Smart Leadership Development Institute and Up & Out of Poverty Now Campaign, c. 1991.

25. Marian Kramer and Willie Baptist, "Welfare Rights and the Leadership of the Poor," University of the Poor, 2022, https://university ofthepoor.org/welfare-rights-and-the-leadership-of-the-poor/.

26. "Philadelphians Campaign Against Welfare Cuts, United States, 1996–1997," Global Nonviolent Action Database, https://nvdatabase .swarthmore.edu/content/philadelphians-campaign-against-welfare -cuts-united-states-1996-1997.

27. Elizabeth Palmberg, "A Toxic Battle for Justice," *Sojourners*, March 2009, https://sojo.net/magazine/march-2009/toxic-battle-justice.

CHAPTER FOUR: THE RIGHT TO NOT BE POOR

1. Paul Gordon Lauren, *The Evolution of International Human Rights: Visions Seen* (Philadelphia: University of Pennsylvania Press, 2003).

2. Carol Anderson, *Eyes off the Prize: The United Nations and the African American Struggle for Human Rights 1944–1955* (Cambridge: Cambridge University Press, 2023), 5–6.

3. Martin Luther King Jr., *Where Do We Go from Here: Chaos or Community?* (1967; repr. Boston: Beacon Press, 2010).

4. Larry Cox, "The Power of Religion and Human Rights: Larry Cox at the Bernstein Symposium at Yale University," Kairos Center, July 6, 2017, https://kairoscenter.org/power-religion-human-rights/.

5. Joan Roelofs, "How Foundations Exercise Power," *American Journal of Economics and Sociology* 4, no. 4, The Hidden Hand: How Foundations Shape the Course of History (September 2015): 654–75.

6. Shailly Gupta Barnes, "Kairos Center Policy Briefing #9: From Austerity to Abundance," Kairos Center, Febuary 8, 2021, https://kairos center.org/policy-briefing-9-from-austerity-to-abundance/.

7. Hilary Beaumont, "Flint Residents Grapple with Water Crisis a Decade Later: 'If We Had the Energy Left, We'd Cry,'" *The Guardian*, April 25, 2024.

8. Cecil Angel, "Official Recommends Bankruptcy for Highland Park, Mich.," *Detroit Free Press*, April 19, 2002.

9. Christopher Caruso, "A New and Unsettling Force: Information Technology, Popular Education and the Movement to End Poverty,"

CUNY Academic Works, 2019, https://academicworks.cuny.edu/gc
_etds/3103, 86.

10. Christopher Caruso, "Chapter 6: A Case Study on Organizing: The Struggle for Water in Postindustrial Detroit," in Willie Baptist and Jan Rehmann, *Pedagogy of the Poor: Building the Movement to End Poverty* (New York: Teachers College Press, 2011), 91

11. Caruso, "A New and Unsettling Force," 87

12. Lucia Litowich, "Coalition Warns of Possible Water Riots in Detroit," Michigan Independent Media Center, Febuary 7, 2004.

13. Joint Press Statement by Special Rapporteur on Adequate Housing as a Component of the Right to an Adequate Sandard of Living and to Right to Non-Discrimination in this Context, and Special Rapporteur on the Human Right to Safe Drinking Water and Sanitation Visit to City of Detroit (United States of America) 18–20 October 2014," Office of the United Nations High Commissioner for Human Rights, October 20, 2014, https://www.ohchr.org/en/statements/2014/10/joint-press-statement-special-rapporteur adequate-housing-component-right?

14. Caruso, "A New and Unsettling Force," 90.

15. "2005 Water Affordability Program," People's Water Board Coalition, https://peopleswaterboard.org/water-affordability-program/, accessed September 19, 2024.

16. Caruso, "A New and Unsettling Force," 89.

17. Brian Allnutt, "Advocates Hail Progress with Michigan Water Affordability Bills," *Planet Detroit*, October 5, 2023, https://planetdetroit.org/2023/10/advocates-hail-progress-with michigan-water-affordability-bills/.

18. Mia DiFelice, "How Corporate Greed Leads to Utility Shutoffs for Millions," Food and Water Watch, Febuary 7, 2023, https://www.foodandwaterwatch.org/2023/02/07/utility-shutoffs-corporate-greed/; Kelly L. Smalling et al., "Per- and Polyfluoroalkyl Substances (PFAS) in United States Tapwater: Comparison of Underserved Private-Well and Public-Supply Exposures and Associated Health Implications," *Environment International* 178 (August 2023).

19. Caruso, "A New and Unsettling Force," 66.

20. Caruso, "A New and Unsettling Force," 68.

21. "Partners," Fair Food Program, https://fairfoodprogram.org, accessed September 19, 2024.

22. *Voices of the Vermont Healthcare Crisis: The Human Right to Healthcare*, Vermont Workers' Center, December 10, 2008, https://workerscenter.org/wp-content/uploads/2022/11/Voices_of_the_Vermont_Healthcare_Crisis.pdf.

23. Steve Early, "Vermont's Struggle for Single-Payer Healthcare," *The Nation*, March 28, 2011, https://www.thenation.com/article/archive /vermonts-struggle-single-payer-healthcare/.

24. "Our History," Vermont Workers' Center, https://workerscenter .org/about/, accessed September 19, 2024.

CHAPTER FIVE: THE STRUGGLE IS THE SCHOOL

1. NPR Staff, "Coal Reignites a Mighty Battle of Labor History," NPR, March 5, 2011, https://www.npr.org/2011/03/05/134203550/coal -reignites-a-mighty-battle-of-labor-history.

2. General Gordon Baker, Speech, US Social Forum in Detroit, 2010.

3. Martin Luther King Jr., *Where Do We Go from Here: Chaos or Community?* (1967; repr. Boston: Beacon Press, 2010).

4. Willie Baptist, *Pedagogy of the Poor: Building the Movement to End Poverty* (New York: Teachers College Press, 2011).

5. "Philadelphians Campaign Against Welfare Cuts, United States, 1996–1997," Global Nonviolent Action Database, https://nvdatabase .swarthmore.edu/content/philadelphians-campaign-against-welfare -cuts-united-states-1996-1997.

6. "Philadelphians Campaign Against Welfare Cuts, United States, 1996-1997," Global Nonviolent Action Database.

7. Myles Horton and Paulo Freire, *We Make the Road by Walking: Conversations on Education and Social Change* (Philadelphia: Temple University Press, 1990).

8. Horton, *The Long Haul*, xx.

9. Myles Horton with Judith Kohl and Herbert Kohl, *The Long Haul: An Autobiography* (New York: Teachers College Press, 1997), 138.

10. Horton, *The Long Haul*, 180.

11. Horton, *The Long Haul*, 114–15.

CHAPTER SIX: THE BATTLE FOR THE BIBLE

1. Aaron Scott, author interview, April 2024.

2. Scott, author interview.

3. "Projects of Survival," Chaplains on the Harbor, https://chaplains ontheharbor.org/ourwork/survivalprojects/#.

4. Louis Krauss, "Federal Lawsuit: Aberdeen Tosses Permit System for Homeless Camp Visitors," *The Chronicle*, January 4, 2019, https:// www.chronline.com/stories/federallawsuit-aberdeen-tosses-permit -system-for-homeless-camp-visitors,12009#googlevignette.

5. Scott, author interview.

6. Scott, author interview.

7. Carey Daniel, *God the Original Segregationist*, pamphlet, published by the author, 1955.

8. Martin Luther King Jr., "Our God Is Marching On!" March 25, 1965, at the Martin Luther King, Jr. Research and Education Institute, Stanford, https://kinginstitute.stanford.edu/our-god-marching.

9. Poor People's Campaign: A National Call for Moral Revival, "State Fact Sheets (2023)," https://www.poorpeoplescampaign.org/resource/state-fact-sheets-2023/, accessed September 19, 2024.

10. Kevin M. Kruse, *One Nation Under God: How Corporate America Invented Christian America* (Princeton, NJ: Princeton University Press, 2015), xiv.

11. PRRI Staff, *A Christian Nation? Understanding the Threat of Christian Nationalism to American Democracy and Culture*, February 8, 2023, https://www.prri.org/research/a-christian-nation-understanding-the-threat-of-christian-nationalism-to-american-democracy-and-culture/.

12. Randall Balmer, "The Real Origins of the Religious Right," *Politico* magazine, May 27, 2014, https://www.politico.com/magazine/story/2014/05/religious-right-real-origins-107133/.

13. This writing is drawn from Liz Theoharis, "Christianity Will Fail If We Don't Stop Christian Nationalism," *Waging Nonviolence*, January 17, 2023, https://wagingnonviolence.org/forusa/2023/01/christianity-will-fail-if-we-dont-stop-christian-nationalism/.

14. Project 2025, Heritage Foundation, April 2023, https://www.project2025.org/, accessed September 12, 2024.

15. Maura Casey, "Project 2025: The Blueprint for Christian Nationalist Regime Change," Charles F. Kettering Foundation, August 19, 2024, https://kettering.org/project-2025-the-blueprint for christian-nationalist-regime-change/; Chris Lehmann, "The Terrifying Christian Nationalist Crusade to Conquer America," *The Nation*, March 13, 2024, https://www.thenation.com/article/politics/christian-nationalism-trump-republicans/.

16. Ian Smith, "Project 2025 Has Become Significantly More Unfavorable Since Trump Attempted to Distance Himself from the Plan," Navigator, July 23, 2024, https://navigatorresearch.org/project-2025-has-become-significantly-more-unfavorable-since-trump-attempted-to-distance-himself-from-the-plan/.

17. Tim Reid, "Trump Tells Christians They Won't Have To Vote After This Election," Reuters, July 28, 2024, https://www.reuters.com/world/us/trump-tells-christians-they-wont-have-vote-after-this-election-2024-07-27/.

18. Liz Theoharis and Shailly Gupta Barnes, "The Christian Nationalist Vision for America," Tom Dispatch, July 28, 2024, https://tom dispatch.com/project-2025/.

19. "Robert Paul Hartley, "Unleashing the Power of Poor and Low-Income Americans: Changing the Political Landscape," Poor People's Campaign: A National Call for Moral Revival, August 2020, https://www.poorpeoplescampaign.org/resource/power-of-poor voters/; Dan Milmo, "Trump's Victory Adds Record $64bn to the Wealth of Richest Top 10," *The Guardian*, November 7, 2024, https://www.theguardian.com/business/2024/nov/07/trump-victory-adds-record-wealth-richest-top-10.

20. "Exit Polls," NBC News, last updated November 15, 2024, https://www.nbcnews.com/politics/2024-elections/exit-polls.

21. Cedar Monroe, *Trash: A Poor White Journey* (Minneapolis: Broadleaf, 2024), 41.

22. Katie Hunt, "Abortion Is Ancient History: Long Before Roe, Women Terminated Pregnancies," CNN, June 23, 2023, https://www.cnn.com/2023/06/23/health/abortion-is-ancient-history-and-that-matters-today-scn/index.html.

23. *All of U.S.: Organizing to Counter White Christian Nationalism and Build a Pro-Democracy Society*, Kairos Center and MoveOn Education Fund, May 2023.

24. "Zikode, S'bu Zikode in Dialogue with Rev. Dr. Liz Theoharis," People's Forum, April 20, 2020, https://www.youtube.com/watch?v=da6QMo9VOIY.

25. "Zikode, S'bu Zikode in Dialogue with Rev. Dr. Liz Theoharis."

CHAPTER SEVEN: OUR KAIROS MOMENT

1. Sharon Lavigne, "Listen: In 'Cancer Alley,' A Teacher Called to Fight," *Grist*, April 25, 2023, https://grist.org/temperature-check/sharon-lavigne-cancer-alley-industry-formosa/.

2. Sharon Lavigne, author interview, May 7, 2024.

3. Nicole Greenfield, "Advocates Are Sparking a Revolution in Louisiana's 'Cancer Alley,'" National Resources Defense Council, November 10, 2022, https://www.nrdc.org/stories/advocates-are-sparking-revolution-louisianas-cancer-alley.

4. Victoria St. Martin, "In Louisiana's 'Cancer Alley,' Excitement over New Emissions Rules Is Tempered by a Legal Challenge to Federal Environmental Justice Efforts," *Inside Climate News*, May 10, 2024, https://insideclimatenews.org/news/10052024/louisiana-cancer-alley-emission-rules-environmental-justice/.

5. James Bruggers, "On the Frontlines in a 'Cancer Alley,' Black Women Inspired by Faith Are Powering the Environmental Justice Movement," *Inside Climate News*, Febuary 20, 2023, https://insideclimate news.org/news/20022023/cancer-alley-louisiana-environmental-justice -black-women-faith/.

6. Lylla Younes, "A Louisiana Court Just Revived Plans for the Country's Biggest Plastics Plant," *Grist*, January 23, 2024, https://grist .org/regulation/louisiana-court-revived-biggest plastic-plant-formosa/.

7. Younes, "A Louisiana Court Just Revived Plans for the Country's Biggest Plastics Plant."

8. Lavigne, author interview.

9. Center for Biological Diversity, "A Deadly Toll: The Devastating Wildlife Effects of Deepwater Horizion—and the Next Catastrophic Oil Spill," https://www.biologicaldiversity.org/programs/public_lands /energy/dirty_energy_development/oil_and_gas/gulf_oil_spill/a_deadly _toll.html, accessed September 12, 2024.

10. Center for Biological Diversity, "A Deadly Toll."

11. Staff, "US Leads Global Oil Production For Sixth Straight Year-EIA," Reuters, March 11, 2024, https://www.reuters.com/markets /commodities/us-leads-global-oil-production sixth-straight-year-eia -2024-03-11/.

12. "We Are In a Pitched Battle," Kairos Center, November 18, 2014, https://kairoscenter.org/pitched-battle/.

13. Flowers chronicles this reality in her indispensable book *Waste: One Woman's Fight Against America's Dirty Secret* (New York: New Press, 2020).

14. Susan Roesgen, "Protestors Take to the Sky to Fight Bayou Bridge Pipeline," WGNO, August 22, 2018, https://wgno.com/news /exclusive-protesters-take-to-the-sky-to-fight-bayou-bridge-pipeline/.

15. Julie Dermanksy, "Permit Hearing for Taiwanese Plastic Plant in Louisiana Turns into a Referendum on Environmental Racism," *DeSmog*, December 13, 2018, https://www.desmog.com/2018/12/13/formosa -plastics-plant-st-james-parish-louisiana-environmental-racism/.

16. Lisa Friedman, "In 'Cancer Alley,' Judge Blocks Huge Petrochemical Plant," *New York Times*, September 15, 2022, https://www .nytimes.com/2022/09/15/climate/louisiana-judge-blocks-formosa -plant.html.

17. Alexandria Trimble, "Louisiana Court Ruling Reverses Lower Court Decision and Upholds Air Permits for Formosa Plastics' Massive Petrochemical Complex in Cancer Alley," *Earth Justice*, January 19, 2024, https://earthjustice.org/press/2024/louisiana-court-ruling-reverses

-lower-court-decision-and-upholds-air-permits-for-formosa-plastics -massive-petrochemical-complex-in-cancer-alley.

18. This writing on prophets and inaction is drawn from Liz Theoharis, "Plagues Expose the Foundations of Injustice," *Sojourners*, March 18, 2020, https://sojo.net/articles/plagues expose-foundations-injustice.

19. Dan Jones, "Freedom Shul of the Poor Passover Seder," Kairos Center, April 21, 2024.

20. This writing on plagues is also drawn from Theoharis, "Plagues Expose the Foundations of Injustice."

21. Jones, "Freedom Shul of the Poor Passover Seder."

22. Elizabeth R. Earle, "Paul Tillich's Communication Theology and the Rhetoric of Existentialism," 2014, LSU Master's Theses, https://repository.lsu.edu/gradschooltheses/3668.

23. "The South Africa Kairos Document 1985," Kairos Southern Africa, posted May 8, 2011, https://kairossouthernafrica.wordpress.com /2011/05/08/the-south-africa-kairos-document-1985/.

24. Tyler McBrien, "The Struggle Continues: On Vincent Bevins's 'If We Burn,'" *Los Angeles Review of Books*, October 3, 2023, https://lareview ofbooks.org/article/the-struggle continues-on-vincent-bevinss-if-we -burn/.

25. "Poverty Initiative," https://kairoscenter.org/poverty-initiative/, accessed September 12, 2024.

26. Larry Buchanan, Quoctrung Bui, and Jugal K. Patel, "Black Lives Matter May Be the Largest Movement in U.S. History," *New York Times*, July 3, 2020, https://www.nytimes.com/interactive/2020/07/03 /us/george-floyd-protests-crowd-size.html.

27. M. A. Primbs et al., "The Effects of the 2020 BLM Protests on Racial Bias in the United States," *Personality and Social Psychology Bulletin* (2024).

28. "Project Esther: A National Strategy to Combat Antisemitism," The Heritage Foundation, October 7, 2024, https://www.heritage.org /progressivism/report/project-esther-national-strategy-combat -antisemitism.

29. Janine Jackson, "It's the Biggest Assault on Voting Rights Since the End of Reconstruction," FAIR, March 16, 2021, https://fair.org /home/its-the-biggest-assault-on-voting-rights-since-the-end-of -reconstruction/.

30. Adam Freedman, "The War on Protest Is Here," *In These Times*, April 17, 2024, https://inthesetimes.com/article/war-protest-standing -rock-cop-city-repression-criminalize-dissent-political-rights-first -amendment.

31. Freedman, "The War on Protest Is Here."

32. Gabriela Parra, "Vast Majorities of Americans Intensely Support Increasing Funding for Programs," Navigator, November 30, 2024, https://navigatorresearch.org/vast-majorities-of-americans-intensely -support-increasing-funding-for-programs/.

33. Fernando Garcia and Aaron Nofke, "We Are a Human Rights Organization—Interview with Fernando Garcia of the Border Network for Human Rights," Kairos, May 19, 2018, https://kairoscenter.org /fernando-garcia-border-interview/.

34. Garcia and Nofke, "We Are a Human Rights Organization."

35. "Close to Home: Case Studies of Human Rights Work in the United States," Ford Foundation, June 2024, https://www.fordfoundation .org/wpcontent/uploads/2015/03/2004-close_to_home.pdf.

36. American Immigration Council, "The Cost of Immigration and Border Security," fact sheet, August 14, 2024, https://www.american immigrationcouncil.org/research/the-cost-of immigration-enforcement -and-border-security#.

37. Fernando Garcia, "Oversight of the Trump Administration's Border Policies and the Relationship Between Anti-Immigrant Rhetoric and Domestic Terrorism," House Judiciary Committee Field Hearing, September 6, 2019, available at https://www.youtube.com/watch?v=6IU 2cOyklto.

38. Garcia and Nofke, "We Are a Human Rights Organization"; "Fact Sheet: DHS Continues to Strengthen Border Security, Reduce Irregular Migration, and Mobilize International Partnerships," Department of Homeland Security, June 4, 2024, https://www.dhs.gov/news /2024/06/04/fact-sheet-dhs-continues-strengthen-border-security -reduce-irregular-migration-and.

39. Ashley Killough, "El Paso Walmart Shooter Agrees to Pay More Than $5.5 Million in Restitution in Federal Case," CNN, September 23, 2023, https://www.cnn.com/2023/09/25/us/el-paso walmart-shooter -millions-restitution/index.html.

40. Garcia and Nofke, "We Are a Human Rights Organization."

41. Fernando Garcia, "'The System Impacts All of Us . . . So the Solution Has to Come from All of Us,'" Poor People's Campaign, https://www.poorpeoplescampaign.org/we-cry-power/fernando-garcia/, accessed June 11, 2024.

42. In July 2023, then Republican presidential candidate and biotech billionaire Vivek Ramaswamy published an op-ed in the *New York Post*. For more, read Vivek Ramaswamy, "We Must Fix the Sheer Human Misery I Saw on the Streets of Philadelphia," *New York Post*, July 23,

2023, https://nypost.com/2023/07/25/we-must-fix-the-sheer-human-misery-i-saw-on-the-streets-of-philadelphia/.

43. Samantha Melamed, Max Marin, and Dylan Purcell, "How Speculators Fueled a Nightmare for Kensington Residents—and Could Soon Cash In," *Philadelphia Inquirer*, August 12, 2024, https://www.inquirer.com/news/kensington-real-estate-speculators-drug-opioid-crisis-gentrification-20240812.html.

44. Frederick Douglass, "West Indies Emancipation Speech of August 3, 1857," available at https://frederickdouglasspapersproject.com/s/digitaledition/item/10509.

45. W. E. B. Du Bois, *Black Reconstruction in America: 1860–1880* (1935; repro. Free Press, 1999).

46. Diane Bernard, speech, Malcolm X Conference, Highland Park, MI, July 23–25, 1993.